HOW TO STAND OUT
IN THE MIDST OF
COMPETITIVE CLUTTER

◆

THE GUIDE
TO
FINANCIAL
PUBLIC
RELATIONS

HOW TO STAND OUT
IN THE MIDST OF
COMPETITIVE CLUTTER

◆

THE GUIDE
TO
FINANCIAL
PUBLIC
RELATIONS

LARRY
CHAMBERS

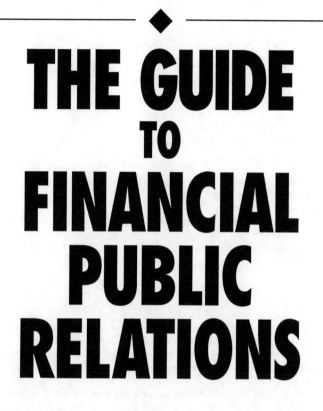

S^t_L

St. Lucie Press
Boca Raton   London   New York   Washington, D.C.

Library of Congress Cataloging-in-Publication Data

Chambers, Larry.
    The guide to financial public relations : how to stand out in the
midst of competitive clutter / Larry Chambers
          p. cm.
    Includes bibliographical references and index.
    ISBN 0-910944-12-1 (alk. paper)
    1. Public relations. I. Title.
HD59.C453 1999
659.2—dc21
                                                              99-25238
                                                                  CIP

© 1999 by CRC Press LLC
St. Lucie Press is an imprint of CRC Press LLC

No claim to original U.S. Government works
International Standard Book Number 0-910944-12-1
Library of Congress Card Number   99-25238
Printed in the United States of America   1 2 3 4 5 6 7 8 9 0
Printed on acid-free paper

Advance Praise

"Written Communication is one of the best ways to gain the trust of clients and prospective clients. This book sets out the guidelines you need to make the written word, whether it is a press release, newspaper article, book, or client newsletter, your strongest ally in strengthening your client base. Any financial advisor looking to differentiate himself/herself from the competition should consider this book a 'must read'."

Ann O'Brien, President, Integrated Concepts Group, Inc.

Pre-publication endorsement *The Guide to Financial Public Relations*

"We started a brand new company and turned to Larry Chambers to help us get our name known in the industry. Within two years, we've become a household name. We hold that a big part of our success is due to Larry's efforts and the use of Larry's strategies to publicize our firm."

Len Reinhart, president, CEO and chairman of Lockwood Financial Group

"Getting articles published is paramount to becoming well-known by your target market. I believe that writing articles and books and being in the media are the most important strategies for building credibility for financial professionals today."

Bill Bachrach, popular keynote speaker and author of *Values Based Selling: The Art of Building High-Trust Relationships for Financial Advisors*

"Just a quick note to say thanks. I just got off the phone with an advisor who called me to let me know that he used my book to help close a $1.4 million sale with a new client. Writing a book was a long-term strategy but has already paying off.

Thanks Again, Larry!"

Michael Lane, Director, Advisor Resources Division, Aegon Financial Services Group and author of *Guaranteed Income for Life*, McGraw-Hill

"We recently completed a tape session where Larry shared his PR business model for using articles and media with our advisors and representatives. We found his ideas and concepts invaluable in growing a financial practice."

Deb Hansen, Marketing Manager, American Securities Advisors

"Larry Chambers has skillfully mastered the art of PR. His book, just like his articles, captures the true essence of what any professional needs to know to be successful in the area of public relations."

Jeffrey H. Rattiner, Editor-In-Chief of Financial Advisory Practice and president of JR Financial Group Inc.

"As a consultant and market researcher, knowledge of both the financial securities and publishing industries, I realize how rare it is to find a how-to book that really addresses a need the audience has and offers solutions that readers can and will be motivated to implement. This one makes the grade."

Russ Alan Prince, expert on the psychology of the affluent, is author of *Cultivating the Affluent and Building Your Business.*

"After hearing Larry Chambers speak on PR I put together a folder of articles, some I had written and some about me. I now hand them to prospects when we first meet. It takes me past the initial awkward phase of a first meeting. Instead of me saying, "I'm an expert," the articles say it for me. They become my credentials. It really breaks the ice. I no longer have to sell them on me. I'm pre-sold."

Leon Spheeris, First Vice President, Dain Rauscher, Chairman of Advisory Board of IIMC and past president.

"Getting good public relations means client referrals"

Lynn Hopewell, President, The Monitor Group Inc.

"Nobody is going to know your name until *you* get the word out. This book will show you how."

Louis Schiff, creator of the *Armchair Millionaire* website

"I've seen first hand the power of a positive media image in building business success. Today it's a matter of survival. Larry Chambers' book can put you on top of the pile."

Woody Gair, former advertising agency executive vice president

"Public relations is one of the most important products of business success, and Chambers' book is clear, concise, and infinitely helpful."

Chris Bunch, former publicist, and best-selling author of *The Seer King Trilogy*

"Having worked with Larry as his editor on several books, I have witnessed first hand Larry's extensive knowledge of what it takes to become recognized as an expert. That's what you will learn in this book."

Kevin Commins, Senior Acquisitions Editor, CCH Inc.

"I never realized the time involved in trying to self-publish. Larry Chambers convinced me there was a better way. I'm very thankful to Larry for helping us find a publisher and editing our new book, *Financial Planning in the Year 2000 and Beyond.*"

Tom J. Nohr, CFP RFC

"A published article is better than a brochure. People associate a level of competency with you that may go far beyond your actual skills and knowledge."

Gary Pia, a financial advisor in Pasadena, CA

"Larry Chambers is the secret weapon behind many of the most successful financial service companies in North America."

Steve Moller, President and CEO, American Business Visions

"In 1973 Don Shula led the little known Miami Dolphins out of obscurity into the history books. Let this be the year Larry Chambers leads you out of obscurity into the light of a higher media presence."

Bo Cornell, Regional Director, Dimensional Fund Advisors

Larry Chambers knows the media and knows what is important for them. With a wide range of by-lines and several successful books under his belt, he knows how to get the attention of editors.

Gregory Bresiger, editor, writer

Preface

Here's the challenge: Today's consumers, especially the affluent, are more sophisticated than ever before. They want to know who you are before doing business with you, and just how you are going to help them. There must be a compelling difference for them to choose you over your competition.

Most of us don't have a system to tilt the scale in our favor. We may see our competition winning out in a coveted target market when we know we are the better choice. The difference is often not in skill level or expertise or knowledge, it's in marketing and communicating. To be recognized as a leader in your field, you're going to have to be seen in the media, read about by your prospects, and heard by the investing public. You'll need to develop your promotional, writing, and speaking skills. But where do you begin?

That's precisely where this book comes in. This book will lay out, step by step, how to work with the media and become recognized as an expert in your field—attracting an endless stream of pre-endorsed, pre-qualified prospects in the process. Okay, I may have gotten a little carried away. Maybe I can't guarantee prospects will knock your door off its hinges; but what I do know is, this book will help you showcase your talents and knowledge in a way that will make potential customers want to contact you.

This is not a pie-in-the-sky theoretical book. It's the result of real world experiences that the author, Larry Chambers, has had helping many of the most successful leaders in today's information-cluttered business world to stand out as experts. I know these strategies work. With Larry's help, my partners and I have built a two-billion-dollar business—and we're just getting started!

I believe this book can cause a breakthrough in your own marketing campaign and help you reach your own next level of success. By following Larry's methods, you can start your program today and begin to see results immediately.

John Bowen
President and Chief Executive Officer (CEO)
Reinhardt Werba Bowen Advisor Services

About the Author

Larry Chambers is the financial service industry's #1 writing and media coach. His unique approach involves coaching members of the industry to write and place their own material. His clients have been published by major publishing houses—including Irwin, McGraw-Hill, Random House, Times Mirror, Dow Jones, and John Wiley and Sons—as well as featured in major national trade magazines.

Chambers is a former long-time member of the same audience he addresses. After attending the University of Utah, where he received bachelor's and master's degrees and was elected to the Phi Kappa Phi honor society, he joined E.F. Hutton. At E.F. Hutton, he gained experience in managed money consulting for over 500 private and institutional accounts, including pension and profit sharing plans, foundations, state retirement funds, and university endowments. He achieved an outstanding track record and was named one of the top 20 brokers out of more than 5,000, and received numerous awards and acknowledgments.

Now a full-time writer, Chambers has authored, contributed to, and ghostwritten over six hundred investment articles, and is on the advisory board for the *Journal of Investing,* an Institutional Investor publication.

Larry Chambers
PO Box 1810
Ojai, CA 93024
phone: 805 640-0888
Lchamb007@aol.com

Acknowledgments

It was Thomas Stanley, the author of *Marketing To The Affluent* and his "New York Times" mega hit, *The Millionaire Next Door*, who started me writing. He told me, "Larry, if you want to have a major advantage over your competition, you've got to write. It shows the world that you are the expert. Just remember, anyone can print up a fancy brochure, but a reprint of an article you authored is your calling card of credibility." Thanks, Tom.

I'm deeply grateful, too, to John J. Bowen, Jr. at Reinhardt Werba Bowen Advisory Services for his generosity in making this book happen and also to Doug Carter for his coaching and to Bill Bachrach and his "Trusted Advisor Coach Program".

I would like to thank Russ Prince for his academic research and guidance; and Michael Lane, President, Advisor Resources of Aegon Financial who always follows my advice and whose new book is now a Money Book Club selection.

To my friends at *Financial Planning* magazine, Evan Simonoff and Tom Johnson; Jed Horowitz, editor of *On Wall Street*; Cheryl Cooper at *Registered Representative*; and Jeff Rattiner at *Financial Advisory Practice* magazine. To Michael Jeffers at Glenlake Company, to CRC Press LLC, and to Drew Gierman, publisher at St. Lucie Press; and Meritt Lewis at ML Publishing Services.

To the guys at the iVillage's *Armchair Millionaire* website, Louis Schiff and Doug Gerlach; Steve Moller at American Business Visions; Peter Neves at USAWorks for his help in building a great looking website; and Anne Bachrach for her repackaging reprint service.

Also to John Kramer, author of *1001 Ways to Market Your Books* and editor of a great resource, "Book Market Update." Jack Canfield and Mark Victor Hansen, co-authors of the *Chicken Soup for the Soul* for teaching me how little I know about selling. Jerrold Jenkins, author of *Publish to Win*, for his knowledge and insights in the publishing business; and to Robert Bly, author of a great book *Target Public Relations*.

Acknowledgments

Thanks to my staff, Karen Johnson and Mayo Morley, Jari Chevalier my writing coach and, the Ojai Roasting Company, for endless cups of coffee.

And lastly to Charles E. Merrill. Sixty years ago he was out educating potential investors through lectures, seminars and an endless stream of newspaper and magazine articles. You recognize him more readily as the Merrill in—Merrill Lynch.

Table of Contents

Preface

Acknowledgments

About the Author

Introduction 1

Part I—Building Your Publicity Program

Chapter 1—The Media Opportunity 9

Chapter 2—How to Position Yourself in the Right Marketplace. . . . 15

Chapter 3—Add the Media to Your Marketing Plan 23

Chapter 4—How to Get Your Message Out Fast 35

Chapter 5—Building a Top-of-Mind Awareness System 47

Chapter 6—Credibility Marketing Strategies 57

Part II—Writing a Publishable Article

Chapter 7—How to Write the Problem/Solution Magazine Article . 79

Chapter 8—More Things You can Do to Look Like a Pro 95

Chapter 9—Breaking into Print the Easy Way 105

Chapter 10—Where to Find the Right Trade Publication 109

Chapter 11—Trade Magazine Guidelines. 121

Chapter 12—How to Leverage Your Articles. 125

Chapter 13—Present Yourself on a Website. 129

Chapter 14—Making Your Newsletters Sing 137

Part III—Writing an Investment Book

Chapter 15—The Master Investment Book Template. 145

Chapter 16—How to Sell Your Book to a Publisher—Before
You Write It 153

Chapter 17—How to Make It Look Even More Professional 159

Chapter 18—How to Turn Your Old Articles into New Books. . . . 165

Chapter 19—Titles That Send a Message. 169

Chapter 20—Writing for Permissions 173

Chapter 21—How to Promote Your Book 177

Chapter 22—How to Land a Spot on a National Television
Talk Show. 193

Part IV—The Circle of Publicity Activities

Chapter 23—Advertising and Public Relations—How to Make
Them Work. 209

Chapter 24—How to Turn a Trade Conference into a Gold Mine. . 217

Chapter 25—How to Turn Your Expertise into a College Course. . 225

Chapter 26—Yellow Gold: Revisit the Yellow Pages. 233

Contents

Chapter 27—Speak Like an Expert—Unforgettable Presentations . 243

Chapter 28—Help! 251

Conclusion.. 269

Appendix I—Marketing Studies......................... 271

Appendix II—Media Comparison: Pros & Cons 277

Appendix III—Sample Client Letters...................... 283

Glossary.. 293

Suggested Resources................................. 313

Index 317

Introduction

Why did you pick this book off the shelf? Are you looking for a proven way to build your business, or to increase the size of your financial practice? Do you need to know how to create a professional image that will give you instant credibility in your hometown? Do you want to become recognized as an expert? Would you like to be invited to speak at meetings of your clients' business associations? Do you want to learn how to reinforce relationships with existing clients? Do you want to learn the secrets of referral prospecting? Do you want to stand out as a leader in the midst of all the competitive clutter out there?

If your answer to any of these questions is "yes," you've bought the right book!

What if—in just three months, six months, or a year—you could see a marked growth in new and existing business? What if prospecting could become a fun game you enjoy rather than a laborious chore you dread? This book will give you tools that strategically shorten the sales process and increase sales. In fact, the promise of this book is to get you started on the right track and then help you—every step of the way—to systematically build your own dynamic publicity plan. You will become an expert at organizing your own resources and taking confident steps toward your own marketing success.

During the past 10 years, I've written and placed more than 600 articles in trade magazines throughout the country and had 16 financial books published by major houses, including McGraw-Hill, Ivy Books (a division of Random House), Times Mirror, Richard D. Irwin, and John Wiley and Sons. I've taught the techniques of writing problem/solution articles to financial advisors in workshops across the United States and provided one-on-one advice to some of the securities industry's biggest players.

How was I able to beat out other, more experienced, writers, journalists, and so-called public relations specialists? Because I started as one of you, spending over 20 years on main street's front lines as a stockbroker and financial advisor during some of the best and worst markets we've ever seen. I've capitalized on that real world experience, using my passion for our industry to get media to work *with* me.

Even though this is aimed at financial professionals because of my point of view, these techniques are valid for anyone selling a product or service. Take advantage of my experience, combine it with your own knowledge, and you'll be on the road to a successful promotional campaign.

Marketing Challenges

Following are the four marketing challenges you face.

Challenge One

We live in a world full of look-alike competitors. Due to the substantially similar choices available, it has become ever more difficult for clients, customers, and prospects to find objective reasons to choose one advisor over another. Since the alternatives are basically alike to the average consumer, there are no wrong choices—only unfamiliar ones.

Challenge Two

Today's consumers don't want you to make contact directly. They want to initiate the contact. This puts you, today's financial professional, squarely on the horns of a dilemma: "If I contact prospects directly, they'll think of me as a salesman. If I don't, I could go out of business waiting for them to find me."

Challenge Three

Many of us mistakenly believe that making things happen, our drive to be successful, is what *makes* us successful. Consider instead that we attract success into our life by preparing for it.

Challenge Four

Financial advisors with the highest marks and those with the worst records all use the same title. Consumers can't tell who's competent and who's not, so how do they choose? The smart consumers get their advice from an expert. And by today's standards, an expert is anyone whose advice appears *in print*. Bingo! The way to break through the clutter and stand out to prospects is to become recognized as an expert by getting into print!

Most Financial Advisors Have No Marketing Plans

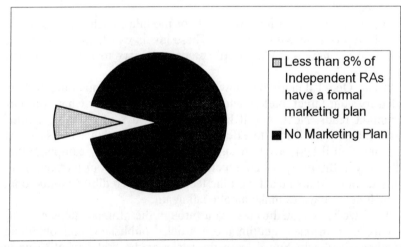

Source: Prince & Asscociates, 1997 Independent RA (Registered Advisors) Survey, pg. 53

It's up to you to separate yourself from the pack.

Here's where this book comes in. It's written for those who aspire to be the best in their profession and to be recognized for their efforts. It presents a simple, easy-to-follow system that will showcase your talents, knowledge, and skills in their best light. This book was written to deal with the realities of self-promotion, and to give you an alternative to traditional public relations.

The basic goal, then, is to get your expertise published in the media. All you need is the persistence to follow through.

Follow the steps in order. They are designed to give you incremental, predictable results—small marketing successes that together form a strong foundation and give you the validation and encouragement to proceed. Each success will move you one step higher above the valley floor, where hordes of look-alike competitors fight over the kill of the day. This book will show you how to find your way to a new plateau, the one where the big game roams undisturbed!

When you use the information in this book, something truly amazing will happen. You will learn to leave a "visual scent" so powerful that the market you are hunting will actually seek you out. You'll be pursued by the very prospects you've spent a career trying to attract. That's when marketing really becomes exciting!

Do you remember a time when you felt totally motivated, when you knew you couldn't be stopped? With a little effort, you can be again the best of the best.

The book is divided into four parts or modules, each representing a level of involvement with publicity. These levels will help you pinpoint where you are now and the specific steps necessary to reach your next goal.

In Part One, I'll begin by showing you how to position yourself, how to identify your target market, and why you need to know what your target market reads. Next, you'll learn the best ways of creating a compelling message and how to effectively communicate that message. At this point, you'll be ready to design a proactive publicity campaign that will give you the image of an expert—no writing on your part required. In this section I'll also teach you the techniques of credibility marketing, so you'll never have to make a cold call again.

Part Two is designed to take you through the ultimate steps of writing your own articles, getting those articles published, and obtaining immediate feedback. You'll learn the tricks of the trade: what to write about, how to write effective magazine articles, a way to rewrite the same article for different markets, how to make your manuscript look professional, what to say in a stay-behind piece, and how to write a query letter that will get you noticed.

The goal is to write and place two articles a year. Don't be put off by this. You can always hire someone to help write the articles (a local writer, an English teacher, an assistant). You can even go a step further and use your own experience to qualify you to write a monthly magazine column. This is for the more adventurous, but the rewards are huge.

At this stage you'll have a publicity campaign proceeding at full speed.

Part Three is how to write a book. It requires a larger commitment of time. It's not necessary for you to move to this next level at all, if levels one and two are working to your satisfaction.

This module leverages everything you've learned and accomplished to this point. You'll learn how to turn your magazine articles into a full-blown book, and how to write that book in as little as ten days by following a master investment book plot. You'll learn how to write the perfect book proposal and how to promote your own book. And you'll learn how to find a publisher who may even pay you for your publicity program, and how to get the media to point to you as an expert in their news stories.

Imagine yourself at a presentation, handing out a book you have written about your area of expertise. This accomplishment, a published book, moves you into the status of an expert, recognized by your industry. Imagine how that feels and what a difference it makes to how the audience perceives you.

In Part Four, you'll learn how to make winning presentations using your reprints, and how to capitalize on your exposure in thousands of bookstores across the country. This is an exciting level that multiplies the original advantage of writing a book. Your book can even become the basis of a college course! The possibilities are endless. Where you take it and how far are for *you* to decide!

So, before you spend another dollar on advertising and publicity, or make your next cold call: Stop! Read this book. The path it maps for you can take you to unknown trade routes where fortunes await!

Part I
Building Your Publicity
Program

In this section, you'll learn:
• How to build your publicity program around your expertise;
• How to position yourself as a media source;
• The best ways to create a compelling message;
• How to communicate that message;
• How to become a problem solver for your clients;
• How to build a top-of-mind awareness system;
• How to create an endless stream of pre-qualified prospects;
• How to reinforce your relationships with existing clients; and
• How to build your image and credibility.

Publicity Building Blocks

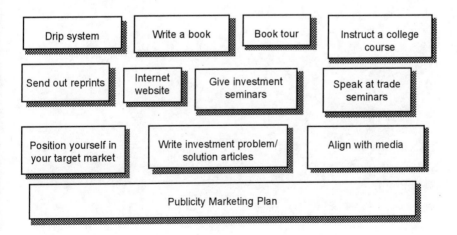

Chapter 1
The Media Opportunity

In this chapter, you will learn:
• How the media works
• Why the media absolutely needs your expertise
• What is credibility marketing and why it works
• Why you don't have a program

You already know this, but being an investor today is much more difficult than it was just 10 years ago. In today's financial marketplace, size plus complexities equals confusion. The Dow Jones industrial average has doubled in the past two and a half years, and 10,000 on the Dow seems less a fantasy every day. Money keeps flooding into the market; the New York Stock Exchange's daily trading volume is four times what it was in 1990. There are infinitely more choices and investments to sort through. Today, there are more mutual fund choices than stocks listed on the New York Stock Exchange; over 1,500 of them were created since 1995.

Technology has given ordinary people complex tools, without good advice on how to use them. Never have so many Americans experienced such control over their financial futures, yet felt such a need for help. Often the most conservative advice nestles right up against market predictions and stock touting, without investors having any way to evaluate their choices. Most people become investors without the wisdom of experience, but having to apply lessons learned from mistakes made along the way is a hard and discouraging road.

Now, more than ever, you have an opportunity to share your knowledge with prospects and clients through the media. The media are desperate for your help. Don't believe me? Let me quote what *Modern Maturity's* senior articles editor John Wood said in *Writer's Digest* (July

1998): "I'm desperate for writers who can handle financial topics for the lay person," he said. "We need financial advice for columns and features that aren't so technical as to be obscure." *Modern Maturity* happens to have the largest magazine circulation in the country, with over 30 *million* readers. Do I have your attention yet?

The print media desperately need your stories and articles to fill space. Editors don't get pages of market analysis every day as a lot of us do from our firms or compliance departments. If you have something to say, hungry readers are ready to consume your knowledge and know-how. The most desirable article in magazines today is the "how-to." Advice and service are the battle cries not just of the '90s but into the next century. Armed with knowledge of how the media work, you'll be powerful in getting your message out.

Another advantage of this approach is that you will *not* be seen as a salesperson. Although it's common knowledge that anyone who actively pursues customers is regarded as an intrusive salesperson, financial professionals continue to make initial contact either by phone or direct mail, when most people definitely prefer to get a referral from someone they trust at the time they need that service.

Credibility marketing can definitely help you rise above the competitive clutter. Every time your name is by-lined on an article, or you're mentioned in a magazine, it increases exponentially the number of times your name will come to mind when people think *investment advisor.* Prospects and clients will view you differently. You're the expert.

Colleges and universities actually apply a ranking system according to how many times each faculty member is published. You, too, can set yourself apart from competitors by writing and being profiled in magazine articles. The coverage gives you a higher profile. You feel better and more confident about yourself, and then it becomes easier to find other ways to make yourself even more visible.

This process should become an integral part of your marketing efforts. Instead of—or along with—business cards, send out a "calling card of success" piece, such as an article with your viewpoints that appeared in a prominent national trade magazine. Article reprints can be sent out to prospective clients or used in a presentation, giving you credibility that most advisors only dream about.

Though scores of financial experts crowd every aspect of the market today, most don't promote themselves. The same goes for accountants, lawyers, and others in service professions. Marketing experts consider that type of non-action to be career suicide.

In today's expensive, cluttered, media-filled world, shooting for free coverage makes especially good sense. Writing and placing an article or writing a book about your particular specialty allows you to target that small percentage of consumers who need your services. Once they read it, they will seek you out.

Many investment advisors spend their time picking stocks, researching investments, and waiting for the phone to ring with a new client on the other end. It rarely does. Marketing is necessary, and it's up to you. But if you think there are no alternatives to old-fashioned cold calling and direct marketing, you're wrong. The public relations process can turn cold calls into warm calls, even motivating pre-qualified prospects to contact you to sign up.

Writing has other benefits, too. It forces you to think logically and lay your thoughts out in a manner that the audience can follow. This book will enable you to compose your own marketing message in a way that will get through to your target audience and expand your opportunities for repeated media exposure. That message can be built into a powerful presentation, whether you use it one-on-one or with groups.

Throughout the book, you'll encounter examples of real investment advisors who have effectively used the methods I'll describe. These low cost, high impact strategies are powerful, and you can use them immediately. This book is designed to become an integral part of both your marketing plan and the public relations arm of your business. Keep it on your shelf and refer to it often. You'll find helpful, down-to-earth advice on each aspect of the process.

What keeps most financial advisors from initiating their own public relations programs? Russ Alan Prince asked a number of them.

The most common reason was that it was too difficult.[1] That was the overwhelming response of 81 percent of those queried. My mission over the next few hundred pages is to *kill* that reason.

Lack of time was the second excuse. But the program I describe is something that you can do in-house, in just a few hours each month. Besides, since the different techniques I show you can be integrated for use in all aspects of your marketing, including speaking and giving presentations, they will actually save you time.

---

[1] Russ Alan Prince, Karen Maru File, *Cultivating the Affluent and Building Your Business*, HNW Press, Fairfield, Ct 1997.

Figure 1-1 Common Reasons for Not Having a Public Relations Program

Reasons	Attorney	Accountant	Insurance Agent	Broker	Financial Planner	Total
Implementation is very difficult	70.2%	85.4%	89.4%	77.1%	87.1%	81.1%
PR programs are too expensive to implement	58.1%	74.4%	76.5%	62.9%	73.5%	68.3%
Lack of time	74.7%	76.7%	62.2%	23.5%	71.2%	59.0%
Material does not lend itself to a PR effort	28.7%	20.9%	10.6%	21.6%	1.1%	17.5%
Corporate restrictions (e.g., compliance)	4.2%	11.3%	25.3%	35.3%	2.3%	16.7%
Not an expert	0.3%	3.7%	9.7%	11.1%	0.8%	5.3%
Other	0.3%	1.0%	2.8%	4.1%	0.0%	1.8%

Source: Russ Alan Prince, *Cultivating the Affluent and Building Your Business*

It's also interesting to note that those queried believed that their material didn't lend itself to a public relations effort. I think they simply misuse it. This book will help you arrange your material in a compelling vision of success that you'll be glad to share with your clients.

It seems to me that most advisors have their priorities out of order. Get clear about your public relations goals. Decide what you want most: A campaign to enhance your career? to build an image with your clients? to attract new clients? to convert existing clients? Articulate your priorities in order.

Then: What target market are you hoping to reach? Where do you want to be recognized? Nationally, regionally, or locally? There's no sense in being in a national marketplace if your target market is local. One client of mine become nationally known in less than three years; think what you could do if your goals are only local. And finally, what medium will work best? Whatever medium you choose—radio, TV, newspapers, or magazines—this program will help you.

Figure 1-2 Advisors Increasingly See Value In Public Relations Program

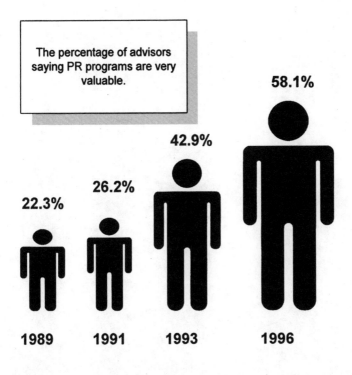

The percentage of advisors saying PR programs are very valuable.

58.1%

42.9%

26.2%

22.3%

1989 1991 1993 1996

Source: Prince & Associates, 1997 Independent RIA Survey

Chapter 2
How to Position
Yourself in the Right
Marketplace

Be Different

In this chapter, you will learn:
• How to differentiate yourself from the crowd
• Why you should write for a trade magazine
• How to write a simple position statement about your business
• Six key elements of positioning
• How to find out what your clients expect from you

I love to visit my favorite bookstore for ideas. On recent visits I've noticed that magazines about money dominated the entire top three shelves. Who would have thought twenty years ago that there would be magazines about mutual funds? *Money Magazine* is filled with fund ads promoting their high Morningstar ratings. I remember when Morningstar was just a star. Anyway, I was thumbing through one issue, trying to find the cover story that had caught my interest, but it was so buried in no-load mutual fund advertisements I couldn't find it. I put the magazine down and laughed.

Advertisers have the same problems you do—getting the attention of prospects. They have three seconds to grab attention before the reader turns the page. Three seconds. That's a lot of pressure. At least it takes ten seconds for a prospect to hang up on your cold call.

There's a better way to compete, a much more subtle one. One where track record or current performance is never mentioned, fees are not an issue, and credibility is instant. It's also a lot better than tossing money down the advertising drain. It's called the "You tell your story and get it in print" game. Jack Sulton from the Institute for PR Research and

15

Education told me a recent example. Crayola Company announced it was going to retire certain long-standing colors from its collection in an article written by the Crayola PR department. It said the reason was that these colors would entice small children to eat them. After the article ran in several national newspapers, a protest group formed, completely separate from anyone connected with Crayola. The upshot was an additional $6 million dollars in profits for Crayola that following quarter. Oh yeah, they kept the colors!

A few years ago a reporter did a story about the writers for *Money.* It turned out that only a few of them even owned a mutual fund. The editor had given such bad advice about buying gold funds, it made you feel embarrassed for him. Too bad there's no consumer group actively following up on the results of his stories.

But though the wealthy may glance through consumer magazines like *Money,* they actually read their own trade magazines, cover to cover, and keep them for reference. Not convinced? What do you read? I bet your trade magazine is sitting somewhere on your desk. Trade magazines are almost entirely written by experts in the field. Few professional writers waste their time writing for these media because they don't pay much.

Trade magazines have a different mission. They can get people who are experts to write for free for the magazine. Let's assume your target market is insurance brokers. These guys read *National Underwriter* or *Best's Review* before a letter from their mother. They want to know about the competition, new equipment, recent technology, who's selling what, and where the next industry convention will be. If the target audience was doctors or accountants, it's all the same. Each specialty has its own trade rags.

The positioning theory is based on you being positioned as an expert in the mind of your target market. It also means that if your prospects read a certain trade magazine, you'd better get into these magazines. No leap of faith here.

I've found I have little competition when I write for trade magazines. Why? It's dollars. Most professional writers can't afford to write for trade magazines. The only professional writers are usually the editor and a few staff writers. Who writes the articles? People like you and me who have raised their hands and said, "I'll write it."

Standing Out From the Crowd

What do most financial advisors, stockbrokers, and insurance agents do to position themselves in the marketplace? They most often take actions that position themselves against one another. That's a big mistake.

Positioning is considered by most to be an "against" strategy. But that's not going to get you above the clutter. Take advantage of what I've been sharing with you about positioning yourself as an expert. Don't fight the competition, differentiate yourself from it. Become a messenger of solutions to your market.

Let me tell you about a very successful seminar program we took on the road last year. I started the seminar off by asking each participant to tell me what he or she does for a living. Without fail, the introduction was the same: "Hi, I'm Bob Smith, I'm a financial advisor with Dean Witter."

Then we came to one guy with a very compelling answer. He said, "Hi, I'm Alex, I help Silicon Valley executives who have created wealth keep it by minimizing their taxes through effective investment management." I almost fell down. I could see everybody writing down what he'd just said, alongside his name. This man had positioned himself in the minds of everyone present. Number one, he worked for Silicon Valley executives; we all knew exactly what his target market was and where. Number two, he helped people who have created wealth. Anyone creating wealth and wanting to keep it is going to listen to this guy. Number three, he minimizes taxes (we can all relate to that one) through effective investment management.

Now picture yourself at the next Rotary Club meeting, and you're a guest. The group asks you, "What do you do?" You stand up and say, "I'm an investment advisor." Nobody is going to be very motivated to run over to you after the meeting and ask for advice. But think what might happen to a guy with an introduction like Alex. Well, you'd be surprised. A well-thought-out benefit statement positions you in two important ways: (1) It turns off the people you don't want to work with, and (2) it turns on the ones who do.

If you're a Silicon Valley executive who's busy creating wealth, and you really want to minimize your taxes, plus you're concerned about your investments, after his introduction you'll think, *Alex is a guy I really want to talk with*.

Do you have a positioning statement, or a verbal benefit statement? Grab some 3 by 5 cards. Let's work on that verbal benefit statement right now.

Six Key Elements of a Positioning Statement

Write a simple position statement about your business. In a good position statement, you effectively articulate your personal, product or market profile in order to create movement in the business relationship. The position statement should answer at least one, if not all three, of the following questions: What are your services and areas of expertise? What are your products? Who is your market?

A position statement must:
1. Present value in the eyes of the customer or prospect.
2. Briefly define your company.
3. Be easily understood.
4. Be believable, yet intriguing.
5. Differentiate your business from the competition.

The inability of most businesses to differentiate their product line or their personal expertise from that of their competitors generates frustration and ineffectiveness. The traditional sales approaches—advertising, direct mail, cold calling, and referral—fall short of meeting the sales and marketing challenges at hand.

Here are the six key elements of a good positioning statement or benefit statement.

1. It's simple and concise.
2. It relates to something already on the prospect's mind.
3. It solves a problem in the prospect's mind.
4. It gives a strong promise of benefit to your targeted prospect.
5. It differentiates you from the competition.
6. It is not just believable but also intriguing.

Number one is to keep it short and simple. Think of being at that Rotary meeting or at a cocktail party where somebody asks you, "What do you do?" You have to keep it short or you lose your listener.

Number two is to relate to something already on the prospect's mind. In that deep and narrow target market that you want to work in, what are the common goals? What are the common concerns?

Third, take a 3x5 card and write out three problems that are likely to be in your prospects' minds. Take out another card and write down solutions to those problems.

Fourth, think of Alex. Alex was promising to help create wealth by minimizing taxes through effective money management. There's a benefit for you.

I did a second seminar in Los Angeles at a major accounting firm, together with the head partner of the financial planning group. All the young CPAs started by introducing themselves, "Hi, I'm Joe Thomas. I'm a CPA." Typical. There are so many CPAs out there that the term is just more clutter. Then it was Jeff Saccacio's turn. He said, "I help wealthy people keep their wealth." Jeff knew exactly what he was doing.

You want to move away from positioning yourself against your peers or being perceived as yet another product pusher. You want to be known as someone who's a problem solver.

Solving your clients' problems will definitely set you apart from your competition. The narrower the niche, the easier to understand the unique needs. For instance, you might say, "I work with ocular surgeons, managing their wealth." It can be that simple.

Finally, create your elevator speech. The elevator speech is what you say when you have 30 seconds at a cocktail party or while riding in an elevator to tell others what you do. I position myself in the financial services industry by telling my audience: "I help people in the financial services industry write and get published."

One of my most successful clients, John Bowen, gave me the idea. He says "I help advisors build hugely successful asset management businesses." That's a turnkey statement. Whatever your point is, you should be able to say it within 30 seconds. And what you say should be compelling.

Scott Cook of Intuit is also a master at this. He began one of his presentations by asking, "How many of you balance your check books?" Nearly every hand went up. "And how many of you like taking the time to do it?" Nearly every hand went down. Then he said, "There are millions of people all around the world who don't like taking the time to balance their check books either. Intuit has a product to solve that problem." Nice. His elevator talk caught the attention of a lot of investors.

Shortcut

Another way to write a positioning statement is to borrow from successful ones. Go through business magazines, pull out advertisements, and make a collage. Separate the ads by service or product categories. Choose the ad copy that you feel has the best statement at the top in each category. Try adapting the concept, theme, or phrasing of the strongest ads to your own situation.

Ask yourself questions: What do I do? Did I tell them what I do? Do they know who my target market is? And what problems I can solve? You goal is to position yourself as an expert in the minds of your prospects.

An expert is defined by *The American Heritage Dictionary* as a person with a high degree of skill or knowledge of a certain subject. Hey, we can all qualify for that one! I read that as: an expert is a *problem solver with a high degree of skill or knowledge* of a certain subject *that is recognized in the world.*

Understand the nature of the business you are in and decide how to position yourself in your marketplace before you begin your marketing campaign. You want to create the perception by the public, and that includes people who work for you, that your company offers the best product or service in your field. But how can you establish that point? You must position yourself as a problem solver in the minds of your customers.

Figure 2-1 What is Expected of a Personal Financial Advisor

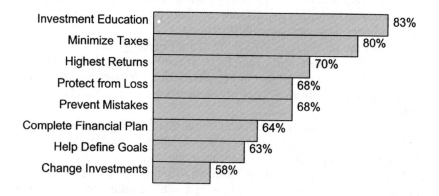

Base: 4,299

Percent of Respondents Who Expect Each Function
(Respondents gave multiple answers)

Source: 1996 DALBAR Series on Personal Financial Advice[2]

---

[2] The 1996 DALBAR Series survey asked 4,299 investors and potential investors what they expect from a personal financial advisor. The respondents all had minimum household incomes of $40,000. Financial advisors and institutions who focus their practice on fulfilling customer expectations for education and minimizing taxes are positioning themselves for success.

Look at Figure 2-1. What that chart tells me is potential investors want to be *educated.* Telling someone that you use a Pentium MMIII computer, for instance, says nothing useful to potential customers. Customers don't care what tools or computer software you use, just as they really don't care what system a bank uses to produce their monthly statements. All they're concerned about is that their bank statements are accurate and easy to understand. Everything else is irrelevant.

Another successful financial advisor, Lucinda Fairfield, has a great positioning statement. She tells prospects, "I help wealthy people keep their wealth." *That* certainly relates to something on the prospect's mind!

This isn't something canned. When Lucinda introduces herself in a seminar, she may vary the statement a bit. She says, *"The one thing I can't do is make you rich, but what I can do is keep you from being poor."*

If you can get these concepts down, it will make a big difference.

Your Positioning Statement (First Draft)

_____
_____
_____
_____
_____
_____
_____
_____
_____
_____
_____
_____
_____

Have you correctly positioned yourself? Ask yourself these questions.

1. Are you concentrating on a specific target market?
2. Can you solve problems within that specific target market?
3. Have you uncovered what your clients need, not just what they think they want?
4. Have you set up a process that challenges you to continually educate yourself?

5. Have you set up a process for educating your prospects in your management philosophy?
6. Are you building a library of proof statements and articles to back up your positioning statement.

Now try rephrasing your position statement.

Edited Positioning Statement

_____

_____

_____

_____

_____

_____

_____

_____

_____

_____

_____

_____

Congratulations! Now let's see how to use your positioning statement with the media.

Chapter 3
Add the Media to Your
Marketing Plan

In this chapter, you will learn:
• What to do when a reporter calls
• How to build a media packet
• How to build a relationship with the media
• How to distribute press releases
• How to write your own press release
• Where to find the media

Even when financial advisors get lucky and get quoted in a magazine, they often highlight the wrong message. No one but your mother cares if you made the "million dollar round table." You want to give the media something that educates them.

Aligning with the media is about being prepared. Always have a media kit on hand for clients or if someone from the media wants to interview you; it will keep you on track. Put in it background information, a bio, an article you've written, a photo, a fact sheet, a seminar schedule, a message.

If somebody is going to interview you locally, you want to have your message there. So include a copy of it. Or give them a copy of your book. It makes their job easier, and you become one of their resources.

They've got to fill the space between the advertisements, but they've got to fill the space with something that's worth reading. So they're looking for good stories. They're looking for the expertise that you've got. If you have something already prepared, you help these people out with a good story. The more of the media process you can control, the better. Being prepared helps you do that.

Any time a consumer magazine like *Money* or *Forbes* calls, watch out. This type of consumer magazines has a combative interview style and getting into them always involves a risk.

When someone hires me, the first question they usually ask is, "Can you get my story into *Forbes, Money,* or *Fortune.*" But that's not really where you want to be. Wouldn't you rather be seen in, say, *Ocular Surgery News*? That's a magazine read by 60,000 ocular surgeons who have an average net worth of over $2 million and an average annual income of $500,000. Not bad prospects. That's the kind of place you want your articles to be seen, articles that address the concerns and problems of the kinds of clients you want to have. Ocular surgeons want to read about the problems that *they* have.

Before you blindly fire off your next press release, though, you might want to find out what the recipients of all this paper have to say. To most editors this strategy is the same as direct mail or mass marketing, with the same result—they end up in the trash.

Los Angeles Times editor Michael Schrage has no mail overflow problem. "I don't have much of a mail problem because I throw it all out." Schrage also has no tolerance for phone pitches from people working off media lists. He feels it's unprofessional.

But don't toss out your press releases, at least not yet. Later, I'll show you how to write an effective problem/solution press release.

The way into the media: Spend time getting to know a small group of journalists. The editors I've spoken to say they are more likely to work with someone they know and trust.

Build a Media Packet

Take the time to prepare a media packet ahead of time—not just a press release. After you have made contact with a reporter, it serves as a convenient messenger that can tell the media assignment editor who you are and what you offer. It's your opportunity to go beyond a simple press release and create a concise and attractive package of information that represents and supports your point of view. A good media kit can therefore greatly improve your chances for placement in a publication—or even get you onto a local TV show.

Figure 3-1 The Media Packet

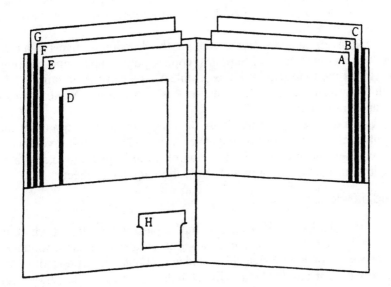

G: Background Information
F: Bio
E: Articles
D: Photo

H: Business Card

C: Fact Sheet
B: Seminar Schedule
A: Message

Be certain that your packet presents you in a way that will enhance your image and open opportunities. When you give editors and reporters an attractive media kit, you impress them with both the quality of your work and your skills at presentation. If you present detailed information in print and communicate with flair, you assure them that you will be able to communicate well with their audience.

The more you reveal in your packet about your credibility, the appropriateness of your presentation, and the appeal of your public persona, the more you assure reporters and editors that presenting you and your story will please their audiences. That's their agenda, and you need to convince them that you can help them with it.

Reporters are always harried by intense time pressures, so they especially appreciate thorough digests of information about special products or services so that they don't have to research facts or devise focus points. Include in your media kit a list of highlights that might interest the audience. You do them and yourself a favor by making it easier for them to present your topic.

One major consideration in making the decision to invest in a media packet, of course, is cost. Supplies, copies, photography, and printing—as well as the time required to assemble a kit—can run up quite a tab in both money and energy. But in media kits, less is more. Make them simple and to the point.

Use a double-pocket portfolio, the kind you can buy at any business supply store. They give you the space to include everything you need to sell yourself as an expert. If, for example, you're planning a seminar or event, your packet might include the following single sheets:

Media Release

Okay, it looks like a press release, but as part of a media kit which was hand-delivered, it takes on a new life. This single sheet may announce an event or say something significant and new about your product or service. Begin with a strong lead that will catch the attention of the editor or producer. Follow with an overview of your services or the event, and why the public needs to know about it.

If you're handling a complex seminar with many different speakers, send the schedule on a separate page.

Fact Sheet

This explains in more detail the significant points of the topic you are presenting to provide credibility. Highlight the aspects that set you apart from other, similar services.

Photograph

Use an 8-by-10-inch glossy black-and-white "head shot"—or a shot of yourself at a seminar event with lots of clients milling about, or in another work-related situation. Choose a professional photographer. Your publicity photo can be used by newspapers along with their story on your business. Only when a photograph is professional looking, in focus, and presents you in a good light is it worth a thousand words!

Previous Articles, if You Have Any

Include a recent article written by or about you—but not clippings from country club newsletters or church bulletins.

Biography

Fight the compelling urge to begin with "I was born in . . ." and then narrating all your life's events to the present. The bio should be a brisk one-page document that weaves facts about your education and background into a scenario centered on your current business.

Briefing or Background Sheet

Use this sheet to explain your product or service. Your goal is to send your media materials in a format that is not only seductive, alluring, and informational, but also easy to handle. This information differs from the Fact Sheet because in it you present your compelling message.

Ask someone to look at your kit and give you an honest opinion. Is it too much of a sales piece? Better to hear it from a friend than not hear from an editor. Sometimes your message can be contrary to the image you wish to convey. Find that out before an editor does. Get feedback.

Building Relationships With the Media

It's important to learn how to communicate with people in the media. Understand their difficulties, pressures and needs, and you will be the trusted expert they call first.

When a Reporter Calls

Ask the reason for their call. And ask if you can call back. (This gives you time to prepare your answers.) But get the reporter interested with a reason to continue the conversation. Make sure reporters know you've done your homework, and that you have something to offer of importance to their readers.

The media depend on advertising to pay for production and distribution. Advertisers only place ads in respected media within their selected markets. What makes a certain form of media "respected" is the quality of its stories. Quality stories depend on quality sources. The media is dependent on experts to provide insight, knowledge, and accuracy. Experts draw the interest of the audience, which draws in advertisers.

You, as the expert, are fundamental to media economics. It cannot happen without you. By providing data or research, you offer reporters credibility and accuracy.

Reporters are evaluated by the quality of their stories. The stories determine a reporter's reputation and space allocation. Reporters are not the experts—you are. They need someone like you to explain the details of a story to them. They are always looking for a fresh angle and for experts to help them create a great story under intense deadlines.

Remember this: You are the industry expert who gives substance and credibility to stories prepared by the media.

Figure 3-2 The Media Needs You: How the News Is Generated

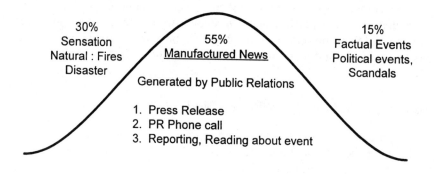

Notice the amount of manufactured news. Have you ever wondered where all these stories originate?

You follow and understand trends in order to serve your clients or customers. The media need your knowledge of your industry. The media will never, in a lifetime of reporting on your industry or profession, be able to match the level of knowledge you acquire by handling the simple investor problems you deal with every day. The questions clients frequently ask create patterns that can be transformed into dynamic story ideas.

The Interview

Whenever you're dealing with the media, remember that they have the capacity to influence and to produce an effect on others. Television, radio and print media are the great teachers of the day. A person contemplating participating in a media event or being interviewed should keep the idea of influence uppermost in mind.

Many people have frequent contact with all three segments of the media. Others have sporadic dealings with one or two. Some are national or regional, but most will be on a local level. But whatever level, from a business standpoint any dealings with the media are important. Never underestimate how much media exposure can benefit or harm you.

Let's say a reporter from a local newspaper or television contacts you for an interview. How do you prepare? You begin by remembering that the media look first at their own needs, and the biggest need is to provide stimulating television or controversial radio or an exciting article or feature. Journalism thrives on sensationalism. Don't assume you know up front who, what, when, where and why you're being contacted.

Many financial advisors are unwilling to adapt their style to fit the media's needs. As a result, they're ineffective in getting their message across. You want to have a specific goal in mind if you're approached for an interview, and that goal is to showcase yourself in the best light—because your ultimate goal is to have pre-qualified, and in this case pre-endorsed, prospects become clients.

Take a moment or two to go back over your positioning statement, what it is that you offer to your clients, and have ready two or three of the major problems that face today's investors, and your solutions. Have some charts or quotes—statements you can use to support the claims that you are going to make.

If you know your subject and have confidence, you can handle the most difficult questions any media contact may ask you. In fact, you may find the experience enjoyable and satisfying. Sometimes it's even exhilarating. And because of your knowledge, you have an unquestionable advantage over your interviewer. You're on your home turf and you know the topic better than a reporter. Here are some tips for an effective interview:

1. Be confident. You know that you have more knowledge of your subject than the journalist does. Knowing you're needed by the media will give you confidence when speaking to them.

2. Be straightforward, pleasant and cooperative. Look and sound professional.

3. Know what you want to get across in the interview. If you're being interviewed about the stock market, know your facts. Know the good news and positive aspects of your business.

4. Anticipate what might be asked. No reasonable question should come as a surprise. In fact, you'll probably be able to think of more questions than an interviewer can even ask. In television or radio, if the interviewer interrupts you, doesn't let you answer fully, or is rude, the audience will know and sympathize with you. Just by virtue of being interviewed, you develop instant credibility and importance.

5. Make positive points to your advantage regardless of the pattern of the questioning.

6. Never speak off the record.

7. Never say anything bad about another member of your industry or firm.

8. You have no obligation to keep the interview moving. That's up to the interviewer. You don't have to keep talking to fill dead air on a radio or television broadcast.

9. You have no obligation to tell something that is damaging to you or to reveal information that could be helpful to a competitor.

10. Have one or two memorable comments written down. These will cast you and your company in a good light.

These are my guidelines for interviews, but there's a lot more that can be said. John Wade in *Dealing Effectively With The Media* (Menlo Park, CA: Crisp Publications) has come up with another useful checklist.

1. Be yourself. Never lie. Don't try to develop a different persona during media interviews. Don't attempt to become what you think you should be. Rely on the strong points of your own character, personality, and experience for the raw material.

2. Stress the positive aspects of your company, your cause, or your ideas. Put out as much good news and helpful information as possible.

3. Think problem/solution. Think of the problems in the industry and the solutions that can resolve them.

4. Keep your message simple. Comments should be brief and to the point, easily understood by the general public that the media people are trying to reach. If you do this, your words are more likely to be remembered or written down and you'll have more time to make your points. Avoid long, rambling answers and comments.

5. Don't use jargon that's particular to your industry. If you must use these terms, simplify them or have definitions available.

6. It's always better to say something important more than once than to say several unimportant things.

7. Don't try to make too many complex points, especially in a television interview.

8. You are not in the interview to defend yourself, don't allow yourself to get into that position. Worse yet, don't assume it.

9. Don't be afraid to *not* answer a question, but do explain why you can't. Viewers and listeners and readers don't expect anyone to know everything. Showing your human side adds credibility. You can say something like, "I don't feel qualified to answer that" or "I'd like to leave that up to the experts" or "I don't have the complete data at this time."

10. Don't be sidetracked. Hold your ground. Don't allow the interviewer to take up valuable time on matters that are unrelated to your goals.

11. Never lose your temper or shout or yell. Always remain calm, but remain firm in your comments. You're in control.

12. Don't volunteer information or opinions that may damage you.

13. Refute incorrect statements immediately. Correct any statement that is inaccurate, especially if the statement weakens your position, whether it's made by another guest, an audience member, or a caller. If you do make a meaningful error, admit it. Apologize quickly and then move on.

14. Don't let the interviewer misinterpret your statements. Politely interrupt and set the interviewer straight as to your meaning.

15. Once you've fully answered a question or made a point, stop talking. Don't be pushed into adding something that's unnecessary.

16. Don't be suckered into hypothetical or leading questions. Just turn to the interviewer and say, "I wouldn't want to speculate on that."

17. Provide evidence that supports your points. Come prepared with charts or citations that you can use.

18. Develop anecdotes, quotes, or metaphors that can make your stories come alive. People love stories. Think of that great investment story that happened to one of your clients and how this particular solution solved a problem for him.

19. Have a ready supply of illustrations, charts, and, for TV, film clips or videotape for television producers. Call ahead to find out if they can be used.

20. For direct television interviews you shouldn't have notes on paper. You want to relax and not read prepared answers or statements. Relax and have fun with the interview.

21. Don't allow distractions such as crew conversations and background noise to throw you.

22. Always treat other guests with dignity and courtesy no matter how they behave.

23. It's always good to show genuine emotion. Get excited. Laugh, show surprise or indignation if there is something you don't agree with. But don't let emotions cause a flood of words. This can detract from your message or image.

24. Don't be afraid to repeat a key point, maybe in a slightly different way.

25. Always try to simplify your comments, and try to have the last word in a television or radio interview.

26. Don't allow the interview to end on a note negative to you or your interests.

27. Sit still and in place at the end of a television interview until you get the off-the-air sign. Don't make any additional comments.

28. After the interview, immediately thank the people involved—the interviewer, the production manager. Most of the time you'll be very motivated to do this; you'll probably be exhilarated. If it's a print interview, ask the writer if you may read the article before it's published. Politely make it clear that you're only checking for

accuracy in what was said or what you didn't say that you might like to add. Usually, the answer will be no, but it's worth asking.

It's also good public relations to let your clients know that you've been interviewed and when it's going to air or when they're going to read about it.

After the interview, get busy with your after-interview activities. Contact other print media or television or radio media for additional exposure. If you now have an audio or video tape, send it to another station or to a trade show convention.

Contact the writer who interviewed you and offer a photo. Have professional photos taken and always on hand in your media kit to send to them. Keep a journal of each media appearance and write down all the pertinent information—what worked and what didn't, what charts you took with you and how they worked, and how you used the interview for reprints. Also, keep track of the people who interviewed you. Sometimes they move up and in and out of other media outlets.

Next, let's look at how stories are generated and how to ensure yours gets into print.

Chapter 4
How to Get Your
Message Out Fast!

In this chapter, you will learn:
• What most do and how to do it correctly
• Press release checklist
• How to write a call-to-action
• How to grab an editor's attention

In the financial services industry there are two types of news. Hard news is a bank take over or the markets crashing in Japan or Russia. The majority of news, however, is soft news: someone is being promoted or receiving an award, a company has an anniversary or other milestone or relocates its offices. These stories are generated through press releases. The problem is that because everyone is competing for soft coverage, conventional press releases—the typical one or two pages of news or information about a company or one of its employees—don't work.

Following is a typical press release:

FOR IMMEDIATE RELEASE
Drew Washburn named Senior Vice President
of SCI Capital Management
in Cedar Rapids, Iowa.
Drew Washburn has been promoted to Senior Vice President of SCI Capital Management. In his new position he will be responsible for Midwest managed money operations as well as long range strategic planning and institutional accounts. Before being promoted to Senior Vice President, Mr. Washburn spent five years as a representative of Aegon, USA in Cedar Rapids. Mr. Washburn holds a BS degree. He currently resides in Cedar Rapids with his wife and two children.

Most publications receiving this release will simply ignore it. Possibly a Cedar Rapids newspaper might run a short feature article with a photo and the text of the release but generally the result will be minimal coverage, minimal improvement in visibility, zero leads, no inquiries, and no new business at all. In short, there is no return on the investment—on the time and the energy you spend—in preparing and distributing the release.

The sad news is that as many as 90 percent of the press releases distributed in the financial services community are like this example, generating a similar lack of interest, media coverage, or prospect interest. This type of release may be popular, but it's ineffective. The reason for this says Robert W. Bly in *Targeted Public Relations* (New York, Henry Holt & Co., Inc. Publisher) is that the topic is a non-event. People get hired or are promoted every day so there's nothing to differentiate the announcement from the other dozens or hundreds of press releases editors receive.

Second, Bly says, the topic is not meaningful to anyone but Mr. Washburn and his family. There is nothing of interest to the editor or the reader.

Third, the announcement doesn't really help promote SCI Capital Management or his money management services. There's no incentive for the reader to pay attention. There's no benefit in the information presented. Last, says Bly, there's no call to action, no response sought for the reader to do business with Mr. Washburn.

Nine out of ten press releases are structured like this. They include hiring, awards won, honors, corporate reorganizations, opening of new facilities, or company anniversary announcements. Publicists like them for two reasons: they can be prepared quickly, and they don't really take any thought. PR firms that are on a retainer have a contractual obligation to do something for you, and press releases and media kits seem to be the immediate focus of their attention. In terms of market response, it's the lowest use of energy.

A better alternative is what Bly calls the direct response press release. The direct response press release is built around a genuine story, a real event, important new information, or other real news. Using the following checklist, you can analyze a proposed subject or topic to see if it contains within it any of the themes most likely to have a strong media appeal.

Press Release Checklist:

News

Is there an aspect of what you're promoting that's new or improved? Has the product had any recent developments?

Interesting Information

Is there any unique knowledge you can share with the public? Have you collected unique statistics that the reader would be interested in? Have you just compiled information people might want to know about? Have you discovered anything unusual or out of the ordinary about your particular subject?

Useful Information

Are you an expert in the field? Does your service or product solve a problem? improve someone's life? accomplish a specific task? illuminate a need?

Controversy

Have you or your company taken a stand or opinion on a topic currently in the news? Is your topic controversial?

Timeliness

Is there a seasonal trend that ties in with your PR efforts? Is there a tie-in between your activity and a current condition in the economy?

All of these can help you come up with ideas for press releases. Remember, you want to build your story around what would be interesting to your prospects, not to you. Too many people write press releases from their own point of view.

Last, every press release should end with a call to action so the reader is encouraged to call, write, fax, or email to get a booklet, product sample, videotape, or some other item you can distribute free or at minimal cost. Traditional publicists occasionally will make free offers but they don't make a deliberate practice of making an offer most of the time. You should.

Another type of press release that will generate media coverage is a free booklet or report or tip sheet. It's the single most effective type of press release that I know. Give away something and you'll get attention.

Headline your press release "New Free Booklet" or "Tips to Success." Next, repeat some of the highlights in the booklet or report, so that an editor can possibly run your release as a mini-feature article on the topic.

It has been my experience that you can run the entire text of an article that you have written as a report. Why? Because people don't like to tear an article out of a magazine, but find booklets and reports more appropriate media. You can also put excerpts of your booklet into your press release. Your press release should be self-contained, like a mini-article, ending with the call to action: "For a free booklet, contact (*your name, company, address, and phone*)." Many editors will include the contact information; others will not, but you have no control over that. However, if you do not put in a call to action, you will never know.

There are two examples of press releases on the following pages that can serve as articles if editors choose.

There are two basic types of leads for press releases, news and feature. The news lead is the prototype, the traditional who, what, when, where, why, and how—right out of Journalism 101. The other is the feature lead, which I recommend. It's written as an attention-getting device, like the opening of a magazine feature article. The purpose is to grab the editor's attention. After the lead comes the body of the story. The last paragraph of your press release contains response information – who and how to contact—to get a free catalog or booklet. At the end of the story, simply type "END." Try to limit it to one page.

Write the problem, then solve the problem. Then, after you've written your press release, go back and tighten the writing. Less is more. Use subheadings in long stories. Consider adding a fact sheet. Make your release a mini-article. Don't send a cover letter. Let the release stand on its own. Send the release to all the publications that your target market reads.

Photos are not necessary, but can add interest to an article when it's published. Photos should be black and white, glossy, have sharp contrast, and measure at least 5 x 7 inches. Photo captions typed on separate paper should be taped on the back of the photo. Never type or write with ball point pen directly on the back of the photo.

FREE REPRINT. If you reprint an article, offer it as a free special report, or perhaps a tip sheet—anything that sounds better than "article reprint."

PRESS RELEASE
FOR IMMEDIATE RELEASE
Don't Sell That Fund!
Investment Workshop
Hilton Hotel Wednesday, July 22 from 7 - 8 p.m.
Call 805-640-0888 for more information.

The problem with experience is that you get the test before the lesson!
Did you ever sell a stock or mutual fund because you'd heard on the evening news that the market had dropped? You probably felt foolish two days later when the market reversed and went up a hundred points from where you sold. Your decision to sell was based on investment emotion. Don't feel badly. It's easy to understand why investors believe the market may fall off a cliff. Prices seem to be too high, don't they? You may feel that it's not wise to sit and watch the signs that a crash is coming and not rush to the phone and sell the first time the Dow drops 100 points or more.

But let's look behind that strategy. You sell during the downturn, trying to keep your hard-won gains by avoiding the drop, or thinking you can get back even if the market bottoms out, or buy back at a lower price. Or once you sell your current mutual fund you think you can get into a new advertised hot fund. If a global fund appears to be gaining favor over a domestic mutual fund, for example, you could switch into the global fund. Or you could switch from growth to value. Making a move would enable you to sell high and buy low or to make sure that you're in a fund that still is in favor. It sounds easy.

Well, it's not that easy. Not only would you have to be as swift and coordinated as a trader on Wall Street, academics tell us that historically it's impossible to time the stock market.

And you'd have another problem. That is to get back into the market at exactly the right time or else the move you made was in vain. Again, this involves timing the market - and timing has proven to be impossible.

Also, if you sold your stock or mutual fund, you'd have to pay a 20 percent capital gains on your profits. For example, if your fund was up 60 percent, you'd lose a full third of that gain to taxes. You'd also lose the compounding effect that drives your profits that can give it the advantage of long-term investing.

Investment academics say that investors should consider the following before bailing out of stock or mutual funds or trying to time the market or pick market declines. First, the general trend of the stock market for the last 60 years has been upward, and it's likely to continue to climb. According to the newest estimates by the Congressional Budget Office, we are looking at federal surpluses of $1.55 trillion over the next decade. Inflation and interest rates are at an all time low. These are all positive signs of an upward march of corporate earnings which fuel the stock market.

Don't be dismayed. You are going to see downturns. The downturns of the market will be normal, but a 200 point drop in the Dow at 9000 is less than 2 percent. Today, that kind of drop shouldn't scare anyone into selling their funds. Academics tell us the best strategy is to buy and hold a portfolio of different investment asset classes to protect against downturns. A steep market decline offers buying opportunities. When gas goes on sale, I don't stop driving my car, I fill my tank. When the market drops, think of it as a sale. If you've got the money you can take advantage of market dips to add to your holdings.

Larry Chambers will be hosting an evening workshop explaining the stock market at the Hilton Wednesday, July 22 from 7 - 8 p.m. Call for reservations. Meanwhile, check our website at www.makemoney.com or call 805-640-0888 for more information.
End

PRESS RELEASE
FOR IMMEDIATE RELEASE
NEW BOOK REVEALS STRATEGIES FOR INCREASING INVESTMENT RETURNS WHILE LOWERING RISK
Date: July 20,1998
McGraw Hill and Co. announced today the publication of a 300 page guidebook.
Author: Larry Chambers
Title: The First Time Investor

It has been eight years since *The First Time Investor* became a Fortune book club selection. Back then, everyone was selling gloom and doom. Authors were telling readers to hide in the hills, sell their stocks, and buy gold. Bad advice! Against the conventional wisdom of the time, the author forecasted that those economic developments would lead to a 5000 Dow and 5 percent interest rates. And five years later, in December 1995, as if on cue, the Dow passed the 5001 mark and the Fed discount rate was sitting at around 5.75 percent.

By the time you finish reading the first 60 pages of this book you'll know more than 90 percent of the Wall Street experts and 99 percent of veteran investors. You will gain a deeper understanding of how the markets work, and how to implement easy-to-follow investment strategies. The strategies allow the investor to increase returns while lowering risk by combining investments in asset classes and markets which move opposite each other.

Asset class investing is based on nearly 40 years of academic research of Markowitz' Modern Portfolio Theory, first pioneered in the early 1950s. In fact, the academics found that the two strategies Wall Street uses most, stock trading and market timing, historically add the least value over time. The results were the subject of three Nobel Prizes in Economics in 1990—which certainly qualifies as *outstanding.*

Being an investor today is much more difficult than it was just 10 years ago. The size and complexities of today's financial marketplace equal confusion. The Dow Jones industrial average has doubled in the past two and a half years, and 10,000 on the Dow seems less a fantasy every day. Money keeps flooding into the market and the New York Stock Exchange daily trading volume is four times that of 1990. There are infinitely more choices and investments to sort through and be concerned about. Today, there are more mutual fund choices than stocks listed on the New York Stock Exchange, over 1,500 of which were created in just the past three years.

Technology has given ordinary people complex tools, without good advice on how to use them. Never have so many Americans experienced such control over their financial futures, yet felt such a need for help. Often the most conservative advice nestles right up against market predictions and stock touting, without giving investors a way of evaluating their choices.

"In the last three years, everything has worked!" says Larry Chambers, the book's author. "If investment gurus were farmers, they would be taking credit for the sun shining on the crops. The problem is that most investment strategies can't duplicate the results they produce. If they could, you'd be able to duplicate what Peter Lynch did, or anybody else for that matter."

The book is not for a *dummy.* You will learn the strategies of how to build portfolios by combining investments with less volatility and have a greater compound rate of return. For a free copy of an investment policy statement, CONTACT Karen Johnson (805) 640-0888.
End

Follow up. Keep copies of press releases with a list of where you sent them and to whom. If you send out a hundred press releases to the top magazines, you may want to follow up with five or ten of the most important, the ones you really want to get in. First, telephone the editor within a week after the mailing. Introduce yourself and say that you sent a press release and you're wondering if they got it. The editor might say he doesn't remember because he gets so many press releases floating across his desk, but it opens up contact with him. If he asks what it was, you can explain it to him again over the phone. And send him another copy.

When you write a press release, think in terms of the readers and what your prospects want or desire. Think problem/solution.

People want to feel important and successful. They may want to save money, or make money, or have financial security, or improve their investing skills. Look for one small aspect of what's new about what you're promoting. Then use the word NEW in the headlines to make it a new story.

Press Release Checklist

One of the most efficient ways to achieve wide distribution of data is to follow these basic writing rules.

1. Incorporate all the facts that are relevant and accurate.
2. Answer the who, what, where, when, and why.
3. Pose a question to the industry that you're writing about and answer that question in your release.
4. Write clearly.
5. Check to be sure there are no spelling or other errors.
6. Double-space.
7. Print the release on only one side of the paper.
8. Include a dateline or release date and a contact person, the author if the release is based on a book.

So now you have your press release. Where do you go with it?

How To Distribute Press Releases

You can use a press release to support news conferences and media briefings. It's an excellent information piece to give to editors before or after an interview to give them supplementary information on your product or service. The release can be used with a cover letter to solicit an interview, or it can be adapted for general use.

Public relation wires services such as PR Newswire or Business Wire have the capacity for instant access to almost any point in the world. Their services include a range of distribution possibilities. Their charges, based on the selection you make, range from as low as $25 for a 400-word story submitted to all media in Nebraska or Wyoming to $500 to reach more than 2000 newspapers, wire services, magazines, and broadcast outlets across the United States. Distribution can be tailored to your market needs.

Here are seven of the public relations service orgnizations you can use to get your message across to the media:

1. PR Newswire is the leading media distribution service in the world. The first public relations wire service, it now has 21 bureaus throughout the country. PR Newswire's international service covers all of Europe. The company transmits some 100,000 news releases a year. It provides immediate and simultaneous 24-hour delivery.

   Besides carrying financial and business news for the majority of all companies listed on the New York Stock Exchange, PR Newswire also carries releases for thousands of public relations professionals.

   It also offers a research database. All the releases sent over any of its circuits are stored in major databases like Nexis, Dow Jones News Retrieval, Dialog Information Service, Knowledge Index, and Knight Brothers Press Line where editors and writers can access them as needed.

   PR Newswire, 810 7th Avenue, New York, NY 10019, Phone: (800) 832-5522 – good people.

2. Business Wire, based in San Francisco, has 16 regional offices. It delivers to over 2,500 news media and 500 investment firms. Business Wire also sends all its news releases to a number of electronic retrieval services, where they are available to more than a million subscribers worldwide.

   Business Wire's U.S. Super Pack costs $550 for a 400-word story that covers both East and West coasts. The U.S. Pack for $475 includes four regional circuits.

   Business Wire, 44 Montgomery St., 39th Floor, San Francisco, CA 94104, Phone: (415) 986-4422; outside California (800) 227-0845

3. Media Distribution Services (MDS) is the nation's largest public relations media, mailing, faxing, printing, and graphics services company.

   The cornerstone of MDS' operation is its Mediamatic System, a computerized data base that provides access to more than 150,000 reporters, editors, broadcasters, syndicated columnists, and security analysts in the United States and Canada. This information is updated daily.

   Media Distribution Services, 307 W. 36th Street, New York, NY 10018, Phone: (212) 279-4800

4. Burrelle's is the world's largest press clipping service and the publisher of numerous media directories. Its data base has the names and addresses of more than 160,000 editors, publishers, radio and television station managers, and advertising and circulation executives at over 40,000 newspapers, magazines, and radio and television stations.

   Burrelle's can provide you with printed pressure-sensitive labels to do mailings to your target markets.

   Burrelle's Media Labels, 75 E. Northfield Rd., Livingston, NJ 07039-9873, Phone: (800) 631-1160

5. Bacon's Mailing Services has a Media Bank that includes 175,000 editors at U.S. and Canadian trade and consumer magazines, every U.S. and Canadian daily newspaper, every U.S. weekly, every commercial U.S. television and cable station, and every U.S. radio station.

   The Bacon's Publicity Fax service offers a standard same-day service to broadcast media using your own letterhead.

   Bacon's Mailing Service, 332 S. Michigan Ave., Ste. 900, Chicago, IL 60604, Phone: (800) 621-0561, fax (312) 922-3127

6. North American Precis Syndicate (NAPS) of New York City is a feature release service that gets the publicity message to suburban and city newspapers and radio and television news and talk shows. Of the more than 10,000 newspapers in the United States, only 1,645 are dailies. Two out of three of the dailies have circulations of 25,000 or less.

   NAPS can send news releases as camera-ready art to 1,000 dailies and 2,800 weeklies for $2,900. The company estimates that one of its newspaper releases will result in between 100 and 400 placements. The client decides on a story and either writes it or sends the information to NAPS to rewrite in a way that will get the best media pickup. The release is then sent out camera-ready.

Radio Roundup is the name of the NAPS script service that goes to 3,000 radio station writers. The cost is $2,650; NAPS estimates an average of 200 to 300 placements.

NAPS, 201 East 42nd St., New York, NY 10017-5704, Phone: (212) 867-9000

7. Associated Release Service (ARS) began as a one-stop publicity production and distribution service for all media. Its camera-ready releases can be sent to 8,100 small daily and weekly newspapers. A minimum order costs $550. A one-column story 7½ inches deep sent to 1,000 newspapers costs $970 compared to a three-column story for $41,220.

The service has pinpointed 3,000 of the more than 8,000 radio stations in the country that frequently use scripts of recorded releases. A one-page script sent to 1,000 women's and drive-time program directors costs $865 compared to a three-page script sent to 3,000 radio stations for $2,605.

Associated Release Service, 2 North Canal, Chicago, IL 60606, Phone: (312) 726-8693

Date and keep a file copy of each press kit in a master file so you can review and update it regularly.

You must also be constantly updating your media lists and contact people. I've become friends with many editors at trade magazines and with television personalities I've worked with. When they move, I find out where they've gone. One woman I wrote articles for when she was the editor of a financial newsletter is currently a reporter at Forbes. We stayed friends, so I now have a contact at Forbes. You never know where people are going to go. Usually, it's up.

Just as you would compile an extensive list for cold calling target prospects, do the same for choosing editors and producers you'll be approaching. Each magazine, radio show, and newspaper will have specific formats and particular kinds of stories and issues it currently features.

Never send a letter to just "the editor." Call and find out the editor's name. Also, it's very important that your media audience match your product or service. If you're talking about seminars on financial planning, forget about a radio talk show on a station that caters to teens. Choose a news, talk or call-in show, or all news station that has a morning news format, and remember that most working people are not at home for midday news. Make sure you get a slot time when business people are likely to be listening.

Where to Find the Media

The following can help you reach the people who can create business-building positive news coverage. Call them and ask for a media kit.

Bradley Communications Corp., 800-784-4359
Publishers of *Radio - TV Interview Report* and other publicity resources.

Publicity Blitz Media Directory is on disk. Radio and TV Interview Report, Box 1206 Lansdowne, PA 19050, Phone: (800) 989-1400 ext. 411.

Bacon's Media Directories, 800-621-0561
Include most media outlets in the country. Available in libraries and on CD-ROM.

Burrelle's Media Directories, 800-631-1160
Individual directories for print, radio, television, and cable.

Hudson's Subscription Newsletter Directory, 800-572-3451
Sorts out the growing number of professional newsletters .

Who's Who in Association Management, 202-626-2723
Published by the American Society of Association Executives; industry or professional organizations listed by subject and region.

How To Get On Radio Talk Shows, 303-722-7200
Lists 700 radio talk show producers in need of expert guests for telephone interviews.

Now let's switch from getting in the media to how to use your placement reprints by building a top-of-mind awareness system.

Chapter 5
Building a Top-Of-Mind
Awareness System

In this chapter, you will learn:
• How to build an information library and what goes into it
• How to create a legal and compliance file
• How to align yourself with other experts in your field
• How to send out reprints

Today's affluent consumers want to initiate the contact. But if you can't call them, how do you get *them* to call you?

Become easy to be found. How? Set up a continuous drip system of magazine articles, books, or solutions to problems that interest your select groups. The top-of-mind awareness system is the distribution side of your marketing campaign. Here you are going to be sending out magazine reprints, handing them out to customers, and leaving them with prospects.

The articles could simply be relevant stories or ideas that will keep your name in their minds. Highlighting text that you particularly want clients or prospects to read and making notations in the margins conveys the impression that you were thinking of them. This habit requires little time or expense and has proven to yield an enormous payback.

You'll be surprised at the positive spin-offs from this simple action. When you send a highlighted article with a personal note, it says you are interested in your client's best interest—that translates into enormous goodwill and credibility.

Start building your publicity library by collecting every article you can find in every trade and business magazine and book that relates to unique financial problems that your clients have. Look for articles you can use to back up your claims. These proof statements can be anything from a book excerpt to a white paper to a magazine article. I used to store mine in a shoebox; now I have a shelf-lined wall filled with books and articles covering hundreds of financial topics. Materials that most of you toss away or forget about can be turned into magazine how-to articles, newspaper investment columns, and investment books. As in grandmother's stew, almost everything can be used. I use them not just to send to clients, but as you'll see, they're research for the articles and books I write.

Another advantage of writing magazine articles or books is tax deductions that you may not otherwise have had because, in fact, your new marketing venture can actually be a business.

Don't be afraid to piggyback on the coattails of experts in your field by telling their stories. Become their messenger: send clients and prospects articles that solve their problems, written by other experts with whom you are (or would like to be) aligned. While inexpensively adding value, you're keeping your name uppermost in your clients' minds by being interested in their problems.

Building a Strategy

Build the following strategy into your selling.

Keep on the Lookout for Good Articles

Read your target market's publications. You undoubtedly know about investments in general, but what are the specific concerns of your target market? Take time each month to skim them for articles you can clip. Consistently position yourself as an expert. People respond favorably to an informed professional offering solutions to real problems.

When I find a good article, I cut it out, add it to my library, then send copies with a brief note to clients I know will be interested in the topic. They soon get the message that I'm thinking of them and understand their concerns. I use a pre-printed pad with my name, address and phone number, and enough room to write a short handwritten note that reads that reads: "I thought you would find the enclosed article of interest."

Gather the Information Your Firms Send You

Organize them in manila folders; look for cross-connections. For instance, if you find an article on mutual funds that talks about college, put a second copy into your "college" folder.

Ultimately, this activity builds your expertise so you can work with your clients better. While the immediate purpose is send the articles out to prospects, you're also assembling them to use for articles, newsletters, and chapters of the book you will write.

Create a Legal and Compliance File

Type a client's or prospective client's name and company name on a manila file folder. At the top, in bold letters, type: ERISA Legal and Compliance file. Put reprints and related articles in this file along with your business card. Give this to your prospect or client after you've made your presentation, explaining that one of the ERISA requirements is on-going due diligence and review.

A compliance file is one thing most Department of Labor auditors would ask for. This very good PR for you provides a valuable service for your client.

Now, when I'm writing on any subject, besides using the Internet, I lay out articles and proof statements as reference material on a 14-foot-long table next to my computer desk. Let's say you're going to explain something about the efficient market theory. Find various proof statements from books that explain modern portfolio theory and from other academics who have written about the efficient market theory to support your explanation. This reference material can be footnoted in an article or chapter of a book as well as being used in the drip system.

Align With an Expert in Your Field

This could be an academic, professional, or top producer (if you could go on sale calls with him, you'll learn by osmosis).

Build an Information Library

The information library of articles you've already collected can be used for your drip system. Trade journals and newsletters have enormous credibility and prestige among affluent members of various industries. Request reprints of particularly good articles from the magazine, and add these to your library and your drip system.

You want the system to be as automatic as possible. To begin, all you need is a shelf with partitions or large envelopes labeled for each month. Place stamped, addressed envelopes in each compartment along with your reprint piece for the month. Date everything at the beginning of the month. At the end of the month, mail out all of the reprints for that month.

Figure 5-1 Shelf With Partitions

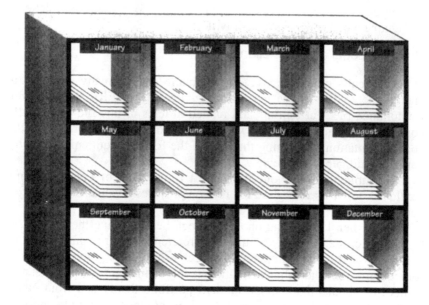

Do the same at the start of each new month for the rest of the year. As you acquire new prospects or clients, put them into the system right away. For example, someone who becomes a client in February would receive the monthly mailings for January as well as February, and thereafter would receive all regular monthly mailings.

To organize the mailings, at the beginning of the year, lay out twelve manila folders on a long table and name each with a month. As you find good articles, place them in the upcoming folder. Insert a list of names to receive the mailings.

Figure 5-2 Manila Folders, Low Tech Organization System

Mutual Fund Articles

Variable Annuity Stories

Investment Planning

Send out the reprints with cover letters relevant to your prospects and clients (some samples to follow on pages 52 and 53). As I said before, you'll be surprised at the positive spin-off from such a simple act. It translates into enormous goodwill and credibility.

Studies show the effectiveness of a phone call added to the process. So after you've sent the reprint, follow up with a phone call. When you say you were reading the latest issue of your client's industry trade magazine and found something that might be of interest, you'll be surprised by their response.

For years I spent time prospecting on the phone. I didn't understand that prospects saw me as a salesman; even when I introduced myself as a stockbroker, the response was often, "Click!!!"

Cover letter 1

To Professionals

Date
Name
Address
City

Dear

This letter is to make you aware that there are solutions available for the most talked-about problem facing [ocular surgeons] today: How you can preserve and maximize the wealth you've accumulated in your practice and in your retirement plan. At _____, we have focused our philosophies and strategies to help you do just that.

I invite you to call or visit my office to learn how I can help you implement these strategies. Also, return the enclosed response sheet for a free copy of my latest article from *Ocular Surgery News*.

Sincerely,
Larry Chambers

It wasn't until I started sending out reprints that my positioning changed. Prospects reacted differently to me; there were fewer hang-ups. My image *really* changed when my name started appearing on the magazine reprints; I was now thought of as a writer. Today in our culture, talkers are hawkers and writers are experts.

Become the Messenger

Does it work? Charles E. Merrill was a true messenger of change. Merrill's message was to sell investments to the country's growing middle class. He was the first to apply mass-marketing techniques to selling stocks and spent heavily on advertising and public relations. Sixty years ago he was out educating potential investors through lectures, seminars and an endless stream of newspaper and magazine articles. You may know him as the Merrill in—Merrill Lynch.

Cover letter 2

To Middle Market Companies

Date
Name
Address
City

Dear

This letter is to make you aware that there are solutions available for the most talked about problem facing [middle market companies] today: how to attract and retain top people.

Over the years, I've found that informed [your target position] are my best clients. I am writing to you because I believe, once you understand the benefits of _____ strategies, you won't be satisfied until we help you tailor these concepts for your company so the top people in your industry aren't going to the competition.

There's no hidden agenda. I'm inviting you to take advantage of our professional consulting services. If you decide to make an appointment, here's what will happen when you arrive at my office: I'll introduce you to the basics of our strategies. I'll start by explaining the fundamentals of [compensation packages].

Then you'll learn about [you fill in]. You'll also discover [you fill in], an institutional tactic for slashing your compensation costs.

I want this to be the best use of your time, and promise that it will be truly an educational experience. Please call my office at _____ to schedule an appointment. Also, return the enclosed response sheet for a free copy of my latest article _____.

Sincerely,
Larry Chambers

The good news is you don't have to be the author of the reprint; just its messenger. A published piece from a periodical that educates, informs, or solves a problem can be very effective in generating new business. It fits with the concept of positioning yourself as an expert in an industry. People respond favorably to an informed professional who is not a salesman pushing a firm or product but is offering a solution to a real problem.

Here is a sample letter requesting rights to reprint. Customize it for your needs, and print it out on your letterhead. Be sure to include the issue, page number, title of the article, and your purpose for the reprints. You may want to call in advance if you're unfamiliar with the publication's reprint policies and prices.

Request Letter Model

June 15, 1993

Miki Thompson
ABC Publications
200 Main Street
Anytown, USA 99999

Dear Ms. Thompson:

We would like permission to reprint an article that appeared in Investors Today in the June issue on page 33. The article was entitled "Saving Money is a Bargain."

We have enclosed a copy of the article for your reference. We plan to use the reprinted copies for promotional purposes.

Please sign below to confirm our permission to reprint this article, and return this letter to me in the envelope provided.

If you have any questions on this request, please contact me directly.

Thank you,
Larry Chambers
Enclosures

Daily Marketing Events

As your business grows and your expertise grows, you need to find ways to leverage your time. In addition to building your expertise, daily marketing events can get you in front of prospects. These steps have the highest probability of getting you seen and heard.

These are the events that the most successful have followed. As in becoming an expert, there are no short cuts. You don't like marketing or calling on people? Get over it. When you stop marketing your service it will be only a short time before you will be gone. Sorry.

Now for those who will do whatever it takes, follow this plan—or some plan, it doesn't matter whose. Market your product or service every day. It will get easier as you become more skillful.

1. The goal is to complete six marketing events every day.

2. Research the problems of your industry or target market.

3. Find someone in your area who is already recognized as an authority. Read articles they've written and start saving them.

4. When you find a relevant story in your target markets' trade magazines, contact the reprint department to request a copy.

5. Send reprints to your target market with a cover letter explaining, "Thought you might be interested in this article."

6. Follow up by contacting prospects by phone to see if they received the article.

7. Arrange at least two speaking engagements or seminars for local civic, social or fraternal organizations. If you are not a good speaker, learn to be one! (See the next chapter.)

Designate a time each week to work on this list. Make it the same day, the same time, with no interruptions, so that you complete your client-building tasks.

Next, we want to revisit the concept of credibility marketing and look closely at the five key strategies to building successful communication plans and why most advisors want the wrong type of marketing support.

Chapter 6
Credibility Marketing
Strategies

In this chapter, you will learn how to:
• Communicate cost-effectively
• Target profitable prospects
• Identify three niche opportunities
• Position yourself to attract qualified prospects by differentiating yourself
• Create a mindset about referrals

There are five key strategies in building a successful credibility marketing action plan.

Step 1: Communicate Your Benefits Cost-Effectively

You need to deliver the right message to the right prospect at the right time. The right message should touch upon a prospect's emotional as well as financial needs.

Select the right channel for communicating with prospects. There are three main channels: the relationship channel, the credibility channel, and the direct channel.

• Relationship marketing is one-on-one, usually through referral or a strategic alliance.

• Credibility marketing is establishing the prospect's concept of you through public relations.

• Direct marketing is achieved through direct response.

Most financial advisors realize that if they could be constantly in contact with qualified prospects, they'd be hugely successful, so they try to do this through mass marketing techniques. That's not effective.

In a survey of independent Registered Investment Advisors (RIAs) by Prince and Associates, financial advisors recognized the need for marketing support in their communications efforts.

Figure 6-1 Investment Advisors Want Marketing Support in All The Wrong Areas!

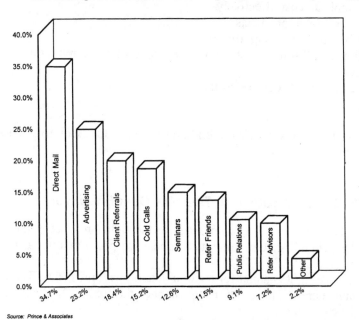

The Percentage of Investment Advisors Putting in Extensive Effort in the Wrong Areas!

Source: Prince & Associates

Investment Advisors Want Marketing Support

Source: Price & Associates. Reprinted with permission.

In Figure 6-1, investment advisors mostly want direct mail support. But look at Figure 6-2. The very same group gives direct mail the lowest marks.

Well over half of those surveyed wanted help in direct mail and advertising. Stop and think about this for a second. Wouldn't it be nice to have a direct mail piece that would bring in multi-million-dollar clients on a systematic basis?

On the other hand, if you were a multi-million-dollar prospect, how would you go about finding your financial advisor? Would it be through a direct mail piece that arrives one day in your mailbox? I don't think so. What about an ad in the local newspaper? No way. So why should you try to contact prospects the way you would never want to be contacted? It's a waste of time and money.

Figure 6-2 Independent Advisors Want Marketing Support

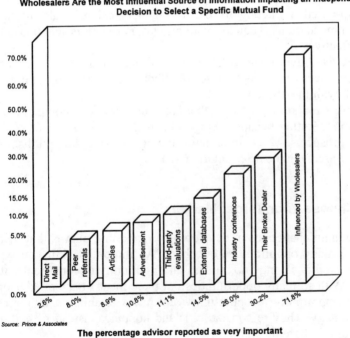

Wholesalers Are the Most Influential Source of Information Impacting an Independent RIA Decision to Select a Specific Mutual Fund

Source: Prince & Associates

The percentage advisor reported as very important

Source: Price & Associates. Reprinted with permission.

Look at Figure 6-2 above. In this chart direct mail has the least impact on your decision to select a mutual fund. Your clients are no different.

The conclusion of the Prince study is that RIAs are too dependent on marketing strategies that are comparatively indirect. Also compare Figure 6.2 to 6.1. Although 34.7 percent of RIAs want marketing support in direct mail, the same RIAs said their own decisions to choose a specific mutual fund were most influenced by wholesalers, not direct mail.

The wholesalers talked directly with the advisors. That creates a relationship. Relationship marketing is built around trust. It's the only way that makes sense.

Fight your instincts. Everyone wants to do direct marketing; it seems so effortless compared to face-to-face contact. When I started in the business as a broker, I did a tremendous amount of direct response, cold calling, mailings, etc. Today, I do no cold calling, mailing, or advertising. Direct mail and advertising can be effective for a firm with an established name that is already a major player, but it's not a good avenue for most individual financial advisors. Instead, concentrate on doing a good job at relationship-based marketing by cultivating personal referrals through client recommendations. Then use your articles, newsletters, and books to be more effective.

The fact is: Advertising, cold calling and mass mailings don't work with affluent investors. In fact, these are effective ways to make sure you won't work with the affluent.

Credibility marketing, on the other hand, does work. It complements relationship marketing because being published gives you instant credibility with prospects. Media interviews, public speaking, and publishing a newsletter are valuable. (See Figure 6-3.)

Step 2: Choose Your Target Markets

One of the main challenges in developing a marketing plan is that there are just too many opportunities out there. An important skill you will need to develop is saying "no" unless an opportunity is consistent with your plan. With so many opportunities out there most financial advisors jump from opportunity to opportunity and never establish a long-term business strategy. They're constantly island hopping, instead of getting the most out of where they are.

Narrow your focus. Work on establishing one marketing sphere and becoming known to one community of prospects. Specialize in a very specific target market. Targeting allows you to focus your resources only on activities that have the highest payoff. Once you've identified a market that you can service profitably, you can leverage your time more effectively. It will also be easy to get referrals because you will understand the deep, narrow issues that affect your target group. You will become known inside this community as "the expert" who really understands their particular issues. Working with only one target market will allow you to become extremely proficient in addressing that group's specific financial challenges.

Figure 6-3 Integrating Credibility Marketing and Publicity
Larry Chambers' 7 Steps to Building Credibility

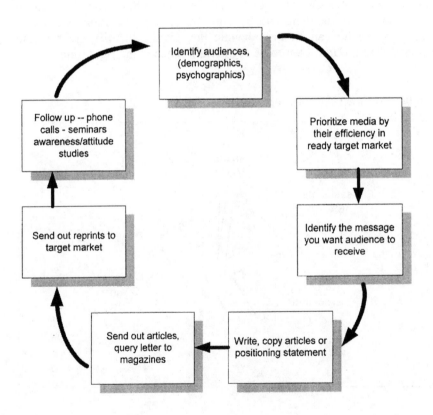

Suppose you decide to become the number one financial advisor in your major metropolitan area of a million people. How long would it take to accomplish that? And at what expense? Five years? A million dollars?

More likely, 20 years and many millions of dollars. You would need to effectively mass market. That requires a huge amount of capital and is not very effective. However, if you decide to become number one in a niche market of perhaps only a thousand people, you will quickly own that market. With very little effort, you can learn a group's unique needs and then help them meet those needs.

Your goal should be to penetrate one niche market accurately and quickly. You need to be there when major life events happen—once-in-a-lifetime events such as selling a business—to the people inhabiting that niche. By systematically getting deeply into your target market, you can identify important events unique to this market. While people in a group have similar needs, there will be slight differences. Position yourself as the person who can expertly handle the details. Identify areas where money is in motion. Plan to be at the right place at the right time.

Figure 6-4 Where's the Money?

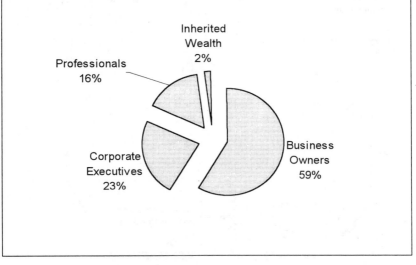

Step 3: Look for Niche Opportunities

A niche opportunity is uncovered by finding a market that's particularly suited to your talents, skills, and interests. All of us have unique talents.

We all have comparative advantages, skills, and interests in different areas. A high quality of life comes from working with a group of people you have an affinity with. Look at the market that you would *enjoy* being in. Make sure, though, that this market has a high concentration of qualified prospects with money in motion or pooled capital available. In identifying a niche, you want to make sure prospects have a shared perception and similar problems, values, and desires for solutions.

Niche opportunities exist everywhere but you have to do your research. There are two types of research: one, internal, where you query your existing client base; and two, external, where you go outside your existing client base to gather information. We have found it extremely effective to interview key clients, centers of influence, local experts, and industry leaders to identify new niches. In the interview process, you will discover many opportunities that you're not yet aware of.

It's okay to jump around at first, looking at all the opportunities out there, but then focus on no more than three niches that you might fully develop. The most successful of these three is likely to end up, long-term, as your only niche.

Start to gain specialized knowledge to work effectively in the niches you have identified. Find out what the inhabitants of a targeted niche are looking for. In interviewing people who aren't yet your clients and finding out what they're looking for in a financial advisor - not trying to sell yourself, just gathering information - people will open up because they won't feel you have a hidden sales agenda that they need to protect themselves from. Explain that you simply want to better understand the financial challenges they face so you can better serve their market. More often than not, you will end up with a client, or at least a referral.

How do You Get Started?

Set out on your research program systematically.

- Identify your favorite clients.
- Develop a set of questions that will both reveal opportunities and lead to referrals. Focus on what you really want to find out.
  1. What do your clients like about working with you?
  2. Are there any problems that they have that you're currently not solving?
  3. What do they think about your existing communications process?
  4. What do they read for their own business insights?

5. How did they find out about you?
6. Are they happy with the job you're doing?
7. Do they have any marketing ideas?

Figure 6-5 Events That Build Your Credibility

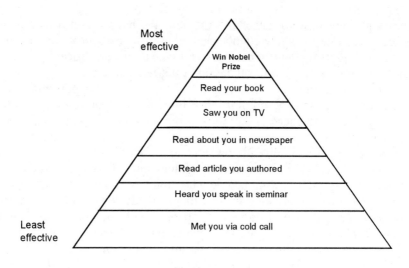

Interview centers of influence in the niche you want to work with, such as CPAs, attorneys, and other professionals who work within that target market. It's easy to get together with anyone in the world; you're simply two phone calls apart: First, a call to set the stage, such as a request for an introduction by someone you both know; and the second, a call to the person directly. When you make those calls, you need to have a deliverable win-win attitude about how you're going to help that person achieve a higher level of success.

In doing research, you want to identify people who need your services. Identify individual prospects and centers of influence. Uncover their values, problems, challenges, and opportunities. Begin building strategic alliances. Commit these steps to writing in your marketing plan.

```
Date _____        Client _____
Interview _____
         _____

Outcome _____
        _____
```

Step 4: Position Yourself as an Expert to Attract Qualified Prospects

Positioning is the art of controlling the perceptions of your clients and prospects.

The goal is to be perceived as different from and better than your competition. Your main challenge is beating your number one competition - the brokerage industry. Fortunately, 53 percent of affluent investors don't trust traditional brokers, so begin through marketing and sales to immediately differentiate yourself from the brokerage industry. Then deliver such high level experiences that your clients are dramatically impressed. (If you're a broker, differentiate yourself by a specialty.)

If you're perceived as a specialist to a particular niche community, you've got a huge advantage. For example, a woman going through perhaps the most traumatic experience of her life, a divorce, has major financial decisions to make. She can work with a general practitioner or she can work with a known specialist in the community who is working with people getting divorced. You've got it beat, hands down, if you're that expert.

Many affluent people view financial specialists as merely product pushers. You want to be perceived, in contrast, as having no bias in terms of particular products. Become known as a person of expertise who enjoys meeting real-world financial challenges. That's your ideal position. It's a powerful one.

In *Cultivating the Affluent*, HNW Press, Russ Allen Prince and Karen Maru File report on a survey of affluent investors to find what they considered to be the most important services provided by a discretional money manager. Number one by far, at 56.7 percent, was asset allocation; the affluent expect good investment advice. Second was financial and estate planning. Next was tax planning. Offer services that the affluent consider important, then add the competitive advantage of understanding your targeted market's specific needs, and you will have positioned yourself as uniquely qualified to assist the affluent.

Capitalize on trends; the asset management business is a trend that is growing dramatically, so go for it.

Develop a unique selling position of benefits that you uniquely offer. Create a strong positioning theme that turns on qualified prospects but turns off people who don't qualify.

State a strong promise of benefit. A good verbal benefit statement can become the subtitle of your business. For example, if you specialize in working with executives, you might state, "I help executives make work optional."

Return to page 22 and write your edited position statement here.

Your Edited Positioning Statement

_____

_____

_____

_____

_____

_____

Make your collateral material consistent with your positioning. The first thing most financial advisors want to do is print up a glossy corporate brochure with matching everything, as if that's the magic silver bullet. One of my clients has a $2 billion investment management advisory business and doesn't have a formal corporate brochure. In fact, these people never mail out any marketing or sales material. Anything that's glossy and looks like mass marketing is sure to turn off the affluent prospect. They meet prospects face-to-face so that they can better understand their issues. Then, they can decide whether the prospect is in fact a good candidate for their services and how best to present themselves.

There are a million different ways to present your services to an individual prospect, but usually only one or two are effective. Customize everything to the individual client; that's what the affluent want, so give it to them.

Step 5: Have a Mindset About Asking for Referrals

The advantages of a referral are obvious. Your credibility is pre-endorsed, the closing ratio is higher, initial transactions are larger, and the sales cycle is shorter. Referrals give you a considerable head start building trust with likely new clients.

When asked why clients wouldn't recommend their financial advisors, the dominant reason clients gave was "Lack of responsiveness to requests." "When a client asks for something it takes too long to get it." "The advisor can't be easily reached."

Most advisors don't even get as far as asking for referrals from their clients. But in a *Success Profile* study[3] of 600 high-net-worth clients, when they were asked, "Would you be comfortable referring your advisor to others?" 80 percent said they would if asked.

That's a huge missed opportunity. Here are some of the reasons why advisors don't ask: They feel uncomfortable; they feel they haven't earned the right to ask; they fear they'll alienate clients; they're concerned they will not appear successful; it's embarrassing; they feel clients should offer and not be asked.

Developing your business through referrals, however, lets you choose who your prospects and new clients will be. The time and resources you once used to court prospects virtually blindfolded can now be much more productively invested in building pre-endorsed referral relationships. Here's how.

Ask yourself, who now buys your program? Who benefits most from what you offer? What kinds of people typically select you over another financial advisor? Why do they do business with you? *Who do you as an advisor mesh best with?* The more specific the description of your ideal client, the better you can hone in on the best referral sources. Identify your best referral sources, those who have influence in your target market.

---

3 *Success Profiles*, "1998 Benchmarking analysis of customer-driven focus assessment." Referrals: *The 100% Solution*, "Tom Olivo Success Profiles and Gaylene Pringle Financial Planning," Oct., 1998.

Figure 6-6 How Do You Find Prospects?

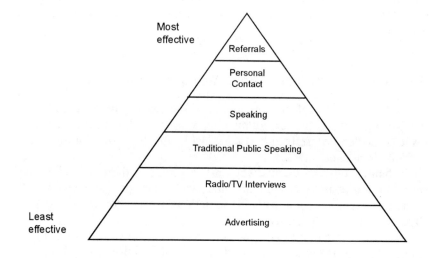

Earn the Referral

Have a sincere interest in your clients. Develop strong relationships so that each referral source is more than willing to refer you to others. Before asking for help, focus on giving. When your clients need help, you want them to think of you first. When you're highly responsive, client retention goes up. Then when you want some help, they're more than happy to help you because you've done so much for them.

Less is More

Focus on your relationship with the fewest number of people who can refer you to the greatest number of ideal prospects. You want to work smart, not hard.

Educate Your Key Clients

Educate your key clients about the type of client you prefer, so they're able to pre-qualify their referrals. People will not refer business to you until they fully understand what you do, so tell your clients exactly what you do best and how. Share your goals with them. Take them to lunch. Make sure to give your clients your marketing brochures and other materials. Develop a single sheet that describes your ideal client and what you can do for him or her.

People remember stories, not facts. One of the easiest ways to educate people is through a compelling client benefit story. If you've done at least one great thing for a client, you've got your own client benefit story. Remember the old sales adage: Facts tell, stories sell. Spread good news about what you do at every opportunity.

Make Referral Requests the Secondary Reason for a Call

It's important to ask for referrals regularly and often. If you don't ask, you may not receive. However, making a referral request should rarely be the primary reason for contacting someone. Call people with new information that is relevant to them, call to ask an opinion, or call to give someone a referral. Again, sincerity is the key to successful referrals.

The most common way to ask, and the way most of us have been trained, is the worst way. We may say, "I earn my money in two ways: I earn it first of all by doing a great job for you, and second, through the referrals that you deliver to me." I consider this one of the worst scripts out there. It's canned, it's cheesy, and it makes clients feel obligated.

First of all, don't use the word *referral*! Ask, "Do you know anyone else who might benefit from my services? Or try something like this:

"Hi Bob, this is Tom. How are you doing? I'm in the process of planning my business strategy for the next year. My goal is to grow my business by 20 percent and I need your advice." Bob says, "Sure, if I can help, I'd be glad to." Tom replies, "Can you sit down with me for 30 minutes? I want to discuss just who my ideal prospects are with you and see if you know anyone who fits the description. If you'd rather not, I understand." Always give people an easy out. If you have a strong relationship, even if you fumble and bumble with your words, on the other end is somebody who's capable and willing to help you.

Propose holding the meeting in your source's office, because that's where phone numbers and information are, so this doesn't turn into a two-step process.

Help your source out with some thought stimulators. You might say, "Bob, who do you know who is really successful and might be spending too much time managing his or her stock portfolio?" Your referral source will feel much more comfortable referring somebody to you who he knows has a problem you might be able to solve.

If you just say, "Who do you know who is a CEO?" you might get the answer, "My friend is a CEO." "Great. Could you introduce me to him?" "Well, let me see if he's interested. I'm not really sure, he's a really busy guy." That's the typical and understandable response. But if you say instead, "Who do you know who's a CEO who's mentioned that he's really frustrated with a certain business or investment problem?" the response may be different. Your referral source is then helping his associate or friend out by giving you the referral. If you say, "That's something I could really help him out with," the bird is almost in your hand. Now your source is more comfortable because it's a potential win for everybody concerned. When you call the friend or associate, you can introduce yourself with, "Hi, Joe. I was talking to our mutual friend, Bob, and he shared your problem with me. He thought I might be able to help you out."

As a result of good thought stimulators, you'll get a few names. Let your source prioritize the list. Ask your source who you should call first and why. Discuss just how you're going to approach your prospects. Your referral source might say, "You know, Tom, don't say that because it touches one of his hot buttons." Now your source has become your coach and you're in this together.

Tell your source, "I'll give this person a call within a week and I'll get back to you." Make sure you follow up and communicate the outcome to your source.

Respond to Referrals Fast

Almost everyone I know has to manage multiple priorities. In managing your own, there is one priority that yields significant results. Respond to anyone who contacts you as a result of a referral from another business contact, and do it quickly. Keeping this a top priority on your "to do" list keeps the referral calls coming. Ultimately, it also saves you time. Even if you know the person contacted you because they were trying to gain your business, respond quickly.

Professionalism is a trait everyone appreciates. Treat all referrals professionally and they may ultimately become yet another referral source!

Approaching the Person You've Been Referred to

When you make that referral call, leverage your source. State the reason your client thought it was a good idea for you to make the call. It will go something like this: "Hi Carol, this is Tom Olivo with Olivo Financial Advisors. I was speaking with a mutual friend of ours, Bob. In discussing what I'm doing for clients, he mentioned that you spend a large amount of time monitoring your company's retirement plan. He thought I could help. He asked me to give you a call and I promised that I would. I just want to know if you'd be interested in sharing the problems you're facing to see if there might be a fit. If not with me, chances are I know of somebody who can help you." Again, always give the person an out.

The underlying theme of the referral process should be to make it easy for clients to refer qualified people to you. Done the right way, it's a seamless process, natural and genuine.

Promptly Acknowledge Referral Sources in Writing

If someone contacts you as a result of a referral, be sure to write promptly to thank the referral source. Written acknowledgments make you indelible in others' minds. There is power in the written word. (In the same mode, always send a thank you note to an editor if your article appears in their magazine.)

People often respond more favorably to written correspondence. Most people remember what they see more easily than what they hear and many people keep the correspondence they receive. Sending a note causes people to remember you. This results in you receiving more referrals from that person.

Other Ideas

Communicate Often

Professional advertisers agree that consistency is a crucial element of a successful ad campaign. It works with informal marketing, too. Communicate often. Be consistent. "One shot" communication will limit your potential to hit anything.

Go the Extra Mile...

In the referral game, the ante for playing is meeting people's expectations of you. To win the game, you must exceed those expectations. People cannot help talking about you when you do more than expected. Give clients service beyond their expectations and you will enjoy continuous referrals.

Return Favors

When people do favors for you, they don't necessarily expect that you'll return them, but they appreciate it when you do! Two good things typically happen as a result of a returned favor: people want to do more favors for you, and they are more likely to refer you when the opportunity presents itself.

Always Come Through

Reliability is a trait that is usually recognized. Unfortunately, being unreliable is equally recognizable. Behave as if your words upon leaving your lips are etched in stone. Give referral sources a reason to be confident in you and the referrals will keep coming.

Let People Know How You've Gone the Extra Mile

Unfortunately, superb efforts don't always garner attention. You can "outservice" your competition, but if your clients do not know it, you are missing key opportunities. Always let people know when you go the extra mile; it will help you retain existing clients and ensure they enthusiastically refer you to others.

Sincerity is Essential

Reflecting on his success, the owner of a multi-million-dollar consulting firm said, "I have a sincere interest in people. I believe that's the primary reason our firm has grown." He went on to say that the more interested he behaved when meeting people, the more interesting they became.

The key word here is "sincerity." He was genuine. He truly wanted to know about the people he met. Knowing that, do you find it surprising that 100 percent of his firm's business was based on referrals?

Avoid "techniques" and focus on the person. Ask yourself, "Do I know how long this person has been in this industry?" "Do I know what motivated this person to join it?" "Does this person have a spouse… children?" If you don't know, ask. Get to know people as people and their business will follow.

Speak With Others' Interests in Mind

The famous motivational speaker Zig Ziglar says, "You can get everything in life you want if you just help enough other people get what they want." A person looking to gain more referrals should call it "speaking with others' interests in mind." If you think more about others, they will think more of you. Constantly focus on others' wants or needs and you will ultimately get what you want, more referrals.

Always Follow Up

Following up with your business contacts usually requires less than an hour a week. A brief phone call or note is all it takes to update your business contacts about the results of the referral or discover what happened with referrals you gave them. Following up is a courteous action that inevitably makes people feel good about referring again because you let them know you took action as a result of their referral. The return on this small investment of your time can be many more referrals.

Reciprocate

When you receive, give. It's a fairly simple, even obvious, principle, but executing it can be the bottleneck. Don't let your busy schedule take your mind off what is important. Remind yourself of those who have helped you. If you received a referral, give a referral. This encourages others to refer you even more.

Listen More Than You Speak

We all have two ears and one mouth—2:1. This is the ratio of how much we should listen versus how much we should speak. No great ideas ever entered the mind through an open mouth. People appreciate being heard and understood. The value of listening is evident to many sales people; however, after an objective evaluation, many are surprised to discover they do just the opposite. Many people who assume they are good listeners don't realize they need improvement until a problem occurs.

Have you evaluated your listening skills lately? When speaking to someone do you *truly* listen? Do you think about what you're hearing? Take notes? Ask questions? Repeat back what you think you heard? Continual refinement of your listening skills enables you to learn about the people who will inevitably like you, remember you, and want to refer you to others.

Separate Yourself From Competition

If you don't have a competitive advantage, don't compete. If you have a competitive advantage, tell everyone! What does your product or service do for your clients that separates you from competitors? Make certain you focus on the benefits of your products or services (how can you save your clients time, money, or aggravation?). People need to understand what makes your product or service different and better so they can enthusiastically refer you to others.

Appear Interested, But Not Desperate

Always be interested in obtaining new business, even excited, but don't act as if you really need the business. What kind of behavior makes you appear in need? Self-deprecating comments about yourself or your business are red flags. How would you feel if you heard the following comments from someone:

"You'll be our first new client in a month of Sundays."
"Our calendar is wide open."
"We need the business."
"Getting to it right away is no problem because things are slow."

Comments like these make people ask, "Why aren't they busy?" If you act desperate for business, people will assume there are reasons for it, like poor service or inappropriate pricing. This image does not win referrals.

Send Your Contacts Information That is Useful to Them

The president of an extremely successful money management firm (85 percent of the firm's new business is from referrals) uses what he calls his "wave theory of marketing." He periodically sends his database of contact information he feels would be useful to them. It's not an advertisement or solicitation, simply useful information. The net result is the referrals come in "waves"! This is like the drip system I described earlier. Send your contacts useful information, and you'll increase your referral business.

Call People Before They Call You

"Thanks for calling; I was just thinking of you," are words you should hear often from quality referral sources. Calling your key referral sources at regular intervals will keep your name at the tip of their tongues, not the back of their minds.

Don't hang out with the invisible. It's time to move up the ladder by writing your own investment article, and becoming a local celebrity.

Figure 6-7 Visibility Reach Pyramid

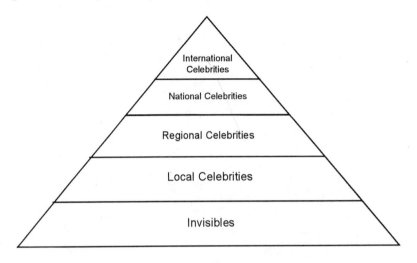

The bottom rung on this chart is unfortunately where you will find most professionals in any field.

Don't hang out with the invisible. It's time to move up the ladder by writing your own investment article, and becoming a local celebrity. How do you become a local celebrity? You'll find out in Part II.

Part II
Writing A Publishable Article

In this section, you will be guided to actually write your own article and learn how to get it published. You will also learn what to write about, how to rewrite the same article for diverse markets, how to prepare a profes-sional-looking manuscript, how to write a stay-behind piece, and how to write a query letter to an editor. We also give you examples of articles and template letters.

Chapter 7
How to Write the
Problem/Solution
Magazine Article

In this chapter, you will learn:
• How to reach thousands of pre-qualified prospects
• What you should write about
• How to structure an article
• The six steps to writing problem/solution articles

Since the beginning of mankind, knowledge has been passed on through telling stories. The storyteller was the village chief, the teacher, the priest, or the elder, and the story usually contained a message about how to solve a problem. Story telling predates writing by tens of thousands of years. The good news is, if you can tell a story, you can write an article. Writing is simply frozen speech.

When people feel good about what they do and who they work for, they are much more productive than when they are merely motivated by monetary rewards. Have you noticed a sense of pride in you and your people whenever an article is published about you or your company, organization, or industry? That same feeling of pride translates into a respect that clients and prospects have for you when they read an article you've authored. Winners like to associate with winners. Your prospects and clients are winners, and they'll want to associate with you.

You may think that writing will take away crucial time from your money-earning efforts. Keep in mind, however, that getting published is a subtle way of prospecting—one where track record or current performance is never mentioned, fees are not an issue, and credibility is instant. An article published in a magazine can be many times more effective than client referrals in generating new business. A referral will introduce you to one or two people, a magazine can reach thousands of pre-qualified prospects. This process becomes geometric if your article is published in a medium that influences a high concentration of opinion leaders—such as lawyers, CPAs, doctors, or advisors.

You could hire a public relations professional, an English teacher, a journalist, a faculty member at a local college, or a screenwriter trying to make an extra buck to help facilitate the writing process. But I think you'll find the process so simple, and so helpful to you in clarifying your own methods or viewpoint that it is actually enjoyable.

What Should You Write About?

Write about what you know. Write about how your product or service can enhance your prospects' knowledge and expertise. Write articles that educate, solve a problem, or set out a successful situation. When you can solve a problem or present meaningful information in a new light, you are regarded with high esteem. Highly educated professionals are always looking for timely information that will increase their wealth. Design articles that explain the increasing complexities of investment products in order to educate the investing public.

Make sure your topic isn't too complicated. If you try to cram too much information into an article, the reader will be confused, so the editor will probably turn it down. This can happen when you're trying to address one article to too many different groups. Begin with one idea addressed to one specific market segment. That will keep your message simple and make your article more effective.

Write your articles as though you were telling a friend about your product or service. Jot down your thoughts on what points you would emphasize to get the friend to order your product or become a client. Then organize the points logically, and you have an outline for an article.

Narrow your focus; write only about subjects you feel will interest your target market. Keep in mind that articles about money are a surefire attention grabber. Almost everyone is interested in money. People with money want to know how to keep it, and people without it want to know how to get it. Your article will establish you as an authority in the minds of the readers.

What's Your Point?

Find what professional writers call a *slant*. A slant is a direction, a point of view. It's a way of cutting a big topic such as the management of retirement assets down to a size that can be explored in detail in 2,000 words.

The stronger the slant, the easier the writing. It defines your topic and helps you organize your thoughts. If your general interest is money management (a broad topic), you'll need to narrow it down to match your audience. You might slant your article to the 401(k) market: "Managing Your 401(k) Assets," or "How to Lower Risk and Increase Returns inside a Retirement Plan."

One slant you can use over and over for years is the transfer of wealth. To borrow some statistics from a book by my mentor, Tom Stanley, *The Millionaire Next Door*, in the ten years from 1996 until 2005, the total net worth of American households will grow to $27.7 trillion, more than 20 percent higher than in 1996. Look for statistics like this to add credibility to your story.

Other Examples

From 1996 through the year 2005, it's estimated that 692,493 people will die and leave estates worth a million dollars or more. This translates into $2.1 trillion dollars. About one-third of that amount will go to their spouses, and almost as much will go to the children—who will eventually probably get what was left to the spouses as well. An article entitled "What Do You Do After the Parents Are Gone," or "How to Manage the Transfer of Wealth," will be timely for the foreseeable future.

An article on minimizing estate taxes or on how parents can reduce the size of their estate for tax purposes by transferring much of their wealth to offspring while they're still alive would also be appropriate. Today's grandparents will give their children and grandchildren more than a trillion dollars in the form of cash, homes, cars, commercial real estate, and securities. An article about how to transfer wealth to grandchildren should have a wide audience.

Ideas are Everywhere; Just Read the Headlines

Congress created a law that allows foreign nationals to obtain permanent U.S. residency if they invest $1 million in a U.S. business—provided that investment creates ten jobs ("Fraud Plagues U.S. Programs that Swap Visas for Investments," *Wall Street Journal*, April 11, 1996, p. B-1). Become an expert on that bill and create an article for a target market on how a foreign national could best invest money.

In your local Sunday paper, sandwiched between news and feature articles you'll find profiles, how-to's, special events, and recipes for leisure. You may wish to use the how-to format, perhaps "How to Invest in the New Millennium," or explain how a certain tax change could affect your reader's investments.

Alex Miller, a stock broker in Nashville, Tennessee, wanted to target physicians but didn't have time to call one physician at a time. He hired me to write an article for a national medical magazine. The article showed how a service like Alex's could benefit physicians, saving them money. The opening was great: "'The last thing I want to do is make an investment decision just before walking into surgery,' said Dr. Jones." That was a powerful hook most doctors could relate to. He didn't have to say, "I have the best product or service." Since the printing of that article, he has had calls from medical professionals all over the country wanting to do business with him.

Articles usually get readers more involved than ads, because readers don't feel they have to defend themselves against being manipulated or "sold" something. The tacit, third-party endorsement in a reputable magazine or newspaper lends credibility that is difficult for a paid advertisement to match.

But some ad supplements do include how-to articles: "How to Hire a Stockbroker," or "How to Survive a Market Crash." Many how-to articles are purchased from news services, but each paper needs stories with a local slant. That's where you should focus your writing. Keep track of the publication dates of these supplements. Make a list of how-to ideas for each one.

Whom Should You Target?

One of the greatest marketing weapons in the securities business is having an image of being knowledgeable about the value of privately held businesses. If you write articles about those and make suggestions in targeted trade journals, this marketing tactic will position you as a source of financial advice for those business owners.

Write about topics of interest to CPAs and lawyers. Over the next 10 years, think about the fees associated with settling estates of a million dollars or more. Though the many CPAs and lawyers who act as co-executors and administrators will receive only a fraction of the net worth of these estates, that still amounts to over $22 billion in executors' fees and $16.9 billion in administrator fees. An article geared toward lawyers on managing estates would be right on target.

All it takes is a little research to find the target market you wish to pursue. What publications do the prospects in your target market routinely read or scan? Look in the Gale's *Directory* (Chapter 10) and find the name of their association and its trade magazine. Write an article for it that addresses a problem, say, "How to Stand Out in the Midst of Competitive Clutter."

Don't Write Advertisements!

Articles that try to sell your product or service make you look self-serving, like someone who does not have the reader's best interest in mind. That kind of article will not get past the editor's desk. Solving the other guy's problem, perhaps by creating a system for passing on a business or developing a strategy for selling a business—being sensitive to the investment needs of the affluent business owner—is far more valuable. Business readers are much more likely to respond favorably to a solution proposed by someone who communicates expertise than from someone boasting.

Focus your articles on the needs of your clients. Far too many PR programs spend too much time talking about the attributes of the product, service, or company, and not enough time about why the customer should care about them. Always develop your articles with a specific application to customer needs. That is the purpose of the problem/solution format.

How do You Structure Your Article?

The structure of a problem/solution article is simple. First, you state a problem. Then, you answer it. You can include an anecdote, as I often do, to illustrate your point. It helps the readers relate to the problem in a personal way and keeps them reading through the details to the solution.

You can also simply state the problem in the first sentence, tell the reader you are going to explain how to solve it, possibly in a series of steps, and then solve it.

From the first line, hit your reader over the head. The first ten lines of an article establish the direction, tone, voice, and pace. The more complicated the subject, the more time you may need to spend giving readers the information they need to become interested right away, but much more than ten lines may be counter-productive.

You might want to insert what I call confidence builders along the way such as "You can easily follow this advice." Sprinkle inspirational confidence builders and encouragements throughout your article to keep readers from feeling overwhelmed.

The article may end with another colorful anecdote, this time with a positive outcome. Or you might have a "call to action," which is an alternate approach to telling your readers that they're now ready to act upon what they have learned. I sometimes include a "quick start," or something like "Five things you can do to start your investment program." I'll even urge the reader to contact me for further information.

Six Steps To Writing Problem/Solution Articles

By following the steps set out in the next few pages, you will write your first magazine article. If you follow the six steps in order, you can't help but produce a complete story. Guaranteed. And it will be *your* story in *your voice*. Voice is the tone you perceive when you read someone's writing—it's what you hear in my writing now.

You can follow the process as I write my own article to demonstrate the techniques. Then you'll work on constructing your own article. You can use this blueprint many times, creating a variety of problem/solution articles.

The Process

Work at your own pace; as you improve, challenge yourself. But first, grab a pen and paper, not your word processor. Plan your story. Try to find some compelling research or data that your reader hasn't heard or seen yet. As an example, at the beginning of this book I talked about how most advisors have been increasingly wanting public relations, but there are several things that stop them. The mind forms the question, "What are those things?" and you read on. I learned this method from fiction writing teacher Jack Bickham in his book, *Scene and Structure*.

Use 3x5 file cards. By recording your thoughts and notes on these cards, you force yourself to work specifically instead of merely daydreaming about the article. The cards also form a permanent reference file that you can use for future articles or as note cards for public speaking.

So the initial task is to gather your thoughts on your file cards. On the first, write what the article will be about. Then card by card, write down points you want to cover, problems you want to point out, your solutions, how to implement them, and, finally, your conclusion.

The cards don't have to be consistent with one another. If, for example, one card shows problems with buying a variable annuity and another mentions the tax treatment of variable annuities, you can choose which to use or which to omit later. Just get everything down at this point.

As you start to define—set up—your story, decide what your slant will be, or the point that you want to get across. Begin to arrange the cards in order. As you think of new subtopics, add those as well. This way you can spot inconsistencies ahead of time and fix them before you begin to write. When you actually write the article, you'll simply expand the notes on the cards into sentences and fill in the blanks.

Everyone is different. Some writers prefer to write on their computers, some use a typewriter, while others dictate their thoughts into a tape recorder. My own best writing happens when I write in long hand on a legal pad.

I then read my story aloud into a mini-cassette recorder. I do this because when you read an article aloud, you can hear both the story and your voice. Remember the tactic of writing as if you were talking to a friend?

Write Your First Draft

It's time for action. It's time for the pay-off, when your planning, thinking, and organizing begin to take more satisfying shape. It's time for you to write your first full draft.

You shouldn't feel too uneasy about it now, because everything's in place, but it's natural to want to delay the challenge of committing words to paper. Use your verbal positioning statement notes to help you organize your thoughts. You have an advantage over most professional writers who are not as well organized. You have investment experience and great story starters, an analogy and your opening sentence.

Keep looking at the cards that describe the problems you want to discuss, and the solutions. That will keep you on track. Refer to your cards often as you move along. Forgetting your cards in a burst of inspiration may send you off course and you'll find yourself writing an entirely different article a few pages down the line. If you do find yourself rambling, look at the cards again and ask yourself, "What's the point of the article?" That'll get you back on track.

Don't make the mistake of skipping around in the cards to write the easy parts first. You want to start at the beginning and write all the way through to the ending.

Now get started!

Step 1. Identify a Problem (pose it as a question)
Write down the primary financial problems of your best clients or targets.

_____

_____

_____

_____

Step 2. Identify Three Related Effects
What adverse conditions are a result of the main problem?
1._____

_____

2._____

_____

3._____

_____

Step 3. Write an Anecdote or an Analogy
Illustrate your point through personal experience or an anecdote that explains in a practical way the effect a given problem will have on the reader, something a reader can relate to. The anecdote will introduce the topic in a catchy, arresting, or amusing manner—or with a bang— establishing a strong initial connection between you and your readers. At its very simplest, you need to grab attention by relating a pertinent thought, insight, or observation that gets your main point across.

You can start with an anecdote and end with another to strengthen your expert stance by showing how your investment advice works in real life. Making the unfamiliar familiar shows that you know your stuff. Just use everyday experiences.

Analogies further simplify the point you're making. *Example*: Hiring a mutual fund organization is like buying a suit off the rack. It might come close enough to a good fit that with a few alterations, it can be made to just about fit your expectations. To be sure of a perfect fit, though, you need have a custom-tailored suit based on your personal measurements. That's what an investment advisor does— tailors your investments to your unique needs.

_____

_____

_____

_____

_____

Step 4. Provide the Solution to the Problem
This is not intended to pitch your service or product, but to give the reader the answer to the problem you described. This is why readers stay with your article. The quickest way to lose your audience is to be vague, or to tell them what they already know.

_____

_____

_____

_____

_____

_____

Step 5. List the Steps to Reach the Solution
These can be how-to components of a solution that build on each other, a list of resources, or examples of results (such as a case study). I like to move my readers through a sequence of instructions for solving the problem in the same order they would perform them.
1._____

_____

2._____

_____

3._____

_____

4._____

_____

And so on...

Step 6. Summary
A bad ending can ruin all your hard work. Sum up your conclusion with information your reader can use. The more clearly and forcefully the conclusion is stated, the greater the likelihood that what you say will be remembered accurately.

Don't forget to use a call to action; invite your reader to call or write for more information. Inviting the reader to take the next step is a critical part of your article. If you've scheduled a seminar, you want your prospects to contact you to make reservations, so tell them explicitly where it will be, when, and whom to call, with a phone number. If it doesn't sound self-serving, most editors have no problem with letting you put your name and phone number in the article.

_____

_____

_____

_____

Now read through what you wrote. See if it rings true and leads logically to the point you intended to make. What's your general impression of your work? Is it understandable? Interesting? Consider the logical flow as seen in this block diagram, study it for pacing, and check your article against it.

Sample Article

Here's an example by John Bowen, CEO, RWB Advisory Services, San Jose, CA, after a little editing:

SHOULD YOU INVEST INTERNATIONALLY?
Was it a good investment decision to invest internationally in 1997? Clearly, after the fact, it wasn't. However, at the beginning of the year, it certainly seemed the right thing to do. **(Started by asking a powerful story question - the problem)**
    You didn't think you made a bad decision buying fire insurance on your home just because it didn't burn down last year. **(The analogy)** Investing internationally could be viewed, in the same light, as a form of investment insurance. It's insurance because when U.S. stocks are weak, foreign stocks tend to be strong; and when foreign stocks are weak, U.S. stocks tend to be strong. The problem is, no one can forecast when either trend will occur.
    So when you begin to build your client's portfolio, you need, first and foremost, to consider effective diversification. **(Evidence)** When Merton Miller, the Nobel laureate, was asked to sum up the most important investment concept individuals should know, he stated, "Diversification is your buddy."
    Over the last 28 years, the standard deviation of the differences between U.S. stocks (measured by the S&P 500 Index) and international stocks (measured by the EAFE Index) is 18.9 percent. **(Proof statement)** Using historical standard deviation, we can calculate the range within which we would expect 95 percent of the differences between U.S. and foreign returns to fall. The size of the range declines with the square root of time.

Sample Article, con't.

The chart below shows that it is normal for international returns to drift far from U.S. returns, even over longer time periods. **(Proof by adding chart)** The data show that there has been significant drift over time, both positive and negative. Yet, remarkably, the returns of the U.S. and foreign markets are within one percent of each other for the 28-year period ending in September 1997.

The recent returns of international stocks have been poor, but well within a normal range of expectations. The poor relative results of recent years have been matched by equally superior relative results in previous years.

Average Annual Returns (%) Ending 9/97

Time Period	EAFE Index	S&P 500 Index	Difference	95% Confidence Limits
1 Year	12.4	40.5	-28.1	± 37.1%
5 Years	12.8	21.4	-8.6	±16.6%
10 Years	7.4	16.1	8.7	± 11.7%
20 Years	17.6	17.6	0.0	± 8.3%
28 Years	15.5	14.6	0.9	± 7.0%
40 Years				± 5.9%
50 Years				± 5.2%

Small cap stocks tend to magnify this effect. Because small companies are more closely tied to domestic markets, they tend to perform best when their domestic market does well. Therefore, although international large cap stocks are a good diversification vehicle, international small cap stocks are even better.

	1982-1990	1991-1997
U.S. Stocks		
Large Cap	16.24	20.06
Small Cap	8.83	25.55
International Stocks		
Large Cap	19.19	9.70
Small Cap	26.29	3.38
International Premium (International minus U.S. Returns)		
Large Cap	2.95	-10.36
Small Cap	17.46	-22.17

During the period from 1982 to 1990, international markets earned a significant premium over domestic markets. We didn't see financial magazines or newspaper articles entitled, "Drop Global Investment Bunk." Instead, the headlines read "Invest Globally—Drop U.S. Stocks." Then the international premium turned negative from 1991 to 1997, and now you are reading "Drop Global—Hold U.S. Stocks".

What does this tell us? **(Now you start to solve the problem)** These two markets move very differently. The good news is, this is exactly what we want in order to effectively diversify. Dissimilar price movement reduces volatility and increases overall portfolio returns on a long-term basis. What that means is, by definition, the highest performing asset class will outperform the aggregate portfolio's return.

Sample Article, con't.

It is normal for investors to question the benefits of diversification when clear hindsight tells them they could have made more money if they had simply invested only in the winning asset class. Of course, only hindsight can tell us which is the highest performing asset class. The consolation is that, over time, both performances tend to balance out.

(Proof statement) For the past 27 years, the S&P 500 and the EAFE Indexes have had an annualized return of 11.1 percent and 12.7 percent, respectively. Combining both takes advantage of their low correlation. Harry Markowitz taught us that when we have two portfolios with the same average arithmetic rate of return, the one with the lower rate of volatility will have a higher compounded or geometric return.

Companies that have the same risk, no matter whether they're in the United States or the United Kingdom, are going to have the same expected rate of return over time. That's because markets reprice according to new information.

Clearly, owning both international stocks and domestic stocks lowers volatility. We believe that the expectations about returns are the same, whether they're domestic or global, given similar risk characteristics. We're not looking to get a premium overseas; but simply looking to lower volatility.

In the short run, though, local economic conditions affect returns and we experience dissimilar price movement, which is what Modern Portfolio Theory investing takes into consideration. Academics Eugene Fama and Ken French determined that the risk, as measured by standard deviation, is roughly the same for all stocks worldwide in a given risk category.

(Here, answer the related problems associated with investing internationally) So why do investors question what the academics know works? "Behaviorists" call it cognitive bias: the belief that whatever we are most familiar with will continue. For example, the sun will come up in the same spot every day. **(Proof statement)** Since 1989, the U.S. markets have been so strong that most investors question why they should include international stocks at all in their portfolios.

It's easier to sell what people want, and people want to believe that what they are experiencing will continue. It would be easier for financial professionals to raise money if they just sold U.S. recent winners and dumped the international allocation altogether. What we need to do ethically is not what is easy, but what is right and will truly benefit our clients.

If you're going to follow the academics' advice to include international, the next question you should ask is, what's the most advantageous allocation? Currently, more than 60 percent of the world's markets, as measured by market capitalization, are overseas. **(Proof statement)** All other things being equal, you should invest based on the market capitalization. Rather than being subjective, let the markets tell you what to do.

Your job as financial planners is to help investors move from being "noise" investors to "information" investors. As noise investors, they get caught up in the emotion of the day. They are encouraged by the media to expect what's currently winning to continue; but the reality is, that will not happen. The idea is to take the best information from the academic community to understand how markets really work and how professionals can apply it for the benefit of clients. That's why you should continue to include the international markets in your portfolios. **(Here you have answered the question in the title)**

Article Checklist

- Does the article have a clear story problem or question?
- Does the question appear early in your story?
- Do the steps the reader must take relate to the story problem?
- Do the steps follow one another in logical order?
- Can you eliminate anything without seriously damaging the story?
- Does your ending answer the question or problem?
- Compare your story with your planning blocks or cards. Have you left anything out? Why?
- Can you think of anything more to include?
- Did you contrive an ending that leaves readers feeling they've learned something?

You may find yourself going back to the cards many times and rethinking earlier decisions in light of the block diagram, but it's worth the agony to produce an interesting, well-structured article. Rewrite anything that seems unfinished in your story.

Charts and Graphs

Use graphs or visuals to support your message. They can add interest to your article, prove a statement, or attract attention. Graphics do take up some space, but most editors like them. Your graphic elements help attract readers and emphasize your copy points.

Titles

Many non-writers spend a lot of time picking out the perfect title, but selecting the title is the least important aspect of getting your article published. Often the publisher will change the title before the story is printed anyway.

Don't get me wrong—a good title can have a positive effect. Just don't let beginning to write your article get sabotaged because you can't come up with a profound title! I often don't title an article until I've finished writing it and a title has become clear within the text. In fact, that was how I titled this book.

Your title should reflect the focal point of your article. Make sure your title and headline (which means your first sentence), include a benefit that appeals to some basic need of your reader. "How to Build a Billion Dollar Investment Business" would appeal to an investment advisor. "How to Increase the Size of Your Portfolio at Retirement" would appeal to a retiree.

Aim for the Timeless When Writing

Never write about something that will be out of date within a few weeks. Sometimes it takes three, four, even six months before your article appears. A timeless subject is one that does not depend on current events, the market, or a particular stock price. A timeless article is as relevant and marketable three years from now as it was the day it was written. How to save on taxes, plant your lawn, manage a retirement plan, or build a log cabin are examples of timeless articles. Really, nothing much has changed in twenty years when it comes to sound money management. If you deal in subjects that are long-lived, you will insure you can use them for a few years.

Rhythm

The cadence of the article is very important. Almost anyone, whether or not they've been in the military, can imitate the rhythmic, sing-song tones of the drill instructor as he calls out instructions. "You will clean, fire and carry your rifle by the numbers. Holding your rifle parallel to your body, take your right hand and pull back on the receiver handle. Once it is locked into place, with the fourth finger of the right hand . .", and so forth.

Readers expect to receive how-to information in this manner. Recipes, instruction manuals, and directions on how to use products are all written in this form. When you use it in problem/solution articles, readers recognize the ring and your writing takes on the voice of authority. Obviously, you can't maintain a military cadence throughout an article. It would sound pretty strange. The best way is to deliver it in short doses.

Don't dilute the impact of your commands with phrases like "I think you should." Keep a direct, competent, and authoritative voice. You want readers to feel as though you're beside them, reassuring, guiding their every move.

Unity of Tense

Present tense works best for a problem/solution article. The reader's problem is very much in the present tense—at least until you offer your solution. Present tense says, *You are there*. Once you make your tense choice stick with it. When you edit, check to see that you've stayed in the same tense.

Escape Route

Consider using outside help, maybe a ghostwriter. Many advisors who are too busy to write their own articles hire an outside writer to help, though I recommend that you write the article and have an editor clean it up. An editor has the skills to correct the grammar, the sentence structure, and the spelling.

Spacing Copy

Keep the story moving smoothly by using short to medium-length paragraphs. Long paragraphs are hard to read and often lose the interest of the reader.

Final Advice

The biggest excuse most writers have for not writing is interruptions. Find a quiet place. Put your phone on voice mail. I sometimes drive to the park where no one can reach me. Block out 30 minutes of time every day to work on your article. The cards will help you re-start where you left off the day before. Your objective is to finalize a seven to eight-page article in a week. That can be just one page a day. At the end of the day, if you haven't done any work, grab one of the file cards and write down your excuse. And if you're tired of that, then finish your page.

Good articles aren't written, they're rewritten. No matter how bad you may feel about the words you've written today, you can fix them later. But the key is to complete a seven-page article. Don't let yourself get hung up every time something isn't perfect. If you're waiting for free time or inspiration, don't! Professional writers establish a habit of writing even when they don't feel like it. Writing because you're inspired is the mark of an amateur.

The Next Day

The next day, read your work aloud to see if all the information is there. Read it line by line, listening both to what is said and how it is said. Do you have all the facts, statistics, quotations, and anecdotes? Did you make your point? Is it persuasive? Read for organization. Does the article answer the question or solve the problem posed in the lead? Does the article flow naturally from beginning to end?

Editing

Don't fall in love with your initial effort, like many inexperienced writers do. Remember that you're doing this to be heard, to stand out from the crowd, *not* to write the Great American Novel. Revising an article can be difficult, but by using a systematic procedure for revising your copy, coupled with a positive attitude, you can make the process less painful.

The first step is to eliminate peripheral points and details—even if they're interesting. If they don't support your story, dump them. Remove wordy phrasing, awkward construction, clichés, and spelling errors. Make sure the verbs are strong. Keep adjectives to a minimum. After you've edited it, perform one last re-read, making any last-minute corrections. Never send the article out until you've edited it, corrected the spelling, and made it neat.

Time spent polishing your article is time well spent. A strong article that delivers a compelling message can become the heart of an effective marketing campaign.

You can also take an article published in a trade magazine where you'd like to see your article printed and lay your article alongside it to make visual format comparisons. Are paragraphs about the same length? Are there graphs or tables?

When you've completed your comparison, prepare the final manuscript for submission to the publication.

Chapter 8
More Things You Can
Do to Look Like a Pro

In this chapter, you'll find:
- Tips on preparing a neat, professional-looking submission
- A self-editing checklist
- Keys to revisions
- How to write a sidebar
- The value of monthly columns
- How to turn articles into stay-behind booklets
- How to monitor your results

When the manuscript you write is in the correct form, publishers perceive the writing as professional from the start—which gives you the inside track over other financial advisors.

Following are some tips on preparing a neat, professional-looking submission that will help your article get accepted. To begin with:

- Use short words; avoid using long words whenever possible. Your purpose is to inform, not to intimidate or impress.

- Use short sentences; avoid long and complex sentences. Singular sentences are easier to read and more personal.

- Avoid excessive use of plurals.

- A professional manuscript should be neatly typed, free of errors, and reflect good editing.

- Use good paper, at least 16 or 25-pound quality bond to make your manuscript look professional.

- I use a Hewlett Packard Laser Jet printer, so every copy is an original. A dot matrix printer is a no-no. It should be as close to letter quality as possible.

- If you're using a typewriter, make sure that you always use black ink. Editors who read numerous manuscripts weekly don't appreciate the eye strain caused by colored inks. If they come across an article that has faded from sitting on a windowsill in the sunlight, they will chuck it.

- Use 12 pt. Courier, Times Roman, or an equally simple typeface. Don't use fancy scroll fonts or print wheels. Editors aren't paid to decipher hieroglyphics.

- Use double-spacing throughout your story to permit easier reading and room for editing.

- Leave a 1-1/4 to 1-1/2 inch margin around the text. When your article moves into the production stage, the staff needs space for marking it up for typesetting.

- In the upper left-hand corner of the first page, type your name, address, phone number, social security number. If the editor decides to use your manuscript and needs to get in touch with you immediately to verify information, he'll have your phone number.

- In the upper right-hand corner of the first page, provide the approximate number of words. Count each word of your manuscript (a computer can do this for you). The average length of an article is from 1,000-2,000 words, although longer or shorter articles will be considered, depending on the publication.

- Near the middle of the first page, type your manuscript title. Skip two lines and type "by." Skip two more lines and type your name.

- At the top of the second page, and on every subsequent page, in the upper left-hand corner put your last name, dash, a short version of your manuscript title, another dash and a page number. (I don't always put page numbers here. I usually use the automatic numbering in my word processor.)

- Check every page for typos and mistakes. One or two small corrections on a page won't disqualify you. If you have more than that, retype the page.

- Make sure you use proper postage. Include a SASE (self-addressed stamped envelope) if you want to have the manuscript sent back. I just indicate on the bottom that it's not necessary. If you do send a SASE, again, make sure you include proper postage.

- Before you send the manuscript, recheck it and make sure all the pages are included.

• Finally, send it off! Write down where you sent it, and then forget about it and go back to work!

Do not:
• Use staples.

• Send pages that are not numbered.

• Insist on copyright or serial right notices. Today's copyright laws no longer require these for protection; anything an author writes is automatically protected. A copyright notice sends a red flag shouting "novice."

Nowadays, although a lot of my submissions are over the Internet or by fax, the majority of manuscripts and queries are still sent on paper. Almost all editors need a hard copy at some point in the submission process. I send a copy on a disk, sometimes by e-mail, but I always send a hard copy with a cover letter. Submit books, articles, or serials electronically only when asked to do so.

Self-edit Checklist

Content

To be ahead of the competition, you should tell a story that shows readers how to solve a problem, improve their financial lives, or make their lives easier.

Sentence Structure

1. Do your sentences have variety? Vividness? Clarity?

2. Do they vary in length? Have a rhythm?

3. Do they engage the reader?

Language

1. Is the language specific? Colorful? Visual?

2. Does it appeal to your target reader? Is it appropriate to your industry?

3. Are transitions smooth? Clear? Do they propel reader along?

4. Have you avoided jargon or clichés? They clutter up the prose.

Power Words: Nouns and Verbs

1. Are your verbs active rather than passive? Do they convey action? Movement?
2. Are your nouns specific?
3. Did you avoid using modifiers to prop up weak nouns and verbs? If you think you have to use an adjective or adverb, find a stronger noun or verb.

Tone, Style and Voice

1. Do word choice and supporting detail add texture and mood to your article?
2. Is the tone consistent (ironic, tough, funny, formal, casual)? Is it right for the intended reader? (I use a more formal tone when writing a financial article or chapter.)
3. Does the narrative voice have authority? Does it flow? Capture the reader's imagination?

Keys to Revision

1. Watch for changes in tense.
2. Cut unnecessary words to strengthen your story.
3. Avoid wordiness and redundancies.
4. Avoid starting sentences with "it" and "there."
5. Don't use that's, which's, where's, and's, who's, etc. too often.

Using Anecdotes

A story-within-a-story is a way to:
1. Show, rather than tell - it's a way to create an immediate visual image.
2. Dramatize the information you want to pass along.
3. Simplify a difficult concept.
4. Illustrate a theme.
5. Deepen characterization.

That's it; not so hard! Now we'll add that little something extra that magazine editors all love. It's called the "sidebar."

Whenever possible, include a sidebar with articles you submit, either a chart, a sequence of steps, or some type of how-to. Sidebars make long articles easier to read by breaking them into different sections.

Sample Sidebar

The National Deficit
The national deficit is one of the least understood economic concepts, yet it's one of the best indicators of long-term economic health. You may be wondering, *who owns the national debt?* The media have led many to believe the Japanese do. *Wrong!* According to Dr. Bob Goodman, Ph.D., Senior Economic Advisor for Putnam Investments, over 80 percent of the total outstanding national debt is in the form of bonds owned by Americans. Americans consider the bonds they buy as assets, not liabilities—and 80 percent of the interest on the national debt goes right back to Americans as income—upon which they pay taxes.

Sidebars can be lists, such as the top ten investments or the top mutual funds. Lists are easy to prepare. Sidebars should not be very long. When there's not a lot of room to say what you want to say, you really must grab your reader quickly. When writing a sidebar, don't worry too much about style. However, like the main article, a sidebar demands structure, research, and accuracy.

A Monthly Column Can Make You an Expert

Whether for a local newspaper, a local business paper, or a trade magazine, writing a monthly column takes more time. Before you get excited about taking on this kind of project, ask yourself why you want to write a column.

The best reason is that it gives your name continuous exposure in your target market. One of my goals for my own clients is to set *them* up with a column. I do this after an editor has already published one of our articles or if the client is already a well-known expert. What the editor will want is a continuous flow of new information that readers can derive benefit from.

To pitch a column, you'll have to write a proposal, a list of column titles, and three sample columns—the editor likes to have at least two months in the bank in case you flake out. The good news with a column is that editors generally print your bio, your photo, and often how you can be reached. The column strategy can be very successful because it forces discipline and consistency.

Turn a Sidebar Into a Stay-Behind Booklet

Now for the fun part: your accumulated articles can turn into booklets, or the premise of a book. Assemble your articles so that they serve as concise, logical steps to making something happen. When you couple this concept with the book template, you can short-cut the whole book writing process. We've all seen the how-to booklets, or the "Six Steps to an Investment Policy." Somewhere between five and eight steps seems to be the magic number. Look at the covers of *Money* or some other magazines. They're always listing five, six, seven steps.

Use each article as a booklet. It's perfect. If you've done a good job, it will explain what you do and your investment process.

And you can use your next article to promote the booklet: In the last paragraph of your article, add "For a free copy of [title of booklet], call or write [your name, address, phone]." Many editors will include that contact information; you will get responses and client leads.

Ann Mahoney, the editor of the American Society of Association Executives' trade magazine, *Association Management,* published an article I wrote entitled "Managing Smart." The article addressed the current state of pension plan management. She asked me if I had other information on the subject. All I had was a booklet from one of my companies, Dean Witter, "Investment Performance Report." It gave the reader a short course in investment management. It was a free guide that included sample reports, defined investment monitoring and explained how monitoring and the selection of an investment manager can help pension plan trustees.

In a sidebar with my article, I offered the free booklet to readers along with an investment policy statement they could get from me. My name, address, phone, and fax were in my bio. After ten phone calls for requests, one of which resulted in meeting with a $7 million pension fund, I realized the value of the stay-behind piece.

That fund was interested in switching managers and wanted to know how to go about doing it. The rest was up to me. I called, made the appointment, and gave my usual sales pitch, just like every other broker. The difference was that I had been *invited* in. I was perceived by them as an expert. When I showed up at the meeting, some people already had copies of not only the magazine article, but the stay-behind piece that I'd sent them, which they were able to show the other members of the committee who hadn't read the article. The rest of the meeting was fun; they were already sold before I'd arrived. They wanted to know how they'd go about transferring the fund to the managers we'd recommended.

Figure 8-1 Free Special Report

Performance Report

NEED A SHORT COURSE IN INVESTMENT management? The "Investment Performance Report" offered by Dean Witter Reynolds, Inc., Los Angeles, may be just what you're looking for. This free guide provides sample reports, defines investment monitoring jargon, and explains how monitoring activities and the selection of an investment manager can help pension fund trustees manage retirement plans.

The company can also provide a sample investment policy statement upon request that can serve as a model in meeting federal requirements. Contact Larry Chambers, associate vice president, investments, Dean Witter Reynolds, Inc., 800 Wilshire Blvd., Los Angeles, CA 90017; (213) 486–4493; fax (213) 891–1917.

You can offer your reprinted article as a "free special report" in your media kit or press release and send it to other publications within the same industry.

A Response Tracking System

A few years ago, I was hired to write magazine articles and deliver a non-selling message that would get the client's name in front of stock brokers and investment advisors. We wanted to see the effects of different messages and their perceived value to our audience. The idea was to get the industry readership to inquire about the client organization and eventually become a member. Each member of the board of directors seemed to have a different idea about how to increase membership. The study turned out to have two results. It not only revealed which articles were more effective; it also compared the response rate of article responses to their other forms of advertising, including direct mail and word-of-mouth referrals.

Previously, the organization had added the names of those who responded to ads to their data base, to be notified of meetings and conferences. When a caller became a member, no one knew how the contact had been generated because they had so many marketing programs running concurrently.

We convinced them to begin keeping source records, so that callers could be identified and tracked back to the magazine and even to the article. We put a response tracking system in place. It was pretty simple: the receptionist simply kept track of the origin of incoming calls on a simple matrix sheet. Down the vertical side of the page was a listing of each marketing tactic.

Before the study, the directors were convinced that the article program was a nice way to get the name out, but had little or no value beyond that. They felt that their referral, advertising, and educational programs were far more effective in attracting new members to join their organization.

Each month we wrote a column for one of the industry's trade magazines and articles for other publications. The results were as follows:

In 10 months our article program had generated 3,919 leads in four categories, versus 813 inquiries for *all* other programs.

Article writing outperformed all other forms of advertising for that time period by a 5-to-1 ratio. In addition, when a compelling message hit home *coupled* with an offer such as a free booklet explaining the subject in depth, that article outdid advertising by a **15-to-1** ratio.

Figure 8-2 IIMC PR Study

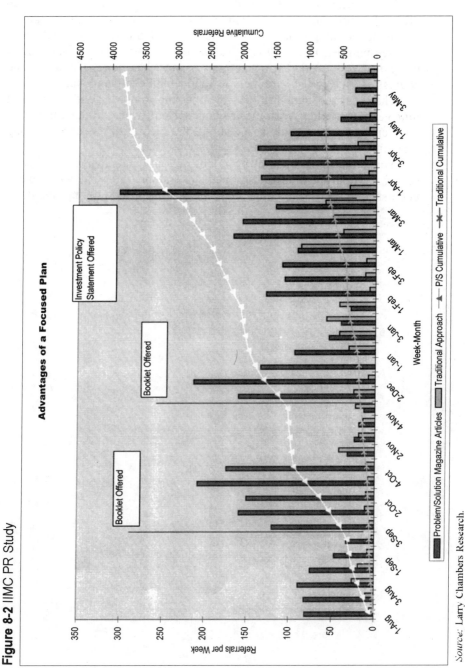

Source: Larry Chambers Research.

We'd write an article about a particular investment problem, then offer: "for more information, contact the organization for a free guide." The editor let us put in the phone number and address. Even without a toll-free number, in one month we had over 900 responses. Their other programs were averaging ten responses; most had none. The name and address of each caller were recorded and a mail campaign was installed.

That year the organization's membership doubled. Within the next four years, it tripled. With the tracking system we could determine that the members came mainly as a result of the success of the article writing program.

Your strategy should now be to look at your whole marketing plan, to see what works and what doesn't in the overall picture. That way you can understand what you're doing and what you need to do to improve it.

Chapter 9
Breaking into Print the
Easy Way

In this chapter, you'll find:
• How to write a pitch (query) letter
• Sample magazine query letter
• Sample newspaper query letter

An easy way to introduce yourself to an editor is with a pitch or query letter that includes any samples you have of your writing. Newspaper editors want samples to prove that you can write or that you're knowledgeable about investing. If you don't have any published clips to send, you
can still send samples that demonstrate how you write. You don't have to
write the actual article until after you get a positive response from the
publication.

First, research your target publication. The monthly issues of *Writer's
Digest* list various magazines with some basic information on their needs.
The annual book, *Writer's Market,* has entries packed with information
and points to look for that will maximize your chances for querying successfully.

Here are two typical entries from *Writer's Market,* the first for a consumer magazine, the second for a trade magazine:

Kiplinger's Personal Finance
1729 H St. NW Washington DC 20006
Editor: Theodore J.Miller
Less than 10% freelance written (only 10%).
Circa 1 million (readers of all segments). Most material is staff-writ-
ten, but does accept some freelance. Query with clips of published
work.

Physician's Management
7500 Old Oak Blvd. Cleveland OH 44130
Editor in Chief: Bob Feigenbaum
Circulation: Circa 120,000 [all potential clients]
75% freelance writers [almost the whole magazine]
Monthly magazine emphasizing finance, practice management, estate and retirement planning. Publishes how-to articles limited to medical practice.

Notice the number of outside writers the trade magazine will use. Your odds of getting in a trade magazine are 650% better than being published in a consumer magazine. Now we're getting somewhere!

Limited circulation, a specialized audience, big percentages of freelance material, a stated desire to work with new writers, purchase of approximately five freelance articles per issue, longevity of publication— these are the kinds of things to look for. Then, when you choose the first publication to query, make a list of what topics you could write on for this publication.

Occasionally, magazines offer guidelines that outline information about the types of article to write. Ideally, review at least three issues of your target publication, looking for patterns in the content that will help you form your own articles or columns. Find out if columns are open to freelancers. If the magazine is not available at the news store or the library, you can call the magazine directly and request sample copies.

Read the articles and take a careful look at the graphics. Does the magazine look good to you? Do you like reading the magazine? Would you be proud to have your work published in it, and would you show these articles to your clients? If the answers are "no," you might want to stop your study right here and search for a different, more compatible, magazine.

Keep a query letter brief. One page is the ideal length. Editors are extremely busy – but they'll read a one-page query letter. It's important to get your idea across quickly and succinctly. After less than 30 seconds of reading, an editor should know everything necessary to make a decision: the subject, the focus, the essential details, and the length. You want to interest the editor, not overwhelm him. Whittle your idea down to the bone so you can summarize it in one or two sentences.

Sample Magazine Query Letter:

June 13, 1998

Xxx Xxxxxx
Modern Maturity
601 E St. NW
Washington, DC 20049

Dear Mr. xxx,

I was amused by your comments in July's *Writer's Digest*. It's true. Shortly after turning fifty, I received the AARP membership form. I felt just about the same as I did when I received that ominous notice from the draft board.

In the same magazine, you were quoted, "I'm desperate for writers who can handle financial topics for the lay person and not make them so technical or obscure." Well, I can relate to that also. My forte is taking complex investment subjects and making them easy to understand.

I've written hundreds of financial articles for various national publications. I write three monthly columns for the main Wall Street trades and just finished my third book for McGraw-Hill. I cover topics from annuities to subjects of special interest to first time investors.

Your age 50-to-60-plus readers are faced with a new complexity in investing that grows exponentially each year. How does a prudent investor sort relevant investment information from the distracting investment noise in order to make investment decisions? This is the subject I would like to address in an article, or with excerpts from my books, for *Modern Maturity*.

I could practically write this 3500-word article in my sleep and have it on your desk in the morning. I look forward to hearing from you.

Regards,
Larry Chambers

Sample Newspaper Query Letter:

Dear Editor,

"What Do You Do When the Stock Market Gets Too High?" My lead is the best place for a beginning investor to get started in mutual funds. The article will cover how to find a mutual fund, how to invest in it, and how to stay in it for the long term. The article will be approximately 1500 words long and can be completed in one week. I am willing to write the piece on spec. I have enclosed copies of other reprints.

Warm regards,
Larry Chambers

Writing a Sample Article

Use common everyday language that people can relate to and everybody can identify with. The average length of a newspaper how-to article is 800 words, which is slightly less than three double-spaced typed pages. Stick to the most interesting highlights. Be thorough. Readers may make investment decisions based on your advice. Make sure your facts are correct and every quote is accurate.

No need to worry if you've never written before. If you're writing an article about investing, and you're the vice president of investments for a major Wall Street firm, that tells the editor that you're qualified.

Okay, but where do you find the right trade publications? Glad you asked, it's the subject of the next chapter.

Chapter 10
Where to Find the Right
Trade Publication

In this chapter, you'll find out:
• Where you should send your article
• What your prospects read
• What's behind the scenes in the trade press
• Why you can re-send the same article to many trade magazines
• Where to go for help

Where should you send your article? Don't make the mistake most beginners make. They try to send their first manuscripts to *Forbes, Fortune, Money* or another consumer magazine. Don't waste your time. These magazines are staff written. They don't buy a lot of outside articles, and when they do, you're competing with every professional writer in the country.

Take a few minutes to peruse the cover stories of the well-known publications on the magazine stands: "How to Get Rich In Funds!", "Mutual Funds Can Improve Your Life," etc.

The good news is that affluent, busy, successful millionaires have more realistic problems. They also see through advertised track records and the magazines you find those in. In fact, most don't read those magazines. It's the guy with a few hundred dollars concerned about an extra 1 or 2 percent who's dreaming of a million-dollar retirement fund. Not a bad person, but a dreamer; that's who's reading these magazines. They're buying dreams. I counted the number of times the word 'dream' was used recently in one consumer publication—over twenty times.

Let's assume your target market is wealthy business owners—a pretty cynical bunch. These guys read their industry trades before a letter from their mother. We've already talked about what they want from what they read: information about the competition and about what's going on in their field, anything that can help them get ahead in their business. These magazines don't pay writers well, so professional writers can't afford to waste their time writing for trade magazines.

That's good news. Your target market doesn't spend a lot of time reading consumer-type financial magazines and reads trade magazines instead; and big-time magazine writers don't write in the trades. So who writes these articles? You do.

All you have to do is identify the publication that serves your targets, then call up the editor and ask for a copy, explaining that you think you can deliver articles that serve the readers and you want to read the magazine to see if they would.

You can even go ahead and order a subscription. My postman thinks I work for the CIA with all the hundreds of trade magazines I receive.

Finding Your Niche

What Do Your Clients Read?

Think of your own trade magazines—*Investment Advisor, Registered Rep, Financial Planning*. Those magazines get read before *Forbes*. Most of the articles in *Forbes* are exposé-type articles. The trade journals are the market that you want to approach. Small business owners are more likely to read *Solutions, Your Company* or *Waste Management* or something that's going to improve their business.

Don't worry about selling your article, your interest should be to get exposure in magazines your clients read.

The readers need information, and the journal provides it. Because they have to help readers do their jobs, trade articles are practical and specific, in-depth or technical. They also lend a lot of credibility to the author. Unlike their consumer cousins, these magazines don't strive to be flashy or entertaining. They look different, too, generally less thick than the mass market magazines and often without the glitz.

There are some 20,000 trade journals published annually. The first job is to zero in on the ones that match your target market. The best places to search are *Bacon's Publicity Checker* (the Business Publication edition), SRDS (Standard Rate and Data Service), the *Writer's Market* (800-289-0963) for a listing of trade journals and associations, and the publications put out by Gale's Research (800-877-GALE).

Figure 10-1 Gale's Research

Source: Gale Research. Reprinted with permission.

Figure 10-1　　Gale's Research, con't.

prevention, and treatment of individual dysfunctions. **Founded:** 1973. **Frequency:** Bimonthly. **Print Method:** Offset. **Trim Size:** 6 x 9. **Cols./Page:** 1. **Col. Width:** 54 nonpareils. **Col. Depth:** 103 agate lines. **Key Personnel:** Edison J. Trickett, Editor. ISSN: 0091-0562. **Subscription Rates:** $435 other countries; $370.
Circulation: (Not Reported)

Remarks: Accepts advertising.

⊞ 20310　The American Journal of Dermatopathology
Liptencoct-Raven
1185 Avenue of the Americas　　　　　　　　　Phone: (212)930-9500
Mail Stop 3B　　　　　　　　　　　　　　　　Fax: (212)575-1160
New York, NY 10036
Journal offering state-of-the-art coverage of the rapid progress in studying skin diseases. **Subtitle:** Official Publication of the Society for Dermatopathology. **Founded:** 1979. **Frequency:** Bimonthly. **Trim Size:** 8 1/4 x 11. **Key Personnel:** Rita Scheman, Publisher; Clifton R. White, Jr. M., Editor-in-Chief; Phyllis C. Noyes, Advertising Mgr. **Subscription Rates:** $124; $161 other countries; $168 Industry; $205 Industry other countries. $34 single issue.
Ad Rates: BW:　　　$785　　　　　　　　　**Circulation:** 2,500
　　　　　　　4C:　　　$900

⊞ 20311　The American Journal of Drug and Alcohol Abuse
Marcel Dekker, Inc.
270 Madison Ave.　　　　　　　　　　　　　Phone: (212)696-9000
New York, NY 10016　　　　　　　　　　　Fax: (212)685-4540
　　　　　　　　　　　　　　　　　　　　　　(800)228-1160
Medical journal. **Founded:** 1974. **Frequency:** Quarterly. **Trim Size:** 5 7/8 x 9. **Key Personnel:** Edward Kaufman, Editor. ISSN: 0095-2990. **Subscription Rates:** $247.50; $495 institutions.
Ad Rates: BW:　　　$640　　　　　　　　　**Circulation:** 1,500
　　　　　　　4C:　　　$1,401

⊞ 20312　American Journal of Economics and Sociology
American Journal of Economics and Sociology, Inc.
41 E. 72 St.　　　　　　　　　　　　　　　Phone: (212)988-1680
New York, NY 10021
Journal emphasizing interdisciplinary approach in research of the social sciences. **Founded:** Oct. 1941. **Frequency:** Quarterly. **Print Method:** Offset. **Trim Size:** 6 x 9. **Cols./Page:** 1. **Col. Width:** 51 nonpareils. **Col. Depth:** 94 agate lines. **Key Personnel:** Frank C. Genovese, Editor-in-Chief; Susan Klingelhoefer, Business Manager. ISSN: 0002-9246. **Subscription Rates:** $40 institutions; $25.
Circulation: ‡2,300

Remarks: Advertising not accepted.

⊞ 20313　American Journal of Family Law
John Wiley and Sons, Inc.
Subscription Dept.　　　　　　　　　　　　Phone: (212)850-6000
605 3rd Ave.　　　　　　　　　　　　　　Fax: (212)850-6799
New York, NY 10158
Jouranl on family law issues for judges, paralegals, and law practitioners. **Frequency:** Quarterly. **Key Personnel:** Laura E. Shapiro, Esq., Editor. ISSN: 0891-6330. **Subscription Rates:** $148.

⊞ 20314　The American Journal of Forensic Medicine and Pathology
Liptencoct-Raven
1185 Avenue of the Americas　　　　　　　　Phone: (212)930-9500
Mail Stop 3B　　　　　　　　　　　　　　　Fax: (212)575-1160
New York, NY 10036
Journal presenting up-to-date coverage of forensic medical practices worldwide. **Subtitle:** Official Publication of the National Association of Medical Examiners. **Founded:** 1980. **Frequency:** Quarterly. **Print Method:** Sheetfed offset. **Trim Size:** 8 1/4 x 11. **Key Personnel:** Rita Scheman, Publisher; Vincent J.M. DiMaio, M.D., Editor-in-Chief; Phyllis C. Noyes, Advertising Mgr. ISSN: 0721-6798. **Subscription Rates:** $178 institutions; $178 other countries. $62 single issue; $140.
Ad Rates: BW:　　　$800　　　　　　　　　**Circulation:** 2,500
　　　　　　　4C:　　　$995

⊞ 20315　American Journal of Hematology
John Wiley and Sons Inc.
605 3rd Ave.　　　　　　　　　　　　　　Phone: (212)850-8800
New York, NY 10158　　　　　　　　　　Fax: (212)850-6021
　　　　　　　　　　　　　　　　　　　　　　(800)225-5945
Medical research journal. **Founded:** 1976. **Frequency:** 12x/yr. **Print Method:** Offset. **Trim Size:** 8 1/4 x 11. **Cols./Page:** 2. **Col. Width:** 85 nonpareils. **Col. Depth:** 130 agate lines. **Key Personnel:** Ananda S. Prasad, Editor; Roberta Frederick, Advertising Mgr. ISSN: 0361-8609. **Subscription Rates:** $480.
Ad Rates: BW:　　　$625　　　　　　　　　**Circulation:** 1,325
　　　　　　　4C:　　　$1,570

⊞ 20316　American Journal of Human Biology
John Wiley and Sons, Inc.
Subscription Dept.　　　　　　　　　　　　Phone: (212)850-6000
605 3rd Ave.　　　　　　　　　　　　　　Fax: (212)850-6799
New York, NY 10158
The official journal of the Human Biology Council. **Subtitle:** The Official Journal of the Human Biology Association. **Frequency:** Bimonthly. **Key Personnel:** Robert M. Malina, Editor-in-Chief; Gaston Beunen, Review Articles Editor; Leslie Sue Lieberman, Book Review Editor. ISSN: 1042-0533. **Subscription Rates:** $432; $492 Canada and Mexico; $525 other countries.

⊞ 20317　American Journal of Industrial Medicine
John Wiley and Sons Inc.
605 3rd Ave.　　　　　　　　　　　　　　Phone: (212)850-8800
New York, NY 10158　　　　　　　　　　Fax: (212)850-6021
　　　　　　　　　　　　　　　　　　　　　　(800)225-5945
Industrial medical journal. **Founded:** 1980. **Frequency:** Monthly. **Print Method:** Offset. **Trim Size:** 8 1/4 x 11. **Cols./Page:** 1. **Col. Width:** 48 nonpareils. **Col. Depth:** 133 agate lines. **Key Personnel:** Irving J. Selikoff, Editor; Roberta Frederick, Advertising Mgr. ISSN: 0271-3586. **Subscription Rates:** $672.
Ad Rates: BW:　　　$625　　　　　　　　　**Circulation:** 780
　　　　　　　4C:　　　$1,570

⊞ 20318　American Journal of Medical Genetics
John Wiley and Sons, Inc.
605 3rd Ave.　　　　　　　　　　　　　　Phone: (212)850-8800
New York, NY 10158　　　　　　　　　　Fax: (212)850-6021
　　　　　　　　　　　　　　　　　　　　　　(800)225-5945
Medical research journal. **Founded:** 1977. **Frequency:** 16x/yr. **Print Method:** Offset. **Trim Size:** 8 1/4 x 11. **Cols./Page:** 1. **Col. Width:** 80 nonpareils. **Col. Depth:** 130 agate lines. **Key Personnel:** John M. Opitz, Editor; Roberta Frederick, Advertising Mgr. **Subscription Rates:** $1,344.
Ad Rates: BW:　　　$725　　　　　　　　　**Circulation:** 1,000
　　　　　　　4C:　　　$1,670

⊞ 20319　The American Journal of the Medical Sciences
Pharmaceutical Media Inc.
30 E. 33rd St.　　　　　　　　　　　　　Phone: (212)685-5010
New York, NY 10016　　　　　　　　　　Fax: (212)685-5010
Journal publishing developments in the treatment of diseases. Includes research reports, reviews, commentaries, and special reports. **Subtitle:** The Official Journal of the Southern Society for Clinical Investigation. **Founded:** 1820. **Frequency:** Monthly. **Print Method:** Sheetfed offset. **Trim Size:** 8 1/8 x 11. **Key Personnel:** Suzanne Oparil, MD, Editor; Marcia E. Serepy, Publisher; Susan Eidson, Advertising Dir. ISSN: 0002-9629. **Subscription Rates:** $120; $165 other countries. $20 single issue; $230 Industry; $260 other countries' industry.
Ad Rates: GLR:　　$11　　　　　　　　　**Circulation:** 2,041
　　　　　　　BW:　　$550
　　　　　　　4C:　　$1,345

⊞ 20320　American Journal of Medicine
Excerpta Medica, Inc.
655 Avenue of the Americas
New York, NY 10010
Medical journal. **Founded:** 1946. **Frequency:** Monthly. **Print Method:** Offset. **Cols./Page:** 2. **Col. Width:** 41 nonpareils. **Col. Depth:** 140 agate lines. **Key Personnel:** J. Claude Bennett, M.D., Editor; Randolph Nanna, Publisher. **Subscription Rates:** $66.
Ad Rates: BW:　　　$1,975　　　　　　　**Circulation:** ‡53,751
　　　　　　　4C:　　　$3,500

Remarks: Accepts advertising.

⊞ 20321　American Journal of Nursing
American Journal of Nursing Co.
555 W. 57th St.　　　　　　　　　　　　Phone: (212)582-8820
New York, NY 10019　　　　　　　　　　Fax: (212)586-5462
Journal for staff nurses, nurse managers, and clinical nurse specialists. Focuses on patient care in hospitals, hospital ICUs and homes. Provides news coverage of health care from the nursing perspective. **Founded:** 1900. **Frequency:** Monthly. **Print Method:** Offset. **Cols./Page:** 3. **Col. Width:** 30 nonpareils. **Col. Depth:** 140 agate lines. **Key Personnel:** Martin DiCarlantonio, Editor; James Nagle, Advertising Mgr. ISSN: 0002-936X. **Subscription Rates:** $35.
Ad Rates: BW:　　　$5,420　　　　　　　**Circulation:** 205,884
　　　　　　　4C:　　　$7,420

⊞ 20322　American Journal of Orthopsychiatry
American Orthopsychiatric Association
330 Seventh Ave., 18th Fl.　　　　　　　　Phone: (212)564-5930
New York, NY 10001　　　　　　　　　　Fax: (212)564-6180
Journal on an interdisciplinary and interprofessional approach to mental health treatment. **Founded:** Oct. 1930. **Frequency:** Quarterly. **Print Method:** Offset. **Trim Size:** 6 3/4 x 9 3/4. **Cols./Page:** 2. **Col. Width:** 29 nonpareils. **Col. Depth:** 112 agate lines. **Key Personnel:** Ellen Bassuk, M.D., Editor; Joan Alder, Managing Editor. ISSN: 0002-9432. **Subscription Rates:** $45; $65 Industry.
Ad Rates: BW:　　　$500　　　　　　　　**Circulation:** ‡14,000
Alternate Formats: Microfilm.

⊞ 20323　The American Journal of Pediatric Hematology/Oncology
Liptencoct-Raven
1185 Avenue of the Americas　　　　　　　Phone: (212)930-9500
Mail Stop 3B　　　　　　　　　　　　　　Fax: (212)575-1160
New York, NY 10036
Journal with reports on major advances in the diagnosis and treatment of cancer and blood diseases in children. **Subtitle:** Official Publication of the American Society of Pediatric Hematology/Oncology. **Founded:** 1979. **Frequency:** Quarterly. **Print Method:** Sheetfed offset. **Trim Size:** 8 1/4 x 11. **Key Personnel:** Rita Scheman, Publisher; Carl Pochedly, M.D., Editor-in-Chief; Phyllis C. Noyes, Advertising Mgr. **Subscription Rates:** $116; $150 other countries; $160 Industry; $198 Industry other countries. $50 single issue.

Ad Rates: GLR = general line rate; BW = one-time black & white page rate; 4C = one-time four color page rate; SAU = standard advertising unit rate;
CNU = Canadian newspaper advertising unit rate; PCI = per column inch rate.
Circulation: ★ = ABC; △ = BPA; ◆ = CAC; ● = CCAB; □ = VAC; ⊕ = PO Statement; ‡ = Publisher's Report; Boldface figures = sworn; Light figures = estimated.
Entry type: ⊞ = Print; ▲ = Broadcast.

Source: Gale Research. Reprinted with permission.

Each magazine has a particular editorial viewpoint, one that addresses a special interest or concern of its readers. It's also how an editor evaluates whether your story matches the profile of its readers. There are 122,000 trade associations, each with their own magazine.

What Do Editors Think?

I asked Evan Simonoff, editor-in-chief of *Financial Planning* magazine, to talk about how editors think.

"A local newspaper may be looking for something of a little more general interest, but whether you're writing for the *San Jose Mercury* or *Truck Driver Today* or *Fortune* or *P.C. Monthly*, they'll be looking for somebody who is going to tell something new. You tell clients they need to save money for their retirement. Well, they've heard that. They know it. They're probably not doing enough. But you've got to tell them in such a way that it catches their attention."

How Should it be Written?

"Something with a slightly different slant. Maybe an aspect of saving for retirement that people don't know that much about, such as what are the implications of a cut in the capital gains tax?"

"A big sale for the insurance industry is selling survivorship policies, to pay off estate taxes. For many upscale Americans, it's a big issue. If the estate tax is raised (it really doesn't kick in until you get to about $2 million), a lot of people are going to have more survivorship insurance than they need."

"Saving money for your kids' college education, they already know. You've got to come up with an angle that's new, different."

If You Have a Good Story, but Can't Write It?

"I'll take the idea to a top personal finance correspondent, and they're likely to grab it. If someone brings me an idea that's pretty good and says, 'I'd like to write this story' and I want to have someone who's a professional writer do it, then I'll tell the writer, 'This guy knows a lot about it. You really need to contact him.' Because he came to me with the idea, it's only fair."

How Do They Get in Touch With You?

"I get so many query letters and press releases. I try to see the ones that are new or interesting, that have some relevance. I'll give them to someone else to read. It's become a huge industry. I'm constantly amazed when I hear that someone hired some PR firm for $4,000 a month to send out two or three press releases a month."

"There are some people out there who are good at their own public relations. John Bowen is a classic example of someone who knows what he's doing. When he travels to New York, he makes it a point to have breakfast with reporters and editors. He'll write to say, 'I'd like to meet with you, discuss things, maybe you can use me, maybe you can't.'"

"Don't call an editor with, 'Here's the story you should publish,' because that's a turn-off. Or, someone says, 'Here's my picture.' And the editor says, 'Well, what do I put on the rest of the page?' There are some people who think that will get them published."

Then What *do* You Say?

"You've got to have something that's worthwhile to say. We're all in the information and (to some extent) entertainment business. If you have something to say in a different, new way that will make the reporter's or editor's eyes open, or ears perk up, or that will make the editor's readers stop and say, 'Holy smoke,' then you're doing them a favor."

"Or you come up with some very strange way of doing something. Or invent a mutual fund, the 'Anti-Bill and Hillary Mutual Fund'."

"There's a really sharp guy in upstate New York, Phil Johnson. He worked for years for the New York State University system. He's an expert at helping people put their kids through college and getting them aid breaks. This is a guy who knows how to work the aid system. He's spent 15 years doing this. I'll print his articles because of his unique niche and experience level."

"If you're an expert at something, the reporters will find you. If you're out there just touting yourself because you want to give a quote, you may be able to snooker someone into quoting you once or twice. But it could end up backfiring on you."

Shortcuts to Getting Published

1. Send for the magazine's guidelines. Review them and the ones in the next chapter so that you write the article in a clear, logical, straightforward manner that fits in with the style of that magazine. Trade journal readers are very busy people. They read not for entertainment, but for information that can help them.

2. Once you've done this homework, determine what story you want to tell. You can start by recording one of your sales presentations

or going through the product brochure and outlining specific points you want to cover. Journalists call this focus the "hook" or the "angle" of the story.

3. Make your article concise and to the point, concentrating on getting all the facts. Trade magazines stories seek out articles that show the reader how to save money and time and improve their lives.

4. Be specific. Support claims and statements with statistical examples, studies or explanations. If somebody says that one fund outperformed another fund, the editor is going to want to know by how much.

5. Be objective. Your article should contain useful, accurate and honest information and advice, not rewritten corporate bulletins and press releases. If you do a story on money management, talk to several different money managers, not just one. If you're giving a new management perspective, give the pros, as well as the cons. One-sidedness doesn't interest editors. They want the disadvantages spelled out, as well as the advantages.

6. Write for the magazine's audience, not for the editor or yourself.

7. Introduce a problem and describe its solution and the results, or discuss the latest developments in the industry and reasons for them, and finally, organize the structure so it's easy for the reader to understand and follow. Follow an orderly, sensible progression. One structure I like is to present ideas in a series of numbered points such as "Ten tips to better investing," or "Seven rules for successful investing."

8. Double check your facts and make sure they're complete as well as accurate. If in doubt, make sure. Also, make sure the article goes through your legal and compliance department if you have one. Be thorough and ethical. People who read your articles may make decisions or procedural changes based on what you've written. Keep your notes and source materials for at least six months after the article has been published.

What are My Chances of Writing for One of These Magazines?

You have at least a hundred times better odds of getting into print in a trade magazine than in a consumer magazine. We've discovered we have no competition from most of the professional writers. And a magazine article is a hundred times more powerful than an advertisement in the same magazine.

How to Find the Best Target Publication

1. From a core group of your clients, find an influential member of the industry who is willing to give you an entree into that market. Find the person first, then pick that market as the one that has the best potential.

2. What are the typical wants, needs, desires, and problems of the wealthy people in this market? You should have already identified the most common problems of the people in this industry.

3. Make a complete list of all the problems, and the specific solutions you can offer. Also, list all the best people (specialists) who could be used (through a strategic alliance) to implement the solutions.

4. Become a specialist. You can't fake it. To serve a market success-fully, you have to develop a specialty. Therefore, either match your skills to the market or match the market to your skills: there's no in between!

   Being a person with many skills, but a master of none, gives you the reputation and credibility of a master of none. So position yourself as a specialist and a professional expert in solving the problems of a targeted market; then prove it with your solutions.

5. Identify key organizations that represent this market segment (e.g., a trade association, a club, a civic group, etc.). Do the associations or organizations have an information package that you could get?

6. Identify centers of influence and strategic alliances. Who are the centers of influence for your targeted market? Is there someone who could help you identify qualified prospects and perhaps intro-duce you to them?

   Centers of influence can be directors of trade associations, presidents of social clubs, or community leaders. Many others become influential either by occupation, personal trust, or popu-larity. The best way to get centers of influence to work with you is to solve problems for them. Sell the person with the greatest influ-ence first, and the rest are likely to follow. This is a good way to position yourself and communicate your expertise all at once.

Centers of influence can have a dramatic influence on mass decisions. The center of influence could be a minister or a rabbi, a well-known athlete, a public official, or a local individual who through community service has earned many people's trust. A center of influence might even be one of your own top clients. If you don't know who the center of influence is for a given market, just ask. Get many opinions, because there may be more than one person.

7. Identify publications. Does this market have its own newsletter or publication? Would the editor of that publication print an article from you if it addressed the needs of the people in the association and was not a sales pitch? Call the director of the association and get the criteria or rules for outside authors.

8. Identify the biggest financial concern or challenge. What can you say that will exactly identify the problems or needs of the market, and how you will resolve them?

9. Decide what else differentiates you from the competition. What do you offer that's different from other money management or portfolio management services? It must be something unique, something people want, and something your competition doesn't offer.

Summary

By writing an article for a trade magazine you can communicate directly to pre-qualified (preferably pre-endorsed) prospects without having to go to the masses to find your perfect, qualified prospect through sheer luck and great expense. The problem with mass mailings and other mass advertising efforts is that unqualified people respond to you in mass, causing you to waste time sorting them out. To go directly to your wealthy targeted market is cheaper and more efficient. The results—less time, less cost, richer clients—add up to higher profitability and a whole lot less frustration.

However, you still need to find the most efficient way to communicate your unique problem-solving capabilities. Studies have shown that it generally takes eight communication impressions over time to turn an ordinary prospect into a client. It takes this time to gain trust when major decisions are at stake. Unfortunately, most sales people only make about three efforts at communicating and then quit. Instead of trying to make multiple impressions on a thousand unqualified prospects in a random market (e.g. radio, mass geographic mailing, etc.), try making 10 impressions on a hundred qualified prospects in a specified target market.

For optimal results, combine as many different types of communication as possible for each prospect: targeted mailings, trade association speeches or news articles, endorsements from centers of influence, workshop notifications, telephone follow-ups, etc. Consider using as many of these options as possible with each of your targeted prospect groups:

- The fastest and most efficient way to communicate to your market is to speak to an association, club, or organization that represents that market segment (being introduced by someone they already trust). It takes the same hour of time to speak to 100 people as it does to speak to one. If you're a good public speaker, it's a good way to leverage your time. If you're not, either develop the skill required, or find a strategic ally with whom you can share the podium. Public speaking helps to rapidly elevate your credibility as a problem solver. *Caution*: Do not use this speaking opportunity to sell your product! This is generally not allowed by associations. It would not be appropriate anyway because you want to position yourself as a problem solver, not a product pusher!

- Write an article for the target market's newsletter. We've already laid the groundwork for that. If the article addresses a real need of the group without pushing a product, it will be readily accepted— and the reprints can be used to build credibility with current and future clients.

- Give workshops or seminars to a select segment of your market. For your seminar to be successful, you need a list of pre-qualified people to invite. You should be targeting, not randomly "shot gunning" by using expensive mass media campaigns in the vain hope that you will reach a few wealthy prospects. Huge numbers are not necessary—ten very wealthy clients could make your year. However, a hundred very wealthy clients in one room does elevate your chance of great success!

- Put yourself in places where there are high concentrations of people in your targeted market. The best places are trade shows. If you look like them, talk like them, and do the same things they do, they'll get to know you very fast.

- Target mail a valuable problem-solving reprint with a telephone follow-up. Use your key contacts to help you define a list of qualified prospects within the market segment. Mail a personalized letter to these prospects addressing a problem that you can solve for them. Always make it a call for action by inviting them to a workshop or offering them a free half hour of consultation time. Follow up your letter by telephone within three or four days.

- Send your prospects articles by other people that substantiate your knowledge of investment methodology and your problem-solving capabilities. These should be done on a regular schedule.

A database is necessary to track your progress through the various steps of initial communication, follow-ups, and final sales with each client. As you're going to make between five and eight distinct contacts with a prospect (possibly by combining all the above-referenced options), you have to keep track of them so that no prospect is lost through the cracks of your memory.

To do timely, sequential impressions with each client requires a scheduled follow-up system with an automatic reminder alarm for each subsequent step of your tactical sales plan. To miss an appropriately timed follow-up could waste all the effort that's gone before.

Media Relations

1. Make a list of financial publication journalists and editors: names, phone numbers, and addresses. Build your data bank.

2. Set up a mailing system to keep them informed. Become a resource for local editors and journalists in your area.

3. When and if your name is used in a story, call and thank the writer.

4. Make copies and send them as reprints to clients and prospects.

5. Call prospects and ask if they saw the story. Send a reprint with a note: "thought you would be interested."

Don't expect miracles from your first article. Frequency is the important element of a successful PR module. If you run an article once in your daily paper, it's not enough. Try to write a column or work it out with the editor that you send in articles once a month. You have to have enough frequency. The same with sending out reprints: your customers are exposed, and the more often the better. While the decision of how often is going to be determined by your budget and time, if you can't afford to do it right, perhaps you shouldn't do it at all.

Most likely this will be the first time your client has worked with somebody who actually believes in what he's recommending and can prove it. Clients will respect you tremendously for following through on your knowledge and convictions.

Chapter 11
Trade Magazine
Guidelines

In this chapter, you will learn:
• What editors don't want
• Trade magazine tips
• What every editor wants to read

Let the trade magazine editors help you write your article. How? Send for a copy of the magazine and its guidelines. Editors are more than happy to send them, because that way neither of you waste your time. Read an issue or two. The biggest complaint magazine editors have is writers who do not understand the magazine.

Following are the actual writer's guidelines for prospective contributors who wish to write for *Dental Economics*. I thought you might like to see the real thing.

Keep a copy of all material submitted: Nothing is more frustrating than spending precious time preparing material only for it to become lost (this does happen). Make sure you send the original and keep the copy for yourself.

Things to Remember:

• When you start to write, do just that. Don't wait too long to tell readers what your story is all about or you'll lose their interest.

• Because most of you aren't professional writers, editors prefer a roughly written manuscript with good material and accurate facts to one with wonderful format and style with inaccurate information. Most important, be sure the information you provide is accurate.

DENTAL ECONOMICS
COMBINING TODAY'S CLINICAL, PRODUCT & MANAGEMENT SKILLS
WRITER'S GUIDELINES FOR PROSPECTIVE CONTRIBUTORS

Dental Economics is a practice administration magazine (circulation approximately 112,000) directed toward practicing dentists.

Issues: Most articles are on current issues affecting dentistry. Articles directed at consumers or clinical aspects of dentistry are not used. Other materials not accepted include fiction, poetry, news, or clippings.

Articles: We buy North American serial rights only, and pay honorariums of $100 to $400 for feature articles, depending upon quality, how in-depth the article is, and importance of the subject matter to DE. We also require your social security number on all submitted manuscripts. We pay upon acceptance.

Topics: We are always interested in articles that will help dentists to upgrade their practices and improve their professional standing (e.g. patient and personnel relations, professional image, practice administration, taxes, investments and insurance).

Query letter: We encourage query letters of no more than one page from new authors. It should briefly describe the subject matter.

Length: Average length of articles from 1,000-2,000 words is preferred although longer or shorter articles will be considered.

Enclosures: Clearly identify all enclosures submitted with your manuscript.

Floppy disks: We do accept and encourage manuscripts submitted for review on a floppy disk. Formatted disks using Microsoft Word are preferred. Please include a "hard copy" of your manuscript with the disk.

All articles are sent to us on speculation for review by our editorial staff. Assignments are rare. If your material is rejected, once again, don't take it personally. Instead, re-write your story and look at it from a different angle. Don't be afraid to try again. In addition, just because one article is rejected doesn't mean future articles will be. Don't hesitate to tell us of another idea you have for a story.

Source: Dental Economics. Reprinted with permission.

- Choose subjects that will have national appeal. If it's a national magazine, the material must be of interest to those across the nation.

- If you're writing for *Dental Economics*, write for the dentist, not the patient. Use an informal, conversational style of writing with a lot of anecdotes and quotes. Talk to your readers, not down to them.

- Research your subject well enough that you can provide an objective view of the situation. Giving only your opinion will lessen your credibility.

- Good editing improves writing and should be viewed as helpful hints for future writing endeavors. The editor has, and takes, final responsibility for everything that goes into the magazine. Copy that doesn't require editing to meet magazine style is rare, so don't take changes personally.

Articles will not get published if you write about how your firm does this or that. Likewise, statements you make in articles should never be directed so as to sell yourself or the product. If you're working for a major firm, compliance will be an issue. One of the ways to ensure that your article will *not* make it through compliance is to start quoting a lot of numbers and statistics of funds or making bold statements such as "stocks always go up."

The one way around compliance problems is not to write articles like the type you read in consumer magazines or newspapers. The life of those articles is only a few days. If you talk about how to do something—how to invest money or how to buy a municipal bond or invest with a money manager—that information is timeless. Those articles don't go out of date and are easier to get through compliance because of the steps involved in doing it, not whether or not you're going to make any money—which you can't guarantee anyway.

Chapter 12
How to Leverage Your
Articles

In this chapter, you will learn:
• How to reuse existing articles you've already written
• How to use your reprints to sell your expertise to new markets
• How to leverage your time

There are two basic ways to turn your original premise into multiple articles. One is spinning off ideas. The other is repackaging the same material for a different audience. Usually this means keeping the basic concept the same, but taking a different approach.

One of the people I respect most in the investment field is Dan Bott. Bott has built a multi-million-dollar money management business using public relations and magazine reprints as his marketing tools. In fact he has repackaged one investment article over twenty times in different versions.

You can take an article specifically written for small business owners, for example, and on your word processor replace references to small business owners with doctors or dentists.

The same basic article can be used in various trade magazines. Since trade magazines aren't like mainstream commercial magazines, there isn't necessarily a conflict of interest in writing the same article for various trades.

Most ideas lend themselves to at least several different variations. Some can spawn literally hundreds of different pieces or alternate points of view for different intended target audiences. Repackaging the same material to a different audience means keeping the basic concept the same, but taking a different slant.

Suppose you've written an article for doctors who are concerned about their retirement plans. Your article explains how to find a money manager. A logical place for this article might be medical journals such as *Ocular Surgery News*, or magazines that not only offer medical news but also have a financial news slant.

With a minor rewrite, this article might be appropriate for small business owners, or maybe contractors, who have the same problems with managing money. Notice, by the way, that these are non-competing publications. Each trade publication has its own unique readership, its own needs, concerns, and expectations. Your networked article must match its intended audience before you can send it out.

Sequels are another way to leverage your articles. Write a sequel article based on a theme or premise. You might have an article on "Ten ways to save money for retirement." The sequel could be, "Ten more ways to save money for retirement." Almost any article or story can lend itself to several different types of sequel, depending on the approach you want to take. One drawback in writing a sequel is it often takes as much time and effort as writing the original article.

The etiquette for sending articles to trade magazine editors is no different from selling an article to a consumer magazine: Don't sell the same or a similar piece to publications with overlapping readerships. In other words, you wouldn't want to send an article on teaching stock brokers to both *Registered Representative* and *Financial Planning*, because many of the same people read both magazines. Mention in your cover letter where your work on the same topic has already been published or is scheduled to be published. This also demonstrates that you could write a publishable piece. Treat each rewrite as a new unpublished piece. If, however, it only has a few minor changes and is largely identical to the piece you've already had published, then you must treat it as a reprint.

One thing about sending reprints with your queries: Editors tend to trust each other's judgment, so once a piece has passed the test of publication, editors are more inclined to think highly of it. In fact, most of *Reader's Digest* is reprinted. Reprint opportunities also exist in magazines and newspapers, though many general interest magazines never publish reprints.

The criteria include the magazine's readership will be interested; the reader is unlikely to have seen the piece in its previous appearance; the magazine has run nothing similar recently; and a reasonable reprint rate is available. If an editor likes your manuscript and all these questions are answered, you've got yourself a reprint.

Newspapers are probably the best places to resell your work. An article that appears in the *Army Times* can be resold to the *Los Angeles Times*, the *Ojai Observer*, and so on. There are dozens, even hundreds, of papers from big cities to rural and suburban weeklies. But with few exceptions, newspapers generally do not reprint material that was previously printed in national magazines or in regional magazines in the same city or area because of the overlap in readership. Newspapers also don't reprint material that has appeared in competing newspapers in the region.

Marketing reprints is no different than sending your original work. Here are some tips for effective marketing:

1. Your cover letter should be virtually identical to the one that you use for original work; however, the letter should state when your piece was first published or is scheduled to be published. It's not necessary to mention that the article has been reprinted elsewhere.

2. When possible, submit a photocopy of excerpts of your article in the published form, rather than a manuscript work in published form. Subtle psychological pressure on the editor will encourage him to publish you again.

3. If you're submitting a revised, expanded, or updated article, it's usually better to submit a typed or computer-printed manuscript.

4. Check with the original publisher about rights. Some publication contracts specifically forbid writers to resell an article until after the initial publication or a period of six months after publication. Even if you haven't been paid for the article, the magazine still owns the article. You may submit the same article to as many different publications at a time as you like; however, do not submit the same material to two or more magazines with overlapping readerships simultaneously. Newspapers work on a very tight schedule and occasionally rushed freelance material gets into print with the paper neglecting to inform the author until the day of publication, or even a day after. You don't want two newspapers with similar readership publishing the same article.

Let's look at the finished product. Gary Pia's article was published in the American Cancer Society's magazine. Talk about credibility! How would you like to have this reprint in your marketing packet?

Figure 12-1 Financial Health

BY GARY PIA

A Prudent Way To Put Your Money To Work

No mutual fund manager has been able to consistently beat the stock market averages. In any given year, only half the U.S. stock mutual fund managers do better than the overall market, the so-called benchmark average. What's worse, those "upper-half" managers have only about a 50% chance of repeating their results in the following other year. The random nature of these results adds to the conclusion that these active managers do not add sufficient value to justify their cost. In fact, no major academic study has been able to document any added value above the benchmark averages from active management.

Why don't we hear about this? Because active managers are paid huge salaries for buying and selling stocks and bonds and have hypnotized investors by presenting them with meaningless performance figures. Until now, nobody other than a handful of "academic" types has questioned their value.

Here's the problem

Active managers are either market-timers or stock pickers. Market-timers have to be right twice. First they must get out of a particular market before it declines. Then they must get back in early enough to catch the next market rise. Stock pickers attempt to select the best individual stocks through research and analysis. But, because of today's advanced information technology, it just isn't possible for a stock picker to be smarter than the market.

Contrast these strategies with a simple asset class management approach. Asset class management uses index funds to represent the asset classes and entirely avoids both market-timing and individual stock selection. Think of it as a

"passive strategy." Asset class managers couple a strategy of diversification and discipline with a strategy of investing in index funds that reflect various benchmark averages. (Index funds are mutual funds that own all or most of the stocks or bonds in a given segment of the financial markets.)

Index funds attempt to emulate a particular market by owning a large portion of that market's stocks. These funds typically have significantly lower management costs. They also may attempt to add value through trading strategies gained through the economies of scale, but not by forecasting market movements.

Still, index investing does not completely eliminate benchmark risk. Index funds or asset class managers will have some spread from the benchmark they try to track. Even so, by using index funds an asset class investor can narrow the benchmark risk. (Benchmark risk is simply the risk that an investment doesn't do as well as the benchmark.)

By investing in a wide range of index funds which tend to move in very different cycles, it is possible for the portfolio manager to lower the overall risk of investing.

An asset class investment approach can be a healthy solution to your main investment problems. Most academic studies have shown that asset class portfolios have outperformed about 75% of actively managed funds over periods of ten years or longer. Asset class diversification implemented with index funds is an academically sound approach for individuals to pursue.

Twenty years ago, institutional investors had less than $50 million invested in index funds. Today, institutions have somewhere over $500

billion invested this way – a ten thousand fold increase! The point is, you do not have to take leaps of investment faith to get results. There is a body of academically sound knowledge available and by adhering to its principles, shortening bond maturities, and adding small U.S. companies plus large and small international companies, it is possible to increase investment returns while lowering investment risks.

Switching from active management to asset class investing.

An eight step plan:

Step One: Work with an investment advisor who constructs portfolios using asset class strategies.

Step Two: Select an advisor who is paid on a fee-only basis rather than by brokerage commissions.

Step Three: Determine your investment time horizon for investing.

Step Four: Determine your level of risk, particularly on the downside.

Step Five: Set target rates of return for your entire investment portfolio to achieve your objectives.

Step Six: Write an investment policy statement providing specific directions to an investment advisor.

Step Seven: Rebalance your portfolio periodically.

Step Eight: Measure your investment performance quarterly.

Gary E. Pia is the President of G.E. Pia & Company, an investment advisory firm in Pasadena, California. Specializing in world-class portfolio management for prudent investors, Mr. Pia has served the needs of private and institutional investors for over 15 years.

Source: G.E. PIA & Company. Reprinted with permission.

Chapter 13
Present Yourself on a
Website

In this chapter, you will learn about:
- Advertising on the Internet
- How to get started
- Where to go for help

There was a time when simply converting a company brochure to a web page was enough to get you noticed—but in this day and age, that doesn't cut it. Each day, 17,000 domain names are registered. The key is to differentiate yourself from the 200,000 new pages that appear on the Worldwide Web each day.

When we used the Alta Vista search engine to identify websites that contained the words "mutual funds," over 200,000 matches were identified. For the words "financial planning," 800,000 matches came up. The noise on the Internet is increasing all the time. You've got to be different.

One way to differentiate yourself is to place reprints on your site of any articles you've had published or other research material you have permission to use. Have a place to answer people's questions, interact with them, and provide needed services.

Chances are investors aren't merely going to surf your website, then call you up and hire you as an advisor. If you're simply displaying a web page and users happen to come across it, chances are they won't be ready at that moment to make an investment and you won't have made enough of an impression to motivate them to come back to you when they are.

An American Management Association (AMA) study[1] featured the results of two concurrent 1997 surveys—an assessment of personal use of the Internet for business purposes by 3,466 executives and managers in major U.S. firms, and an evaluation of organizational practices, policies and plans for Internet use by 656 systems and administrative managers. The findings:

Home Page Activity and Internet Expenditures: 60 percent of respondent firms currently have a home page on the Internet. This percentage is expected to increase to 82 percent within 24 months. These sites are most frequently updated either weekly (26%) or monthly (26%).

At this time, 87 percent of business professionals who do not have a website are interested in developing one; 82 percent want to develop a website for customers; and 50 percent are planning to implement a website over the next nine months.

Advertising on the Internet: More than 66 percent of respondent firms advertise their products or services on the Internet, with an additional 18 percent currently considering this. However, few companies currently advertising on the Internet are entirely happy with the results (34% rate the Internet as a somewhat successful advertising medium, and half have yet to make a judgment on the effectiveness of Internet advertising).

Potential customers can only find you if they know you're there. Strategically placed banner ads and keyword search purchases should be an essential part of your Internet strategy.

How to Get Started

Step One

To get started on the Internet, first choose an Internet provider. The provider will supply you with the browser software. Use either Microsoft's Internet Explorer or Netscape's Navigator. Three Internet service providers you might try are Netcom (800-NETCOM1), PSI (800-827-7482), and AT&T (800 831-5259). If you get stuck at this point, hire a teenager to get you started; they can be remarkably proficient and inexpensive. You may even have a teenager in your family who would love to get you started.

Programs such as HTMLed, FrontPage and others allow a relative novice to design websites, but do not allow you to learn how to spot mistakes or make minor modifications which could have a great impact on the final appearance. They also create extra code on every page, which will delay the download of your site to visitors.

---

[1] American Management Association (AMA) and Tierney & Partners, a Philadelphia-based communications company.

A do-it-yourself website program typically creates a website that looks good on one browser, but does not necessarily look good on other browsers. If you create a site for yourself and only check the site with one type of browser, you surrender control of your site's appearance. You will have no idea exactly how your site will appear for at least 50 percent of your site's visitors.

Step Two

Allocate several hours over the next couple of months to just browse. Spend time exploring various financial and non-financial sites. Look for what you would like to display on your own site. Three of my favorite financial sites to search through are *The Wall Street Journal, Financial Planning Online,* and *Advisor Link.*

Surf the Internet. There are more current resources on the Internet than anywhere else. Spend as much time as possible researching your competitors on the Internet. This is truly the only way to be competitive. If there are specific products you want to feature, get written permission to use those names on your website. The most important thing here is to ensure you will not ruin what could otherwise be a harmonious relationship.

If you plan on using images from print collateral of a company, get written permission from the company to do so. Ask them to specify in the letter a specific time period during which you're authorized to use the images. Failure to do this could result in a sudden demand that you remove the images from your website. If you relied heavily on the images, your website would be pretty barren.

Step Three

The time you dedicate to selecting the company to design and host a website for your business is critical to its success. It's important to research the firms who are candidates to build your site. It's not simply a matter of calling all the companies in the phone book and finding the least expensive.

Most small business owners who have websites are dissatisfied. Don't join their ranks! Contact current clients of a site design firm and ask if they're satisfied. Are they getting the results they expected? If not, do they know why? Take the time to do the homework required to connect your business with a technologically competent and sincere development firm.

Visit several websites the firm currently hosts. If you have direct access to the Internet via an ISDN or larger data line, make the visit using a modem. Would you feel comfortable with your site being delivered at that speed?

Examine the code used in client sites of the firm you're considering. Using the pull-down menu on your browser, select "View/Sourcecode" or something similar to display the HTML code for the page you are viewing. Does one of the first ten lines include the word "Generator" followed with the name of a website software package? If yes, then you should consider other firms that do not rely on code generators. They slow your visitors down.

Find a company where 100 percent of server time and bandwidth is available to deliver client sites to the public. The result is a really quick server response and a short download time for persons visiting the sites of their clients. If you've visited really slow sites and consider the wait drudgery, then you know exactly what I'm talking about. Dedicated client bandwidth, as is available on the servers of both USAWorks and Aztech Cyberspace, minimizes this wait.

Checklist

Here is a checklist to help you out:

- Will you begin with a basic site, then build a site with greater complexity at some future time?
- Does the firm you're considering have the resources to add new features such as visitor response forms, a database for serving information, or secure on-line ordering systems?
- Are these capabilities in-house or available through a strategic partnership?
- Is the response you receive on who will develop those features specific and confident?
- How much bandwidth is available? Is it shared with an Internet Service Provider?
- Is the bandwidth purchased from a single provider or multiple providers? Multiple is better since this provides true redundancy.
- What type of server will be used? Unix servers, including Linux, Solaris, and Irix, are the most reliable and secure servers available.

- Does the firm repeatedly refer to a complete site using the term "home page"? If yes, move on to the next candidate.

- When meeting with the firm's representatives, do they talk about opportunities to use the Internet to create new opportunities for your business, or do they just want to put your information on the web? A really good firm will become a strategic asset to your business and provide you with insight to achieve results you did not think of yourself.

- Are there important deadlines critical to your success? If there's a specific time frame required, have it included in your contract. If you're a small client and are in a hurry, have reasonable expectations when approaching firms that produce high-quality sites. They typically will already have sites in development for larger firms. The best way you can help yourself is to deliver your end of the site—information about your business, copy writing, and images—on time. Make your needs clear and let the firm do its job.

- Ask about the graphic designers who work for the firm. They should have received formal training. Make an appointment to meet them to discuss your project. They are usually very creative people and will recommend designs that you did not consider yourself. My experience has been that such a meeting will result in a higher quality site. Be sure to ask them what they would do if it were their site.

- If there are customer feedback, database, or secure transaction features, agree on how they'll function before making a commitment on them. Ensure that the firm understands exactly what you want the result of this visitor interaction to be. There are different ways to accomplish the same result, and different firms will propose different solutions for the same problem. Make sure the solution the firm is using will work for your visitors. If you want customers to be able to reach specific information from any location in the site, make sure this is understood.

Costs

Set-up costs for an integrated site, which includes basic information about your business, contacts, information, brief history and industry overview, will cost you between $600 and $2,500.

Today, there are numerous national and local Internet Service Providers (ISPs) that can provide reliable connections at affordable prices. These usually cost $19.95 per month for a regular analog dial-up account (up to 56Kbps) and $30-40 for ISDN service (up to 128Kbps).

Expect to make a down payment of 30 to 60 percent of the site up front. The work produced for your site cannot be used for anyone else, so this is totally reasonable and should be anticipated.

Before you sign up:
1. What are the terms for maintaining the site? Will you have to pay a fee for minor modifications? Make sure you have a site maintenance plan that you are comfortable with.

2. Who will own the work once it's created?

3. Do you have rights to reuse any of the content in other literature your firm distributes?

4. Can you get a back-up copy of the site on CD-ROM to protect your investment?

Step Four

Reserve the domain name for your company, e.g., Nature's Standard (http://www.naturesstandard.com), write the HTML code for the entire site, and register the site with search engines.

Build your website. You won't get it right the first time. The Internet is constantly changing, and your site should also. Plan a systematic review every few months to see how effective it has been and what you can do to improve it. The Internet must become an integral part of your overall marketing structure.

Once work on your site has begun, let the developer do the work without a lot of interruptions. You should have all your questions answered before that point. If you still have a lot of questions when the site is already in development, either you didn't take the time to ask the right questions or you were rushed through the process by the developer. Being hurried through the process is highly undesirable and will usually result in a site that's quite different from what you envisioned.

Step Five

When your site is complete, you need to wait a while to make improvements. Review the responses you've received periodically to ensure that you're getting the results you wanted when you began.

It would also be beneficial to review where your site is listed on search engines. Realize that not every site can come up as number one on every search engine. If your hosting and maintenance contract doesn't provide for extensive follow-up meetings, expect to pay a consultation fee.

Use an FAQ document (Frequently Asked Questions with answers) that you can e-mail to each person who inquires about your product. You can use a program called an autoresponder to do this for you. If you don't have an automatic response form, keep a record of the responses you've been sending out and develop either a Frequently Asked Questions document or some standardized responses you can personalize for visitor inquiries.

These are just some of the steps that can be taken to ensure that the process of developing a site for your business meets your expectations. While you shouldn't have to be involved with every little detail for creating, hosting and maintaining the site, you can prepare yourself for this endeavor by knowing what questions to ask. Write out your own plan on what you hope to achieve before calling anyone.

Additional recommended reading: "*Secrets of Successful Web Sites, Project Management*" by David Siegel is very thorough without getting involved in too many technical details.

Where to go for help: Peter Neves, 702-324-6857, USAWorks! (http://www.usaworks.com) provides design services to small businesses.

Figure 13-1 USAWorks

Source: USA Works! Reprinted with permssion.

Traditional media send information in one direction, a website can also collect it!

While it's sometimes difficult for a financial advisor to measure the success of traditional media campaigns, there are methods for gauging the effectiveness of a website. If your service depends on constant media exposure, an Internet website is a great complement by which to collect client feedback.

Chapter 14
Making Your
Newsletters Sing

In this chapter, you will learn:
• What should go into a newsletter
• Tips for running a newsletter program
• Examples of successful newsletters
• Where to go for help

Newsletters are one way to accomplish your public relations and marketing goals. An effective newsletter will impart interesting information to readers, thus enhancing your credibility and expertise in the eyes of clients and prospects. Every time clients or prospects see the newsletter, they will think about you even if they don't call or comment on the newsletter. The more often they think about you, the more likely it is that they'll call when they need help with a financial matter.

You can use newsletters as a major part in your top-of-the-mind drip system as a way to be systematic and consistent in maintaining contact and building relationships with clients and prospects.

They're also an excellent way to inform your clients and prospects of the services you provide, demonstrate your expertise, and build credibility. A newsletter can be used to explain complicated financial information in an easy-to-read format.

Professionally written newsletters provide information in an editorial format, which is perceived to be more objective than other advertising formats, and generally more believable. It can have a long shelf life; readers may retain the newsletters for a long period of time, producing inquiries months after the newsletter is sent. Before starting a newsletter program, consider the following:

1. *Send your newsletter consistently*—at least quarterly, so that your clients and prospects realize that they're receiving it on a regular schedule and begin to look forward to receiving it.

2. *Be patient.* Newsletters are a subtle, indirect marketing tool that requires time to adequately evaluate their effectiveness. Continue your newsletter for at least 18 months to two years to give it adequate time to make an impression on your clients and prospects.

3. *Determine your goal for the newsletter.* You may simply want to keep in touch with your current clients . . or market additional services to your clients . . or use the newsletter to prospect.

4. *Keep your goal in mind when writing your newsletter.* If you want people to call you, make sure the articles are written on subjects of specific interest to your readers, and ask them to call. Make it easy for your readers to contact you by including a reader response card.

5. *Tell your readers about your website,* its features and how to access it.

6. *Many clients and prospects won't be familiar with the total range of services* you provide. Include a list of your services in your newsletters periodically to remind them.

7. *Highlight articles of particular interest to certain clients.* A handwritten note on the front of the newsletter is an effective attention grabber and will be sure to get your newsletter read.

8. *Only reluctantly delete names from your mailing list.* It may take a prospect a year or two to decide to do business with you. The cost of sending a newsletter to that person over that time period is nominal compared to the revenue you may lose if that person forgets about you.

9. *Keep an extra supply of newsletters.* You can leave them in your office lobby, pass them out at seminars, or mail them to new prospects and clients.

10. *Periodically ask people how they like your newsletter.* At the same time, ask if they know anyone who would like a free subscription.

11. *Send copies of your newsletter to professional referral sources.* Ask them if they'd like additional copies to give to their clients. Keeping your name in front of referral sources is a good way to ensure that they think of you when they have business to refer.

Producing a newsletter yourself is no small task, easily taking 40 to 75 hours to research, write, edit, and print. A newsletter provider is a cost-effective alternative to maintain regular contact with clients and prospects and not spend the time personally to write the piece. There are several companies that prepare newsletters for the financial services industry. The number of options and personalization features offered vary, but some offer so many options that most of your readers will think you produced the newsletter yourself.

Figure 14-1 Integrated Concepts Group, Inc.

Confused by so many choices?

Don't let the amazing number of investment choices confuse you. While it is tempting to spend most of your time selecting individual securities or timing the market, studies have shown that your asset allocation strategy accounts for 91.5% of your total return (Source: *Secure Your Future*, 1996). An asset allocation strategy provides several benefits:

It provides a disciplined approach to diversification.

It encourages long-term investing. While you will need to make changes from time to time, this strategy is designed to control the long-term makeup of your portfolio.

It eliminates the need to time investment decisions. With an asset allocation policy, you don't have to worry about timing the market, you just have to

ensure that your investments stay within the proper percentages.

It reduces risk in your portfolio. Asset allocation allows you to combine risky investments with those that are less risky. This combination reduces the risk of being fully invested in riskier investments, while increasing the return that would be obtained from investing solely in less risky investments.

It provides a means to adjust the risk in your portfolio over time by changing the allocations for different categories of assets you hold.

It keeps you focused on the big picture. Rather than investing in a haphazard manner, it gives you a framework for making investment decisions.

Please call if you'd like to discuss the role of asset allocation in your investment portfolio. ∞

Tackling Inflation

Over a period of years, even 3% inflation can have a dramatic impact on your purchasing power. After 5 years of 3% inflation, $1 is worth 86¢; after 10 years, 74¢; and after 20 years, 55¢. Consider these steps to tackle inflation:

✔ Choose investments with returns greater than the rate of inflation.

✔ Select investments with tax deferral of contributions and earnings.

✔ With many retirements now lasting 15 to 30 years, retirees should choose investments that will hedge against inflation.

✔ Review the limits of your insurance coverages periodically, especially homeowners, renters, and umbrella coverage.

✔ Don't buy into the argument that it is better to borrow and spend money now, paying the debt later with "cheaper" dollars. ∞

Ten Tips

Continued from page 1

7 Take advantage of all retirement plans available to you. Be sure to invest in your company's 401(k), 403(b), or other defined-contribution plan as soon as you are eligible.

8 You need to be concerned about the effects of inflation, even at the current moderate level of 3%. See the article "Tackling Inflation" for more details.

9 Reconsider your views about retirement. Although many people typically consider retirement a time for rest and leisure, 30 years of this can be a bit overwhelming and very

expensive to finance. Instead, you may want to ease into retirement by starting a business or working part-time.

10 Don't touch your retirement savings for anything other than retirement. It is difficult enough to fund a long retirement, without making that task even more difficult by raiding your funds for other purposes.

It is important to get started with your retirement plans now if you hope to have a comfortable retirement. Call today so that together we can design retirement strategies to achieve your retirement goals. ∞

Figure 14-1 Integrated Concepts Group, Inc., con't.

Put Time on Your Side

Consider the savings habits of this 20-year-old couple. The wife starts putting $2,000 per year into a tax-deferred investment when she is 20. After 10 years, she decides to stop investing and just let her money grow until she retires.

The husband decides to start investing when his wife stops. He invests $2,000 a year in a tax-deferred investment from the time he is 30 until he retires at age 65. If they both earn 8% on their savings, who will have more money at age 65?

Time and compound interest favor the wife. She will have $462,648 at age 65, while her husband will only have $372,204.

Use time to your advantage — start saving early. ◯◯◯

```
          $462,648
■ Wife
■ Husband          $372,204



        $70,000
$20,000 ■
Contributions   Value at age 65
```
This example is provided for illustrative purposes only and is not intended to project the performance of a specific investment vehicle.

Most people dream of a secure financial future. Yet your dream will remain just that unless you take steps to accomplish it. Setting specific goals is a critical element in achieving financial success. Keep these tips in mind as you formulate your goals:

✔ **Set exciting goals.** Your goals must keep you motivated to reduce your current spending in order to save for the future. "Financial security when you retire" may be an accurate statement of your goal, but may not be sufficient motivation to delay purchase of that new sports car. A goal of "retiring when you are 55 with $500,000 in investments so you can enjoy your afternoons golfing at your favorite golf course in Florida" is a far more exciting goal.

✔ **Make sure your goals are meaningful to you.** When you are getting started, setting goals that you are motivated to achieve will help you understand the importance of the goal-setting process.

✔ **Put your goals in writing in order to clarify them and to give you a means to assess your progress in meeting them.** Think through your goals carefully. What are your expectations for success? How much time do you have to achieve the goal? How committed are you to the goal? How diffi-

cult is the goal to achieve?

✔ **Prioritize your goals.** Most people have five or six goals; prioritize them to ensure that you achieve those that are most important to you.

✔ **State your goals in measurable terms.** In addition to quantifying your ultimate goal, quantify interim goals. If you need $500,000 in 20 years, how much do you expect to have after one year, two years, etc.?

✔ **Don't be afraid to set ambitious goals.** Just because a goal seems difficult to achieve doesn't mean that you should avoid it. It does mean that you'll have to develop appropriate strategies to achieve the goal.

✔ **Reward yourself when you make progress toward your goals.** Financial goals often take years to achieve. In order to maintain your commitment to the goal, it is important to have interim goals and to reward yourself when you achieve those interim steps.

Setting goals is only the first step toward achieving your financial objectives. You also need strategies to achieve those goals, plus a mechanism to help you measure your progress on a periodic basis. Feel free to call if you would like assistance in this process. ◯◯◯

Source: Integrated Concepts Group, Inc. Reprinted with permission.

This newsletter is offered by Integrated Concepts Group, Inc. 29777 Stephenson Highway, Madison Heights, Michigan 48071 (800)-338-4329); fax (810) 583 3417; phone (810) 583-2646. Integrated Concepts offers a family of 12 different four-page newsletters targeting various areas, such as general financial planning, investment planning, retirement planning, insurance, and 401(k) plans. Two are printed in full color, the others in two colors. Several options are offered. Your information is printed on the top of the front page, including logos, photos, addresses, phone numbers, etc. Current prices range from 80 cents a copy for 50 to 100 copies down to 35 cents a copy for over 2,000 copies; you can subscribe to the service on a monthly, bimonthly, or quarterly basis.

You can date the newsletters any way you wish. They can be set up as self-mailers or folded to fit in a standard business envelope. Integrated Concepts will send you a proof copy of the newsletter before it is actually printed.

The newsletters should be filed with NASD Regulation, and you can arrange to submit the newsletter to compliance departments.

If you prefer to do it yourself, here are some other sources for newsletter publishing:

Mark Beach, *Editing Your Newsletter*, Coast to Coast Books, distributed by Writer's Digest Books, 1507 Dana Ave., Cincinnati, OH 45207; (800) 289-0963.

Frederick Goss, *Success in Newsletter Publishing*, Newsletter Publisher's Association, Suite 509, 1501 Wilson Blvd., Arlington, VA 22209; (703) 527-2333.

A good marketing program resembles a military campaign. The most important thing: plan for it. If you're ready to do battle, armed with your positioning statements, articles, reprints, query letters, websites and newsletters, turn the page and let's meet the rest of your troops. The big gun—the investment book.

Part III: Writing an Investment Book

Become a celebrity to your target market!

The goal of Part III is to leverage everything you have learned so far. You'll learn how to take those magazine articles you've been writing and turn them into a book. You introduce your topic, develop it, and conclude it using an outline filled in with the research you've already been doing. It practically writes itself!

Chapter 15
The Master Investment
Book Template

In this chapter, you will learn:
• The steps to writing a book
• Master book plotting
• How to use a template

Over the years, I've noticed similarities in how-to books. I've read nearly every new one that hits the stands. Not just investment books—psychology, fixing your house, how to fly-fish, how to run a business. They all follow a similar pattern—a pattern that publishers know will sell. Think of how-to books as just a huge problem-solving article. The first chapter sets up the problem and the rest of the book answers the problem.

The following "master book plot" presents ideas on how a non-writer can achieve a professionally written investment book that inspires the readers to want to put the ideas into action. The goal is a 250 to 300-page manuscript. This chapter demonstrates the kind of planning and thinking that should shape such a writing project.

The Steps

Following are the steps you should consider.

Step 1. The Outline

Some writers feel that the process of outlining limits their spontaneity and leads to dull writing, but using this method will ensure your book gets completed when your spontaneity wanes.

Begin with the Table of Contents. Contemplate your subject, write out topics for four or five major sections, then break each section down into subsections. If it's a how-to book, break each subsection into steps that the reader can perform, as we did in this book.

Step 2. Write a Brief Description of Each Chapter

Using 3 x 5 cards, write a different chapter title on each card. Then turn the each card over and write the points or topics that will go into that chapter.

Step 3. Assemble Your Reference Material in Folders

Label a folder for each topic and fill it with your articles and the reprints and permissions you have collected. Organize your research material before you start writing, so that you know what you are including and where to find it. Don't even start writing until you have all of this organized.

Step 4. Reorganize

Assign each section of your outline a different-colored marker, then go back through your reference material and highlight important information and quotes in the right color for the chapter where you want it. You may find some information is applicable to more than one section, or is more effectively used in a different section than you first assigned it.

Step 5. Start Writing

Get words down on paper or on the computer. If it feels good, keep writing. If you sense that you're getting off track, stop and look at your cards again. Just as with writing your articles, this should be a process of simply filling in the blanks and structuring thoughts into sentences.

Step 6. Polish

Writing is rewriting. The more time you spend polishing the manuscript the better the book is going to look in the readers' hands. My favorite saying is, writing that doesn't keep you up all night, won't keep your readers up either.

The Book Template

A book is composed of the following elements.

The Preface

The sole intention of a preface is to intrigue and hook the reader. It should be short and sweet, not exceeding four or five manuscript pages. It should deliver a compelling promise.

Example: "By following the steps in this book, you can build a million-dollar asset management business within five years." That's the very promise John Bowen used in his book on building an asset management business.

In another best seller, *The Millionaire Next Door*, author Thomas Stanley surprises the reader with the declaration that wealthy people are not the extraordinary and gifted human beings that we think they are. He follows up by offering readers insight into the actions affluent people take to accumulate their wealth. In the last part of the preface, he establishes himself and his partner, William Danko, as experts by demonstrating the comprehensive research they have undertaken. A potential reader who ventures into that preface and is interested in accumulating wealth would feel compelled to read the whole book.

What will you ask or tell readers that will hook them? Don't think about the overall book, only of your opening sentence. Give it a try on these next few blank lines.

The Introduction

Establish the main direction and subject of the book in the Introduction. If this is to be your introductory chapter, set up a problem. After you state the problem, make a promise to solve that problem. Tell the readers what they will learn and how you are going to answer this problem. Establish your outlook on investing and tell readers why you think this way. Quickly outline your concept here.

_____

_____

_____

_____

_____

_____

_____

List related areas or concerns affected by, or affecting your problem:
What can you explain that will support your solutions? *Examples*: You
can show the reader how the stock markets works—volatility and perception vs. reality. You may want to discuss the key concepts of investing, and how to enhance returns while lowering risk—that sort of thing.

1._____

2._____

3._____

4._____

5._____

6._____

Current Trends Chapter

List current trends and why you think these trends will continue or correct. Rethink past advice and why it does or doesn't work today. Lay out
areas of investor concern.

_____

_____

_____

_____

_____

_____

Use Proof Statements: Talk about risk in the different areas of investing.
That will get readers starting to think. Discuss new strategies and why
they work in this new economic environment. Back this chapter up with

proof—charts, graphs, and quotes from top academics or well-known names in the stock market.

_____

_____

_____

_____

_____

_____

_____

Diversification Chapter

Spend some time discussing diversification and how fund managers use it to advantage, plus what diversification means to an investment plan.

_____

_____

_____

_____

_____

_____

_____

Define Different Investments

Cover three or four topics that show how different investments work with each other. Add charts, graphs and backup material, along with quotes from a recognized authority.

_____

_____

_____

_____

_____

_____

Investment Strategies

Shift to a study of global investment strategies, discussing the cost of investing overseas, and how this can add value.

_____

_____

_____

_____

_____

_____

_____

Steps To Investing

Solve problems: Show first-time investors how to build their own portfolios. Use steps to walk them through a logical thought process that leads
to lower risk and higher returns.

_____

_____

_____

_____

_____

_____

_____

Back-up material: Change the pace here and provide technical material.
Tell readers to skip this chapter unless they want a detailed explanation of
how the model you're presenting works.

_____

_____

_____

_____

_____

_____

Tools Readers Can Use

You might slip in a copy of an investment policy statement here, explaining how best to use this tool.

_____

_____

_____

_____

_____

_____

How Different Investments Solve Problems

Give readers more solid proof that your system works. Show how different investment products work to solve financial problems. Perhaps present a selection of mutual funds, with phone numbers and other information on how to reach them.

_____

_____

_____

_____

_____

_____

_____

The Pull-It-Together Chapter

Here you answer the original question you set up in the introduction or first chapters. Think logically, solve the problems, pull it all together here. Explain how to select an investment firm, perhaps, or put together a financial team.

_____

Summary

Summarize your book here. Condense everything you've told readers in the previous chapters into a summary, but in a format that helps them get started now. *Tip:* Boil your sales presentation down to a six-step plan. Follow this with a paragraph explaining how to put these principles to work. You want readers to feel a sense of the story coming to a successful and inspiring closure.

_____

_____

_____

_____

_____

_____

_____

_____

Glossary

Toss in a glossary of investment terms and where you got your information—and you're done.

Appendix

I put the technical stuff here: math formulas, studies, etc.

Subject Index

With all the search tools on today's computer software, an index takes hardly any time at all.

About the Author

Tell your readers who you are and highlight your qualifications, education, and position with your firm. Add a picture. Let the readers know how to reach you.

The Finishing Touches

Now go back through and add research, aiming at a length for each chapter of 10 to 30 pages. Once you have the book laid out, the process becomes infinitely easier. The rest is polish. Voila! A book!

But wait! Before you spend any more time writing, you've got to read the next chapter.

Chapter 16
How to Sell Your Book
to a Publisher—Before
You Write It!

In this chapter, you'll learn:
• What goes into a proposal and what sells—Guidelines
• What editors are looking for
• How the proposal becomes the introduction chapter
• Where to send your book proposal

In the U.S. alone, 500,000 books are written every year. No more than 1 in 10 is ever published.

Publishers buy 90 percent of their books based on a book proposal. The proposal previews your book and makes the publisher want to read your completed manuscript. Even if you've completed your book, a publisher is going to want to read a proposal first. If you can write a good proposal and it sells the book before you write it, it gives you the momentum you need to finish.

Think of the proposal as a sales brochure. Before agents or book publishers accept a work of fiction, they require a complete manuscript; however, nonfiction projects are different—a written proposal can do the trick. They both have the same risk of being rejected; the difference is you're not going to spend five years writing a book to get the same result.

The book proposal will force you to assess whether your book is marketable without wasting a lot of time.

Book proposals differ from a typical article query letter. You must include many more elements in order to persuade an editor to look at a book length manuscript. A lot of similar books are in the market. Why is your information new and different? How many chapters will it take to cover the topic? What are the chapter headings? Essentially you must convince the editor that it would be worth his time to publish your book. One of the most important steps is to zero in on the target audience that you're writing to.

Know the book publisher. Your local bookstore can help. Look at books similar to the one you have in mind. Open the cover and find the publisher's name, then look it up in *Writer's Market*.

Writer's Market lists over 4,200 publishers with basic information about each and points to look for that will maximize your chances for querying successfully. You can find this book in book stores for under $30, or write Writer's Digest Books, 1507 Dana Avenue, Cincinnati, OH 45207.

The Book Proposal

Don't Send Unsolicited Manuscripts

Publishers dislike unsolicited book manuscripts. They are thought of as the homeless, floating around aimlessly from publisher to publisher. The book proposal, on the other hand, is an invitation to dinner. Think of your book proposal as a lean, mean, persuasive machine.

Guidelines

Guidelines should only serve as general parameters. A model proposal (which is also just a guideline) is included at the end of this chapter.

Contrary to the common practice in other industries, book publishers do *not* prefer to receive bound proposals. A publisher who likes your proposal will want to photocopy it; binding is only an impediment. Use a paper clip to secure the pages.

The lean, mean, persuasive machine: Appearance counts. Letter quality printing is best. The manuscript should be on bond paper. Always double space. Make sure your proposal isn't dog-eared or marked up or abused by a previous reader. No publisher likes to get something somebody else has read (and probably turned down). The length of the proposal can be anywhere from 15 to 30 double-spaced pages; typical sample chapters add another 10 to 20 pages. It may be as long as 100 pages, it may be much less. Whatever it takes.

Cover Letter

Start by explaining why somebody would buy your book and what its about, and why you're qualified to write it. A good title can sell a mediocre book, but a poor title can't sell a good book. Provide alternative titles to get editors thinking. Try out titles on lots of people.

The Overview

Write an overview of your entire book. How will your book or article benefit the reader? What information do you plan to provide? Be as specific as possible. You separate your book from the rest by listing those benefits that are unique to your system or your approach or your service. One of the ways to hook your editors with the first few words and keep them reading is by skillfully planting attention grabbers, highlights with a few mouthwatering words:

> "Every Millionaire Spent Years Making the Same Six Critical Mistakes"
>
> "How to Build a Million Dollar Advisory Business"
>
> "The 13 Investment Problems to Overcome"

The hook is the implied promise in each of these sentences. An opening like this guarantees to make a publisher feel that the book or the article is something the readers will want to read. It's an attention-getter that inspires the reader to read more. But don't forget to develop your hook.

There are different kinds of hooks. Here are a few more you can use to stimulate your thought:

- Follow a dramatic statement or question with a list of comic experiences about people with the same problem or who lack the skill you teach.
- Use the negative aspect in your dramatic statement, such as "The One Thing No Winning Advisor Ever Tells Anyone," or "Successful Investors Often Have Frequent Losses." Curiosity helps bring readers in.
- Case histories hook people because readers can relate to someone else's experience and look forward to learning how they resolved it.

Outline the Chapters

This is the meat of the proposal. Here you'll tell what's going on in the book. Each chapter will be tentatively titled, followed by no more than 100 words about what will go into it. On the other hand, don't be too brief to adequately represent the project.

It's also a good idea to preface the outline with a table of contents. That way the editor can see your entire focus at the outset.

Marketing & Promotional Section

This is where you justify the book's existence from a commercial perspective: who will buy it. You wouldn't just state, "My book is for wealthy individuals." You need to be more demographically sophisticated than that. Include a marketing example with numbers, if you can. Give the editor a statement that the publisher's sales reps could say to a bookstore owner. They need a 20 to 30-second sound bite. For example, "How about ordering 10 of a book that will tell investment advisors how to start a public relations program?" Mention how you would promote it: Speaking tours; seminars; book signings; connections; sales to clients; sub-rights and spin-offs—audio, video, articles.

Competition Section

If there are any books like yours, describe them here. How is your book unique? You want to analyze the competition before you leap ahead in writing your book on, say, derivatives. Find out how many other books on derivatives there are in the market place. Don't try to compete until you can offer a new approach on the subject, better information, or something that will fill a niche that has been overlooked. If you have that, spell it out for the publisher.

Author's Bio

Write your own profile on your interests or background. Provide interview questions. Write it in the third person. Tell about credentials that support and match the book. Include any public speaking and books and articles you've published. Self-flattery here is appropriate as long as it's the truth.

Sample Chapters

Three sample chapters will help the proposal a lot. Sample chapters help to reduce the editor's concern about your ability to deliver quality work beyond the proposal stage. You can also send copies of articles you've written as samples, though chapters will be more persuasive.

Great! Now let's make it look even more professional.

Figure 16-1 A Model Proposal

Chapter 17
How to Make It Look
Even More Professional

In this chapter, you'll learn:
• Secrets to a professional look
• Why neatness sells
• Everything you need to know about editors

This chapter consists of tips on preparing a neat, professional-looking submission that will help you get accepted:

• Begin with the correct paper, at least 16 to 25-pound quality paper that will make your manuscript look professional.

• Use a laser printer, so every copy is an original. If you're using a typewriter, make sure that you always use black ink. A dot matrix printer is a no-no. Your book should be as close to letter quality as possible. Editors read numerous manuscripts weekly and don't appreciate the eye strain.

• Use 12 pt. Arial, Times Roman, or Courier print. Don't use fancy scroll print wheels. Editors aren't paid to decipher hieroglyphics

• The exact length and number of chapters comes down to math. If your book is 75,000 words you'll need thirty chapters each the length of a short article (2,500 words). If you only have sixteen chapters, they'll need to be about 4,500 words each. It depends on how many chapters you sketched in your outline.

• Use double-spacing throughout your book to permit easier reading and room for editing.

• Format properly. Leave a 1-1/4 to 1-1/2 margin around the text. When your manuscript moves into the production stage, the editor will typeset and the art department will lay out the manuscript, so you don't have to get fancy.

• In the upper left-hand corner of the first page, type your name, address, phone number, social security number. If the editor decides to use your manuscript and needs to get in touch with you immediately to verify information, your phone number will be right there.

• In the upper right corner of the first page, provide the approximate number of words. Count each word of your manuscript (or let your computer do it for you).

• At the middle of the first page, type your manuscript title. Skip two lines and type "by." Skip two more lines and type your name. At the top of the second page in the upper left-hand corner put your last name, dash, and a short version of your manuscript title. Make sure the pages are numbered.

• Submit books, articles or serials electronically only when asked to do so. When I send a copy on disk, or by e-mail, I always follow up with a hard copy and a cover letter.

• Make sure you use proper postage.

• Include a SASE (self-addressed stamped envelope) if you want the manuscript sent back. (I just indicate on the bottom that it's not necessary.) If you do send a SASE, make sure it has proper postage.

• Before you send the manuscript, recheck it and make sure all the pages are included.

• Although many publishers accept submissions over the Internet or by fax, they may request an additional copy of the manuscript be delivered in paper form.

Things to Avoid

What you don't do can be as important as what you do do:

• Don't use staples or bindings.

• Don't forget to number pages.

• Avoid copyright, or serial right notices. You're protected automatically.

• Check every page for typos and mistakes. One or two small corrections on a page are fine. If you have more than that, retype the page.

Tips for an Outstanding Book

Sitting in a backstreet cafe one dark and stormy night, I opened a new book I'd found, *How To Write and Sell A Novel* by Jack Brickman. My waitress noticed and said in a sarcastic tone, "You're going to write your own novel?"

I looked up and started to answer that I'd already written several books, but before I could, she lifted her right eyebrow and added, ". . . and sell it?" I didn't leave her a tip.

Those two paragraphs are an example of showing what happened, not just telling about it. Notice how you're standing there watching the waitress pour coffee and you can hear the sarcasm in her voice.

You're present to the incident. True, you're not always going to write like this in an investment book, but an anecdote is a great way to start a chapter, make a point, or hook the reader. Try it. You won't believe how it makes "dull" exciting.

In my book *The First Time Investor*, the investor is described as standing in front of a magazine rack full of paperback how-to books, confused about how to invest. He's staring at Donald Trump's latest book, *Manhattan on $4,000 a Day*, when he realizes that he has nothing in common with the author.

Just write the way you would tell some kids a story. Storytelling makes it interesting. Narrative is the heart of storytelling; it's how the human condition is portrayed and enlarged upon. Narrative is actually an overwhelmingly large percentage of the daily dialogue we have with each other. We exchange narrative anecdotes as a kind of game.

Use anecdotal stories any time you wish to demonstrate a technique or principle at work in real life. Share a story about those who have benefitted from your service or program. When your readers relate to people like themselves who have experienced success, they're going to be more eager to read about how your approach can produce the same results in their own lives.

Anecdotes can hit home hard. Focus on one strong point in the anecdote. Most people can only remember or concentrate on a few ideas at a time.

You tell a story when you talk to clients and prospects and tell them about your product or service. But most advisors don't do this in the form of a narrative; their talk on the benefits and features of their product or service is delivered as a monologue. When the drama slips away, the narrative becomes a lecture instead of storytelling. Naturally, the prospect or client loses interest.

A good speaker adds drama and intrigue, which keeps us glued to his speech and sweeps us along with it. The master salesman has learned to use narrative to his advantage in explaining his product or service.

John Bowen does just that. Once, he says, when he was teaching a class on the benefits of modern portfolio theory, a student raised his hand and asked John if he used the methods outlined in modern portfolio theory in his own business. John was caught off guard. He had to answer frankly, that no, he wasn't. He went back to his office, got his partners together and asked some really tough questions like, "Why aren't we using modern portfolio theory for our own clients?" This led to John's search over the next several years to find the best and the brightest to build the business that he has today—which is now over $2 billion.

When John talks to a group of advisors, he tells this story and they're captivated—almost like children listening to their father telling a "killing the giant" story. He delivers information and a supportive testimonial, but he does it in a narrative manner. We learn new things along the way, things about his business and things about how investments work, and we feel a sense of identity with John as he tells us of stumbling for an answer in front of the student. The narrative comes alive when the student raises his hand and asks the question. You feel like you're there in the room with John as it happens.

Work on developing the elements of your own narrative. Think of word pictures. When you add a little incident, or inject drama, it broadens the confines of a lengthy narrative speech and makes it more interesting. It provides something for the audience to imagine and identify with.

Here's a little exercise you can try with your own service or product, or a process that's not too technical. First, explain step-by-step how it works, trying to be as clear as possible. Now think of a threat to that process, such as the student calling Bowen on whether or not he was using modern portfolio theory in his own business. Describe how that threat might interrupt and then describe how the narrator feels about the threat and its consequences.

By mixing drama and narrative you'll have done two important things – (1) develop tension and (2) create an incident. Just as in a well-written novel, you'll hook the reader into what happens next.

You might not think of your own product or service as something that's dramatic and exciting, but if you experiment with this technique, you'll find the results surprising. The technique takes a little time to master, but like anything else in life, you can do it easily with a little practice.

Example:

Step 1. Write a Great Client Investment story here.

_____

_____

_____

_____

_____

_____

_____

Step 2. Make the reader be there with you by describing details and surroundings.

_____

_____

_____

_____

_____

_____

Check to see if you used visual descriptive nouns and active verbs. Can you make them more aggressive? Try to mix kinesthetic (emotional), auditory (sound) and visual words into your story.

The Manuscript Troubleshooting List

When I finish a book, I invite friends who are willing to read and criticize my manuscript to a celebration party. I hand each guest a chapter or two to pick apart for errors. I've found this is the best and fastest way to get feedback. The following is a self-editing checklist I give my guests so that I can understand their comments easily.[1]

---

[1] From Jean Marie Stine, *Writing a Successful Self-Help and How-To Book* (John Wiley & Son, Inc.)

Tear out or copy this list:

Gr   = This passage, idea, or phrase is particularly good or has strong emotional impact.
*   = This is exceptional.
Awk   = Awkwardly expressed, could be more smoothly written.
Bor   = Bored me.
S   = Subject goes on too long and could benefit from being shortened or condensed.
Cut   = This material seems too far off from the point of the book or chapter and might be deleted without impairing the reader's understanding of the main theme(s).
Def   = Please define this term or phrase; I'm not sure everyone will be familiar with it.
Dev   = This is an important point that deserves greater development.
Earlier   = This material should go earlier where it would illuminate what you have been saying better or because the main body of the material on this subject is there. (Indicate where the material should be moved, if possible.)
Exm   = This idea would benefit from being illustrated by an example.
Exp   = Explain this idea more fully.
P   = A problem with grammar.
I/L   = I'm lost and don't see where the material is going.
Jar   = Too jargonistic and filled with professional or academic terminology.
NC   = Not clear to me.
Move   = Material seems out of place here; move to (page or chapter where it belongs).
Rep   = Unnecessarily repetitive.
Sp   = A misspelled word. (Circle the suspect word.)
T/B   = Too textbookish and academic in phraseology or approach.
Tr   = Transition needed here; the switch of topics was confusing or the relation between this idea and the one that preceded it was not clear.
W/S   = Why is this so? Explain why it is the way you say it is, or why it works the way it does.
Weak   = Weak material; seems as if it could be improved or made stronger.
?   = What's the point? Why are you telling me this?

Next, you'll learn a secret that can keep you from wasting time and increase your odds of success.

Chapter 18
How to Turn Your Old
Articles into New Books

In this chapter, you'll learn:
• A strategy to save time and money
• How to test your book idea

Okay, getting published still seems like an overwhelming task. You've heard how writer after writer was rejected and spent years writing books that now sit in their desk drawers. Having done my share of cold calling, I hate rejections. I decided a long time ago I couldn't afford to waste time; I had to find a way to ensure a high degree of success.

I started testing book ideas through articles before I spent a year writing a full-length book. It became my form of market research. If a magazine wasn't interested enough in my topic for an article, then a book publisher wouldn't be interested. That saves me a lot of time. In fact, today most of the chapters in this book are different version of articles I've published over the years. You can start with your problem/solution article, add more stories and examples, and soon turn a 1,500-word article into 10,000 words – add a few more articles and you've got your 75,000-word book.

One of the very first articles I wrote was for a trade magazine called *Pension World*. It was the cover story, "The 1990 Market Outlook—Riding the High Wave." The article, written in 1989, predicted a flood of capital into the U.S. that could set the stage for a 5000 Dow by 1995. I interviewed a group of economists who were saying that we were headed toward an unprecedented long-term economic boom, even though bestselling authors like Dr. Ravi Batra were predicting the end of the financial world. I was sick of reading all the-financial-world-will-collapse doomsaying, so I used my irritation to fuel my passion in the article.

The article was so successful that I decided to expand on it. With the magazine publisher's permission, I used the article as the opening chapters for a book.

I also discovered I had a second advantage. I could send a copy of the magazine article to a publisher, which gave my book idea a third-party endorsement—so I was using the magazine to help get my book published. That became my market test to see if there would be interest in a book. I sent a table of contents, a short book proposal, and my first two chapters (which consisted of the *Pension World* article) to several different publishers. It wasn't long before I had a book contract.

One approach to "building" a book is to create a multi-part magazine series on a marketable topic for a newspaper or magazine. I did this on the topic of different money managers' styles. There were so many different styles, I broke the topic into a three-part article, which was later used in a book called *Wrap Fee Advisor*.

Another approach is to become a co-author: combine your articles and research with another author's articles and research to form a book.

You Still Have to do Some Writing

Three general ways books differ from articles:

1. The topic angle is a lot broader. In *The First Time Investor*, we covered everything you would need to know to be a first time investor; whereas, my monthly columns had just been on managing money.

2. The presentation must be more diversified in a book. Articles may feature a sidebar or a couple of photos to accompany the text, but books demand greater variations of presentation formats. Books can have a table of contents, sidebars, graphs, charts, suggested reading lists, maps, photographs, cartoons, footnotes, indexes, a glossary, tests, and fill-in-the-blanks worksheets. I use pretty much all of them. The publisher expects you, as the author, to develop these reader fulfillment options.

3. The writer's style is less confined in a book. The objective of a good article is to report on the who, what, when, where, and how of a topic. Books go beyond the basic elements by fleshing out the bare bones with deeper research and detailed examples, interesting anecdotes, and quotes.

You can also write about something that has many different perspectives. A good nonfiction book will have chapters on the background of the subject, so you can include the history of the stock market, for instance, or current theories, case studies, and research, or interviews with several experts in the field. Or all of these. Just focus them on your chosen theme.

An additional tip: You can sell excerpts of your book. After your book is published, you can send copies to the same magazine editors you've already written articles for and ask for help in exposing the book to the public. Most publishers will gladly send out review copies of your book because they want to sell books. That's their job, so you're helping them market the book.

Do you want to know how to get your readers to believe they can accomplish what your book teaches? The message is in the title.

Chapter 19
Titles That Send a
Message

In this chapter, you'll learn:
• What titles can sell your book
• How titles identify your target market and send a message
• How to write *subtitles* to broaden your market

Like the first phrase in a song, with your title you have a very brief opportunity to get someone's attention. Books with "how to" at the beginning have always enjoyed good sales. And as with this book, don't be afraid to use a long title.

Before you get too far into writing your book, decide upon a title—even a working title, one you're not sure you'll keep. I don't get too excited about titles and waste a lot of time changing them since the publisher may give the book a different title later. But a working title keeps you focused. If it's a really good hook, your publisher may use it.

So what makes a winning title? Well, name some major titles that you recall (how about *How You Can Pay Zero In Taxes?*).

Titles reveal your overall structure. They tell the reader about the promises and benefits of reading your book. Create titles that are specific, rather than general. Specific titles make the reader believe they can successfully accomplish what your book teaches. Readers want to feel you're writing to them personally, that they're the subject of your book, so put the reader in your chapter titles. Chapter titles like "Making The Most Of Your Retirement" or "Unleash Your Financial Genius" create instant reader identification.

It's crucial that a book target a specific area of interest. A financial advisor looking for a book specifically on selling will look for the cover and title that highlights that subject. The cover and title of Bill Bachrach's book, *Values-Based Selling—The Art of Building High Trust Client Relationships for Financial Planners, Investment Reps and Insurance Agents*, for example, tells you immediately what the book's about and who it's written for.

The title, *Values-Based Selling*, is a little unusual. Although it's on the bookstore shelf with other industry-related books, it catches your eye. Maybe you've never heard of values-based selling. Then you read the subtitle, *The Art of Building High Trust Client Relationships for Financial Planners, Investment Reps and Insurance Agents*. Since high trust relationships are the backbone of your business, you see this book as just for you.

If your service is financial planning for chiropractors, write a book titled, *Financial Planning for Chiropractors*. Include testimonials from chiropractors who are your clients and are big hitters in their field. When you do a seminar, offer a free copy of your book. Before long, you will be perceived as *the* financial planner for chiropractors.

Find a Compelling Message

The title page is the easiest way to effectively communicate your book's concept. The book's premise or concept is nothing more than your original position statement written as a compelling message.

Apply the following strategy to formulate winning titles every time:

1. Write down the compelling promise for your article, chapter or book.

2. Identify a problem the reader can relate to.

3. Offer hope or instruction.

4. Spell out what the book will do to benefit the reader.

5. Be upbeat and positive.

6. Describe the theme of the book, one that, like a struck gong, reverberates in every chapter.

You might possibly use a subtitle or a catchy add-on such as "How to Stand Out in the Midst of Competitive Clutter—*A Guide to Becoming a Recognized Expert*." Other examples are "Think *and Grow Rich*" by Napoleon Hill, "How to Swim with the Sharks *Without Being Eaten Alive*" by Harvey McKay, "The Millionaire *Next Door*," by Tom Stanley.

How to Use Subtitles to Explain Your Book

Adding subtitles helps clarify and define your book. Subtitles can also help you reach a secondary market. Here's a list of some title ideas that have been successful for me over the years. Try to incorporate some of these ideas into your own titles:

"How to Improve Your Investment Portfolio"
"How to Build an Investment Program"
"How to Make a Fortune During a Recession"
"How to Win at the Stock Market Game"
"How to Build an Asset Class Portfolio"
"How to Lower Risk While Increasing Returns"
"How to Pick Winners in the Stock Market"
"How to Be an Investment Advisor"
"How to Pick a Good Advisor"

Most people say that if you can get the two words "made easy" in a title, that's another good hook. For instance,

"The Stock Market Made Easy"
"Investing Made Easy"
"Retirement Made Easy"
"Children's College Funds Made Easy"

A favorite of mine, and a favorite of most advertising copy, is the word "secret".

"Stock Market Secrets"
"Asset Class Investing Secrets"
"The Secret of Winning the Market"
"Secrets of Business Management"

And "revealed",

"Investment Strategies Revealed"
"Secrets of the Stock Market Revealed"

I've used "guide" on booklets:

"Practical Guide"
"Expert's Guide"
"The Guide to . . . "

Some publishers love "practical" guides.

"A Practical Guide to Asset Management"
"A Practical Guide to Sales"
"A Practical Guide to Building Your Stock Portfolio"
"A Practical Guide to Personal Happiness"

A specific number of days in the title is another element that offers a strong promise.

"30 Days to a Successful Portfolio"
"How to Write a Book in 10 Days"
"30 Days to Stock Market Success"

Okay, so now you have a working title for your manuscript, but your book will never get published without the information in the next chapter.

Chapter 20
Writing for Permissions

In this chapter, you'll learn:
• Why you need permission and how to get it
• Sample request letters
• How to assemble a permissions file

Whenever you want to quote more than a few words from another writ-ten work in your book (or article), you have to get permission from who-ever owns the copyright. You'll find where to write in the front of the book or magazine you're quoting from. If the address is incomplete, your local library reference desk can usually give you full information. So can *Writer's Market.*

Start writing for permissions as soon as you make the decision to include material from another source. Sometimes it takes many months to get a reply; this could delay publication of your book. Even if you aren't sure the material will be included, get permission. When a fee is required, you generally pay the full fee only if you actually include the material in your work.

1. When you're writing for permission, be sure to include all the nec-essary information about what you wish to reprint or quote. Send the original letter and a copy to the publisher from whom you're requesting permission. Keep another copy for your permissions file. For books, include author(s)/editor(s) of the source volume; its title; the edition; author(s) and title of the article or chapter, if they're different from the book author; figure or table number, if applicable; page number(s); publisher ISBN whenever possible (it's on the copyright page at the front of books); copyright date; and copyright holder. For periodicals, include author, title of

article, page number(s), name of periodical, volume, issue number, date, and publisher.

2. When you receive the permission from the publisher, read it carefully to see whether it contains any unanticipated or undesirable restrictions. If there appears to be a problem, ask your own editor how you should deal with it.

3. Your completed manuscript should go to the publisher with a permissions file containing all correspondence concerning the permissions (including copies of your requests) and a permission for each item that requires one. Identify each permission by the manuscript page on which the material – quotation, table, illustration, etc. – appears (and by illustration or table number if that applies).

4. Prepare a summary and place it in the permissions file. This sheet summarizes all permissions information so that you and the editor can see at a glance what the folder contains.

Writing for Permission and Preparing Your Permissions File

Following are some sample documentation and letters:

Copyright Permission Request

TO   FROM: Larry Chambers

I am preparing material for: <u>The Guide To Financial Public Relations</u> <u>ISBN 0-910-944-12-</u> to be published by CRC Press, LLC. I hereby request permission for non-exclusive world rights in this and all subsequent editions, revisions and derivative Works, in English and in foreign translations, in all formats including CD-ROM and electronic media, for the following:

Your Publication (title/author/figure/page): _____

_____

Figure(s): _____ Table(s) _____

Will appear in my Publication as:
Figure(s): _____ Table(s) _____

Please sign the release form below. Suitable credit will be given in the use of the material; if you have a preferred statement, please indicate it below. If you are not the copyright controller, please indicate to whom I should apply. Your prompt consideration of this request is appreciated. Unless I have heard otherwise from you within six weeks of the date of this request, I shall assume permission is granted.

Sincerely,
Larry Chambers

I (We) grant the permission requested above:

By: _____Date: _____

Model Permissions Letter

(date)
(inside address)
Dear:
(*Name of other authors, if any, and*) I am/are writing a (*type of*) textbook tentatively entitled (*title of your book*), which is proposed to be published by McGraw-Hill, Inc., in (*month, year*) with a (*year*) copyright. This text will be published as a (250) - page (*soft or hard*) cover. A first printing of ( ) copies is planned, with a total life of edition printing expected of ( ). This text will be distributed (*in the US and Canada or throughout the world, etc.*) in English only.

I request permission to reprint the material below (*chart, graph, text*).

In signing and returning one copy of this request, you warrant that you are the sole owner of the rights granted herein and that these rights do not infringe upon the copyright or other rights of any person or entity. Should you not control these rights, please refer me to the proper party.

Credit will be given to the author, publisher, and/or copyright holder as you indicate below.

Please respond by (*date*). The second copy of this letter is for your files.

Should you send an invoice for this material, please be aware that all payments will be made on publication.

With thanks for your cooperation,
(*your name*)

Release Form

Should contain description of material to be reprinted. For books: author(s) /editor(s) and title of source volume; edition; title and author(s) of article/chapter, if different from book editor; figure or table number, if applicable; page number(s); publisher ISBN whenever possible; copyright date; and copyright holder. For periodicals: author, title of article, page number(s), name of periodical, volume, issue number, date, publisher.

Please see photocopy of material, attached.

Permission is hereby granted for use of the material cited above as specified.

Signature_____Date _____
Name (printed or typed)_____
Title/Company_____
Social Security No._____
Tax Identification No._____
Credit line_____

Permissions File Summary, *First Time Investor*, Larry Chambers

Selection	Page Number	Book or Journal Publisher	Copyright Holder	Distribution Rights
1. The Prudent Investor Guide for Beating the Market	24	McGraw-Hill	J. Bowen	US & Canada

Credit line (exact wording): Reprinted with permission of the author, from *The Prudent Investor Guide for Beating the Market*. Copyright © McGraw-Hill, Inc.

| 2. Weiss Ratings, Inc. | 85-86 | 20 Best VA & Lowest Ratings, Inc. | Weiss | US & Canada |

Credit line:

We've come a long way and by now, your book should be with a publisher...but the work has just begun.

Chapter 21
How to Promote Your
Book

In this chapter, you will learn:
• How to create your own public relations campaign
• How to turn bookstores into your marketing department
• 34 ideas for promoting your book
• Where to send your book for reviews

Now it's time to promote your work. But first, let's get the *bad* news out of the way. Unless you're already famous, most publishers won't have the money for promotion. Unfortunately, most of the promoting is going to come from you and the publicity campaign that you're going to develop. You can go on promoting your book indefinitely. As long as it sells, the publisher is going to keep it alive, and publicizing it will keep it alive.

Book Covers

For very little extra cost, you can have extra covers of your book printed. These overruns can make inexpensive brochures—with strong copy and good design on the reverse side of the cover, they make powerful mail-out pieces. You get a high-quality, high-impact brochure at little cost.

You need permission from your publisher to reproduce your book cover. After getting permission, I took mine to Kinko's, where I had it shrunk and reproduced onto heavy paper, creating an attractive postcard.

Public Relations Campaign

Always keep in mind why you wrote your book in the first place. If you are an investment advisor, your book is your business card. It's part of your marketing plan. On the other hand, publishers have a different agenda. If your book sells, they'll keep pouring money into it. If it doesn't, they'll abandon the book. It's up to you to continue making media contacts and writing articles that support your book and your business.

First, compile a list of names and addresses of local newspaper editors, specialized journals, bulletins and periodicals that deal with the topic of your book. A good place to start is with the magazine editors you've already worked with.

Clip ads, note television shows that present guests who speak on that topic and local radio stations that talk about your topic. Have your media kit ready. Your media kit or your brochure can be the messenger.

Along with your brief biography, in the media kit explain the compelling reason why you wrote the book, emphasizing your special knowledge in the field about which you are writing. You can get endorsements from well-known people in the field. (Endorsements can also help sell your book to a publisher.) Add a copy of the Table of Contents.

Your media kit or brochure, along with a review copy and an invitation to any book parties can be sent to media reviewers. Include publication reviews directed to the book trade, and reviews of newspaper, magazine editors, and columnists. Reviews for readers who are in publications are also important in promoting the book to the public. If you've received a favorable review, you can expect interviews, feature stories, and other attention from the media.

Reviews are most helpful if they appear close to the book's publication date. If not, the publishers will prepare a press release explaining who you are and the nature of your book. A media release should then be sent to book reviewers at the publication date.

A favorable review in *Publishers Weekly*, the key magazine in the publishing industry, can net thousands of orders from book stores. At least 90 days before your release date, the bound galleys should be sent there. *Publishers Weekly* is located at 249 W. 17th Street, New York, NY 10011. This magazine, which almost never reviews books after their publication, is the bible of the book trade.

Kirkus, at 200 Park Avenue South, New York, NY 10003, is another important trade magazine that reviews forthcoming books. *Library Journal*, located at the same address as *Publishers Weekly*, and *The American Library Association Journal*, at 50 E. Huron Street, Chicago,

IL 60611, are also important outlets. For a more complete list, go to page 185, "Where to Send Your Book to Get Reviews."

Never underestimate the importance of pre-publication reviews. These reviews can win you national attention and distribution of your book—and help you promote your book after it's been published.

Spend a morning in the library looking at trade magazines that you would like to review your book. References for finding magazine outlets would be the *Literary Marketplace*, a directory of all stages in book publishing. The *Gale's Directory* of publications, newspapers and magazines is organized geographically. *Bacon's Publicity Checker* comprises several volumes for newspapers, magazines and trade journals. There are also the *Editor's and Publisher's International Yearbook*, *The Encyclopedia of Associations*, and the *National Trade Professional Association Directory*.

Every time you receive a review, make copies and add them to your media package. Send a media package and make follow-up phone calls to attract additional interviews. You've no doubt seen authors come to your town, hit the media—all the radio shows, newspapers, and television stations. Your goal is to hit the media with a blast.

At a minimum, your media package should include a media release, a publication announcement or information sheet explaining the scope of the book, a brief biography of yourself, your picture, and a copy of your book. Because editors receive perhaps hundreds of press releases each day, the first line of your press release should be a killer; the first paragraph should draw the reader's attention to what you have written. If possible, try to connect your topic to a current event in the news.

Tell a Success Story About the Book

John Bowen tells about a man in Budapest who had just received a copy of his book, *The Prudent Investor's Guide*, as a Christmas gift. He had contacted Bowen's firm to see if they could refer him to a financial advisor.

"Obviously, we didn't have any advisors in Budapest," says Bowen. "He worked for a company based out of Chicago; we said that when he was traveling in the States, we'd be more than happy to get together with him. Well, he moved back to the States six months later, called us, and we referred him to an advisor. The advisor picked up a $2 million account."

Figure 21-1 The Media Loves Real Life Stories

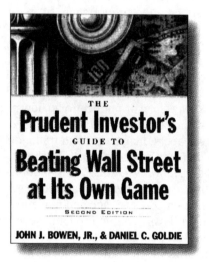

Source: Reinhardt Werba Bowen Advisor Services. Reprinted with permission.

Use Excerpts as Publicity

If your book is a how-to, you can pull out a section of it and use it for an article or an excerpt. The ideal time for an excerpt to appear is as close as possible to the book's publication date.

Getting a book store to have a book signing is probably the easiest thing I've ever done. Call up the manager of the book store, tell him you've got a book coming out and you'd like to set up a book signing. It doesn't cost them anything to get the books in. It gets the traffic to come in. You can put on a presentation in the book store. Sometimes they'll even provide the signage.

Speak at Service Groups

I once spoke at our local Chamber of Commerce luncheon. I invited along the manager of the local B. Dalton's bookstore. After the talk, I had a line of attendees wanting me to sign my book. The manager sold the books to the attendees. It was like having an additional employee. Her enlightened self-interest was to sell books. Mine was finding prospects.

Charity Event or Seminar

Attach your book signing to a charity event or a seminar that you're giving. Give seminars in all the bookstores around your city. Speak on a certain topic in your book, a chapter in your book, perhaps retirement planning or some other aspect that will draw individuals in and attract customers.

Preparing for Interviews and Appearances

Once you've started down this road, it's surprising what will happen. A book takes on a life of its own. Whenever you're asked to speak at a function or go on television, you're looked upon as an expert, so you have to prepare for these events. You need to know all sides of the issue that's going to be discussed. You should be familiar with the topic, especially negative points that might arise. Research who the audience is going to be. The goal is to deliver the same basic message that you've done throughout the book. It will present a positive impression of you. The audience should identify with you, since you're a person whose product or service will provide value for them. Your demeanor and appearance should leave the audience with a feeling of trustworthiness.

Having well-organized material at your fingertips will enable you to cope with any situation you might face. I've written a small, eight-page booklet that was the premise for a larger booklet; I use it when I give a speech. All I have to do is follow the five steps for PR success, so if at any time I lose my place I just look at the next step. It keeps me on track, organized, and focused and it gives me a speech that I can deliver on a moment's notice. It seems to others as if I spent a lot of time on it.

If you're scheduled to be interviewed by a magazine or newspaper reporter, keep in mind they might look for or focus on a controversial or negative point of view. Ask what the story is about. You may be called upon to be an expert and add to a story. Most writers won't share their story until it's published, so it's up to you to ask questions ahead of time.

If you're scheduled to appear on a radio or television show, you'll be assigned a contact person. The contact person is there to assist you in being a success on the air. Establish a rapport with this person and, if possible, meet in advance.

Compile a list of questions about your appearance and thoroughly discuss your concerns. Will your appearance be taped or live? Will you be a member of a panel? Will there be audience interaction? Can you refer to your product or service, or your book? Be cordial, be brief, but be persistent in getting the information you need to perform at your peak.

Additional Ideas

Here are some more ideas to help you promote your book:

1. Position the book as the first one—and the best one—about your specific topic or slant.

2. Develop workshops that could tie into the book.

3. Consider promoting the book as a way to help service groups. This might help the media jump on the story.

4. Consider sending out the news releases on floppy disks.

5. Consider whether this could be the first of a series of books.

6. Send letters to the major review programs in New York, Los Angeles, San Francisco, San Jose, Chicago, wherever, with a kit that's likely to get follow-up. Maybe you can include the promotional schedule that you'll be doing and any innovative publicity plans. Call to follow up each kit.

7. Do your own author's tour. Develop an invitation, inviting the public to hear and meet the author. Arrange with local book stores to do sales at these meetings.

8. Send books for review to *Publishers Weekly, Kirkus Reviews, Book List, New York Times Book Review, Washington Post Book World, San Francisco Chronicle Book Review, Los Angeles Times Book Review, New York News Day, Chicago Tribune Book, USA Today, New York Review of Books*, and *San Francisco Review of Books*.

9. Several services provide major media directories. Use *Bacon's Newsletter Magazine Directory and Radio and TV Directory, Business and Financial News Media List*, and *Talk Shows and Hosts on Radio* to set up your own media plan.

10. With each book send a cover letter that contains the basic facts about the book and you. These facts should answer the questions: (1) what can this book do? (2) what benefit does it offer? (the

33. Use the major media effectively. The most influential financial print medium is *The Wall Street Journal*, followed by *USA Today*, the *New York Times*, the *Washington Post*, and the *Los Angeles Times*. The rule of thumb is to do at least five promotions a day, which requires five contacts a day.

34. Consider developing a business card that's in essence a wallet-sized billboard for the book.

Enough!

Where to Send Your Book to Get Reviews

The major book publisher trade publications review books in pre-publication. Sending bound galleys is encouraged whenever possible.

AMERICAN BOOKSELLER
828 S. Broadway
Tarrytown, NY 10591
Circulation: 11,000
(914) 591-2665; *fax:* (914) 591-2720
Richard Scott, Managing Editor, (914) 591-2665, ext. 272
Published by the American Booksellers Association, this is an excellent venue for reaching booksellers. Its readership consists of book buyers, including college bookstores, major chain buying offices, and especially large and small independent booksellers.
American Bookseller reviews books from galleys and highlights new titles in categories such as business books.

ASSOCIATED PRESS
50 Rockefeller Plaza
New York, NY 10020-1666
Has approximately 1500 members worldwide.
(212) 621-1500; *fax:* (212) 621-1567
Ron Berthel, Book Review Editor - 5th Floor
The Associated Press runs a regular weekly general interest (fiction, non-fiction, how-to, self-help) book column that reviews six to eight books. It mostly features hard cover books, but will consider some paperbacks.

ATLANTA JOURNAL/CONSTITUTION
P.O. Box 4689
Atlanta, GA 30302

Circulation: 715,397 (Sunday). 440,000 (Daily)
(404) 526-5151; *fax:* (404-526-5509
Teresa Weaver, Book Editor, (404) 526-5377

BLOOMSBURY REVIEW
P.O. Box 8928
Denver, CO 80201
Circulation: 50,000
(303) 863-0406; *fax:* (303) 863-0408
Tom Auer, Editor-in-Chief
The *Bloomsbury Review* contains reviews and interviews with writers on
a wide variety of subjects and includes essays and poetry. Send galleys or
finished books to Tom Auer. He wants to see books in all categories,
including fiction and self-help.

BOSTON GLOBE
135 Morrissey Blvd.
Boston, MA 02107
Circulation: 777,902
(617) 929-2000; *fax:* (617) 929-2813
David Mehegan, Assistant Book Review Editor, ext. 2785

BUSINESS WEEK
1221 Avenue of the Americas, 39th Floor
New York, NY 10020
Circulation: 875,000
(212) 512-2511
Hardy Green, Book Editor
Don't assume that because it's called *Business Week,* this magazine is
interested only in business books. The editors recommend reading the
book reviews to get an idea if your book really fits in.

CHICAGO SUN-TIMES
401 N. Wabash Avenue
Chicago, IL 60611
Circulation: 496,030
(312) 321-3000; *fax:* (312) 321-3084
Henry Kisor, Book Editor, Fax: (312) 321-3679

CHICAGO TRIBUNE
435 N. Michigan Avenue
Chicago, IL 60611
Circulation: 1,066,393 (Sunday); 667,908 (Daily)
(312) 222-3232
Elizabeth Taylor, Book Editor, (312) 222-4125

FAMILY CIRCLE
110 Fifth Avenue, 8th floor
New York, NY 10011
Circulation: 5,000,000
(212) 463-1000; *fax:* (212) 463-1808
Kathy Sagan, Book Editor, (212) 463-1240
This is the largest mass-market women's magazine, providing information on how to make both personal and home improvements. Regular editorial features cover personal finance and similar issues.

GLOBE
5401 NW Broken Sound Blvd.
Boca Raton, FL 33487
Circulation: 1,000,000
(561) 997-7733; *fax:* (561) 997-9210
Brian Williams, Executive Editor
This weekly supermarket tabloid provides human interest stories relating to everyday life. Send catalogs, press releases, and press kits first. If Brian Williams is interested, he'll call and request a review copy. *Globe* particularly looks for celebrity topics and really likes books that have "do's and don't's," "50 ways to such and such," etc. A press release entitled "10 Ways to Improve..." will really grab attention at the *Globe*.

KIRKUS REVIEWS
200 Park Avenue South, 17th St.
New York, NY 10003-1543
Circulation: 35,000
(212) 777-4554; *fax:* (212) 979-1352
Sarah Gold, Senior Editor, Non-Fiction
This monthly publication is a major review source for libraries and booksellers. The editors primarily review serious fiction and nonfiction. Even a bad review could prompt other trade publications to evaluate the book.

LOS ANGELES TIMES BOOK REVIEW
Times Mirror Square
Los Angeles, CA 90053
Circulation: 1,400,000 (Sunday). 1,029,000 (Daily)
(213) 237-7778; *fax:* (213) 237-4712
Steve Wasserman, Book Review Editor (assigns reviews), (213) 237-7778
The *L. A. Times Book Review* is one of the largest and most comprehensive newspaper book review sections in the country, publishing about 2,000 reviews a year. It features many paperbacks and some how-to books.

McCALL'S
110 5th Avenue
New York, NY 10011
Circulation: 4,290,216
(212) 463-1000; *fax:* (212) 463-1403
Jane Farrell, Senior Editor
The targeted reader of this mass-market women's magazine is described as sophisticated. Editorial focus is on finance and other personal issues. Books to be excerpted should go to Jane Farrell three to four months ahead of publication. One of the areas *McCall's* is interested in is how-to—especially if it lends itself to being used in a piece like "Ten Ways to Save Money" (pitch it that way in your letter)—though they tend to go for celebrity authors.

THE MIDWEST BOOK REVIEW
278 Orchard Drive
Oregon, WI 53575
(608) 835-7937; E-mail: MWBookRevw@aol.com
James Cox, Publisher/Editor
Diane Donovan, Editor

NEW WOMAN
2 Park Avenue
New York, NY 10016
Circulation: 1,200,000
(212) 545-3500; *fax:* (212) 545-3590
Debra Birnbaum, Senior Book Editor
New Woman publishes about one excerpt per issue of a fiction or nonfiction book. There is a five-month lead time.

NEW YORK REVIEW OF BOOKS
1755 Broadway, 5th Fl.
New York, NY 10009-3780
Circulation: 135,000
(212) 757-8070; *fax:* (212) 333-5374
Robert Silvers, Editor (generally handles nonfiction)
The *New York Review* favors books in the following categories: history, literary novels, biography, reference, science, and art.

NEW YORK TIMES BOOK REVIEW
229 W. 43rd Street, 8th Floor
New York, NY 10036
Circulation: 1,746,707
(212) 556-7464 *Fax:* (212) 556-1320
Charles McGrath, Book Review Editor, Hardcover Books and Paperback Originals
The section reviews about 3,000 books a year. It covers books on general interest topics and general and literary fiction and nonfiction.

NEWSWEEK
251 West 57th Street
New York, NY 10019-1894
Circulation: 3,100,000
(212) 445-4000; *fax:* (212) 445-5439
Ray Sawhill, Book Review Editor, (212) 445-4419
Newsweek, like *Time,* is a weekly forum to keep readers informed of national and international news, the arts, health, current affairs, and the Washington scene.

PEOPLE
People/Time/Life Building
Rockefeller Center
New York, NY 10020
Circulation: 3,449,852
(212) 522-1212; *fax:* (212) 522-0331
Kristin McMurran, Senior Editor in Charge of Book Reviews, (212) 522-2498
Most reviews in *People* are of books from major publishers, but they do some small press titles that merit attention. They consider some how-to and some self-help, but the majority of books they review are Hollywood biographies, music books, and current news.

PHILADELPHIIA INQUIRER
Physical Address:
400 N. Broad Street
Philadelphia, PA 19130
Mailing Address:
P.O. Box 8263
Philadelphia, PA 19101
Circulation: 902,267 (Sunday); 457,932 (Daily)
(215) 854-2000; *fax:* (215) 854-5884
Mike Schaffer, Book Editor

PUBLISHERS WEEKLY
245 West 17th Street
New York, NY 10011
Circulation: 37,726 weekly
(212) 645-0067; *fax:* (212) 463-6631
Widely read by bookstore owners and other book buyers, reviews in this publication are considered important because they are believed to help generate sales. Getting coverage here is extremely competitive.
ADULT TRADE BOOKS:
Genevieve Stuttaford, Editor, Nonfiction (Hardcover Only)
Don't bother sending finished books for review, the editors will not review from them. Galleys should reach editors at least three months prior to the month of publication, but no more than four months in advance.
PAPERBACKS, HOW-TO, MYSTERY, CHILDREN'S AND RELIGIOUS:
Maria Simson, Editor, Paperbacks Only

READER'S DIGEST
Reader's Digest Road
Pleasantville, NY 10570
Circulation: 16,000,000
(914) 238-1000; *fax:* (914) 238-4559
Christopher Wilcox, Editor in Chief
Christine Crisci, Book Editor
Reader's Digest is perhaps the most widely read magazine in the country serving the general-interest reader. Many of the articles that appear in the magazine are reprinted from other major consumer magazines. While competition among book publishers is fierce, the good news is that *Reader's Digest* uses many excerpts from books published by small/independent presses. The kinds of books used most frequently are nonfiction

dealing with true stories of overcoming a major problem or real-life compelling drama (like surviving a shipwreck at sea).

SAN FRANCISCO CHRONICLE
901 Mission Street
San Francisco, CA 94103
Circulation: 652,259 (Sunday); 494,005 (Daily)
(415) 777-1111; *fax:* (415) 896-1107
Patricia Holt, Book Review Editor, (415) 777-7043 Fax: (415) 957-8737

SELF
350 Madison Avenue
New York, NY 10017
Circulation: 1,192,923
(212) 880-6810; *fax:* (212) 880-8110
Katharyn Keller, Lifestyles Editor, (212) 880-6880
Self's readership is the upscale and highly educated woman in her mid-20s to early 30s. Features attempt to serve as a source of stimulation for understanding and developing individual potential. Features regularly include money and career management.

TIME
Time/Life Building
Rockefeller Center
New York, NY
Circulation: 4,000,000
(212) 522-1212; *fax:* (212) 522-0323
Jim Collins, Senior Editor, (212) 522-4366
Time, like *Newsweek*, is a weekly forum to keep readers informed of national and international news, the arts, health, current affairs and the Washington scene.

UNITED PRESS INTERNATIONAL
1510 H St. NW
Washington, DC 20005
Has approximately 2,000 member news organizations worldwide.
(202) 898-8000; *fax:* (202) 898-8147
Cobin Beck, Book Review

USA TODAY
1000 Wilson Boulevard
Arlington, VA 22229
Circulation: 2,181,494 (Friday Edition: 2,500,000)
(703) 276-3400; *fax:* (703) 276-5513
Dierdre Donahue, Book Review Editor
USA Today reviews two to three books and sometimes excerpts a small
amount of material from one of them.

WALL STREET JOURNAL
200 Liberty Street
New York, NY 10281
Circulation: 1,841,000
(212) 416-2000; *fax:* (212) 416-2658
Erich Eichman, Book Review Editor, (212) 416-2487
Though the *Journal* is a daily business forum, it rarely covers business
books. When business books are reviewed, they're done in round-up form
and headed "Business Bookshelf."

WASHINGTON POST BOOK WORLD
1150 Fifteenth Street, NW
Washington, DC 20071
Circulation: 1,200,000
(202) 334-6000; *fax:* (202) 334-5059
Nina King, Book Review Editor, (202) 334-7881
Getting a review here, as in the *New York Times* or *Wall Street Journal*,
can lead to a lot of interest in your book by other media, publishers, cat-
alogs, and subsidiary rights buyers.
The *Post* compiles and publishes its own bestseller list.

Chapter 22
How to Land a Spot on a National Television Talk Show

In this chapter, you will learn:
• How to get on a tv show
• How to design your media kit
• What to do when you get on tv
• List of tv contacts

Your new investment book has just been published. You've followed all the marketing steps and sent a copy of your book to each of your clients. But after six months, your book has sold less than a thousand copies.

Luckily, one copy found its way to the desk of Sue Herera, the host of CNBC's Business Tonight, which has a nationwide audience of millions of viewers. A week later, every copy of your book has sold. Bookstores are begging for more inventory because lots of people who saw your book on Business Tonight are coming in asking for copies. In one week, your book sells 50,000 copies. Suddenly, you're on *The New York Times* Bestseller List. And the best part is, you didn't pay CNBC a penny for the air-time!

A 60-second advertisement on Herera's show would cost you over a hundred thousand dollars. But as a guest on the show, you got an hour of free air-time and reached millions of consumers across the country. So how do you swing a guest spot? You need a great "pitch"—that's publicity slang for when you try to convince a media outlet to book you as a guest or feature your product.

There's no magic formula for creating a pitch that will land you on national television. Talk shows differ in the topics they cover and therefore the type of guests they look for. Nonetheless, there are some basic steps you can follow that will increase your chances of getting on the air.

Do Your Homework

Review the profiles of each show carefully to make sure your pitch is appropriate to the show's format and style. The talk shows often take their lead in reporting the news from major newspapers.

Watch the shows you're most interested in appearing on—there's a list at the end of this chapter. This will help you determine if you should pitch them. It will also give you insight on the host's style and interests.

Have an Angle

You have to demonstrate why you or your product would make an excellent guest or compelling segment. Don't suggest you just talk about your product. Producers don't care about your book or product – what they do care about is creating exciting or informative segments and shows. Try instead to sell the producer on why you'll be a great guest – someone who'll do something of value or interest to the audience.

Don't worry, producers know you're selling something and they'll usually be sure you get a plug. But you have to get on the show first!

Are you an expert who will reveal how innocent consumers are getting ripped off? Or, how the audience can save $200 a month on their grocery bills? Or, how children's safety is at risk when they play with popular toys? Maybe you can share with the audience the secrets of growing garden plants twice the average size, or how to throw an elegant dinner party for under $100.

Make Your Pitch Hard to Resist

Remember, television is a visual media, so any props, photographs, or demonstrations you can do will make your pitch even more desirable to producers.

Talk shows like CNBC's Business Tonight often use investment professionals or panels consisting of several guests on a given topic. Producers spend a lot of time and energy creating panels. Offer a ready-made show to a producer by suggesting other possible panelists.

Use Your TV Media Kit

Your media kit should contain the materials producers use to evaluate potential guests and make booking decisions:

- *A Cover Letter.* Your cover letter must sell producers on why you'd be a great guest. Your opening paragraph must immediately grab their attention and tell them why you or your product would make a compelling guest or segment. Posing questions and answering them, and quoting statistics are two ways to make strong, convincing statements:
  "75% of your viewers are paying too much for stocks."
- *A One or Two-Page Press Release* providing more in-depth information about your hook.
- *A One-Page Biography.* This should list your professional credentials as an expert. Don't ever send a resume. A bio should be more conversational and lend validity to your expertise in a certain area. Be sure to mention previous media appearances.
- *Sample Questions.* Compile a list of at least ten questions that the host or interviewer could ask you during the show.
- *Ideas for Additional Segments or Show Topics.* Pitch a general topic or segment idea, but show how your information and expertise can be applied to create other kinds of segments. For instance, the author of a personal finance book can do separate segments on how to make smart investments in the stock market; helping kids become smart with their money; whether couples should buy homes in this volatile economy; or how to preserve and increase family wealth.
- *A Book or Product Sample.* If it isn't possible to send your product with your press kit, note that samples are available upon request. Include a color photograph of your product. If you're pitching a book that's just being published, include a galley, a sample book, or sample chapters.
- *Print Publicity.* If you have clips from magazine or newspaper articles that were written about you or your product, include two or three of the most favorable.
- *Related Articles from Major Print Publications.* If you're trying to pitch your product or book as being tuned to a rising trend or important social issue, include recent articles on the topic.

Publications like *Time, Newsweek,* and the *Wall Street Journal* can add significantly to the credibility of your pitch.

* *A Professional Photograph.* Your publicity photo should be a black and white head shot taken by a professional photographer. If you're pitching to television, you must include a photograph; don't ruin all your efforts by using an ordinary snapshot.

How Your TV Media Kit Should Look

* Use a brightly colored, durable two-pocket folder to house your materials. A folder with a glossy, coated finish tends to hold up under wear-and-tear better than a plain folder.

* A graphic or headline on the cover will help attract attention. If you're pitching a book, a simple yet effective graphic can be achieved by gluing a sample cover from the book jacket to the front cover.

* Your press release should be the first page on the left with your photograph in front of it.

* Attach your business card to the right pocket of the folder.

* Don't overstuff your media kit because it will look sloppy and unprofessional.

* Use a padded mailing bag or small box to mail your media kit and product sample so they arrive in good condition.

* Most producers prefer that you send materials through the mail, rather than via fax.

* Don't send videotapes of previous media appearances.

Follow-up

* Almost all producers say they hate follow-up calls from publicists and potential guests. At the same time, most experienced publicists will tell you that making polite follow-up calls dramatically increases the chances of landing an interview. A telephone call lets you make a compelling person-to-person sales pitch.

* Wait at least a week before you start calling, so you're reasonably sure your media kit has arrived.

* Never start a conversation with a media person by asking: "Did you get my media kit?" Quickly introduce yourself and promise to be brief: "Hi, I'm from Chambers Financial. I'd like to briefly tell you

about why 75 percent of your viewers are paying too much income tax and what can be done about it. Do you have a minute?" The producer might not have time to stay on the phone, but at least he or she is aware of your name and your pitch. Ask for a more convenient time to talk.

- Don't call anyone repeatedly.
- Don't leave long messages on a producer's voice mail.

Once You're Scheduled on a Show

- Ask the producer or booker to fax you a written confirmation of the date.
- Ask what additional materials you can send them in advance.
- Make sure your booking contact understands what props or materials you will need for any demonstration.
- Verify who will make the travel arrangements and who will pay for them. Don't assume anything. Don't be afraid to ask. If the show makes your flight arrangements and reserves a hotel for you, ask to have a copy of the travel itinerary sent to you.
- Ask what time you need to arrive at the studio and who you should ask for when you get there.
- Find out if the producer will supply you with a videotape of your segment. You can use this tape in other promotions efforts later.

Increasing Publicity and Sales

Before your appearance, don't waste a valuable sales opportunity:

- Contact producers at your local network affiliates and let them know you'll be appearing; they may preview you on the local news.
- Contact editors at your local newspaper and let them know when your appearance is scheduled so they can list it in the television section; they may do a feature write-up about you.
- Fax a press release announcing your upcoming appearance to your major customers, potential customers, and sales reps.
- Fax a press release to potential investors or your financiers.

How to Prepare for Your Interview

- Choose your clothing carefully. If you're a man, wear a suit in a medium tone of gray or blue. Both women and men should wear off-white or pastel shaded shirts or blouses. Solid colors are always best. Never wear stripes, checks, or complex patterns.
- If you normally wear glasses, keep them on for the interview.

Tips for Maximizing Your Effectiveness

- Speak slowly and carefully.
- Avoid unnecessary movements or gestures; they'll distract the audience from what you're saying. Sudden movements are hard for the camera to follow.
- Always look, listen, and speak to the person interviewing you.
- Don't make repeated references to your book or product; you'll sound like a commercial.

Integrate Your National Exposure into Your Marketing Plan

A national television appearance gives you credibility with the public and helps establish you as an expert. Here are some ideas to maximize your future promotional efforts:

- Create a special point-of-purchase display with a header that says: "As Seen On Oprah" or "As Seen On National Television."
- Use it as a sub-heading for your advertisements and direct mail letters.
- Use a quote from the host: "This is an amazing book!" Or print it directly on the book jacket for the next edition.

Good luck—I'll be watching!

Television Contacts

ABC World News Tonight (ABC-TV)
ABC Inc.
47 West 66th Street
Second Floor
New York, NY 10023-6201
Phone: (212) 456-4040; *fax*: (212) 456-2795
Airs: Monday-Friday, 6:30 p.m.
Audience: General adult
Profile: Hard news show with coverage of world events from the day.
They use authors in some segments.
Executive Producer: Kathryn Christiansen
Senior Producer: Stu Schutzman
Booking Contacts for News:
National News Desk Editor: Ms. Kris Sebastian
Booking Contact for American Agenda:
Senior Producer: Paul Slavin

BookNotes (C-Span)
400 N. Capitol Street, NW #650
Washington, DC 20001-1511
Phone: (202) 737-3220; *fax*: (202) 737-3323 or (202) 737-6226
Airs: Sunday, 8:00-9:00 p.m. CST
Audience: General adult
Profile: Interview show featuring nonfiction authors and commentaries
on books dealing with public affairs and history.
How to pitch: They only deal with hard cover, nonfiction books. Authors
must be able to sustain a full hour of conversation. Send all information
by mail.
Booking Contact:
Senior Producer: Hope Lamdy (202) 626-4601

CBS This Morning
CBS News
524 W. 57th Street, Suite 44
New York, NY 10019
Phone: (212) 975-2824; *fax*: (212) 975-2115
Airs: Monday-Friday, 7:00-9:00 a.m. ET
Audience: General adult, over 3 million per show.
Profile: An informational broadcast covering breaking news, weather,
business and personal finance, and consumer affairs.

How to pitch: Mail or fax your material to the producer who handles your subject. Producers want non-flashy press kits and materials that are complete.
Booking Contact:
Book and Supervising Producer: Carol Story (212) 975-4112. The main contact for books, authors, and features, she's open to most ideas.

CNBC Network Programs
2200 Fletcher Avenue
Fort Lee, NJ 07024
Phone: (201) 585-2622; *fax*: (201) 585-6393
Business Tonight
Airs: Mondays-Fridays, 6:30 - 7:00 p.m.
Audience: General adult
Profile: Business news program for executives who want to keep on top of important issues.
How to pitch: Producers look at pitches for segments involving corporations doing things differently. Faxes are the worst way to communicate; mail is the best, preferably very short, one-page pitches.
Booking Contact:
Producer: Robert Ferrarro (201) 585-6366

Cable News Network (CNN)
P.O. Box 105366
Atlanta, GA 30348-55366
Phone: (404) 827-1500; *fax*: (404) 827-1593
Airs: 24 hours a day, seven days a week.
Audience: General adult worldwide
Profile: CNN broadcasts various news programs all day long between other programming.
How to pitch: If you are pitching a book or topic in the area of business, contact the appropriate producer/booker.
Assistant Director of Booking: Diane Durham, (404) 827-1320—the best contact for books and authors.
Producer and Booker: Betsy Goldman—the best overall contact for general interest stories.
Business News Unit:
New York City: Bill Baggitt, Assignment Editor, (212) 714-3340; *fax*: (212) 714-7962

Los Angeles Bureau:
CNN
6430 Sunset Blvd. #300
Los Angeles, CA 90028
Phone: (213) 993-5000; *fax*: (213) 993-5081
News Assignment Editor: Peter Ornstein

Before Hours/Business Day
5 Penn Plaza
New York, NY 10001-1878
Phone: (212) 714-7848; *fax*: (212) 714-7962
Airs: Monday-Friday, 6:00 to 7:00 a.m.
Audience: General adult, business people and investors
Profile: Business news program with up-to-the-minute reports on issues, money management, and people. There are also guest interviews, primarily with prominent investment fund managers and analysts.
How to pitch: Producer Dan Bases prefers that you fax your information to him first and then follow up with a phone call. Keep it short.
Booking Contact:
Business Day Producer: Alex Kaufman (212) 714-7848, 9-11 a.m.

Equal Time
1825 K St.
Washington, DC 20036
Phone: (202) 776-7413; *fax*: (202) 452-8244
Airs: Monday-Friday, 8:00-8:30 p.m.
Audience: General adult
Profile: Political issues program on the cable channel featuring talk, interviews, and listener phone-in. Producers book from day to day, rather than weeks in advance, as they used to do.
How to pitch: Mail, fax, or call. Keep written material to a minimum and, if you are pitching yourself as an author, include book, biography, and credentials.
Booking Contacts:
Producer: Robin Gellman (202) 776-7413
Associate Producer: Mark Allen (202) 776-7427
Associate Producer: Louise Filkins (202) 776-7415

48 Hours
CBS News
524 W. 57th Street
5th Floor

New York, NY 10019-2902
Phone: (212) 975-4848; *fax*: (212) 975-5797
Airs: Thursday, 10-11:00 p.m.
Audience: General adult
Profile: Hour-long news magazine format covers various sides of major national trends and news events from different perspectives over a 48-hour period.
How to pitch: Producers prefer to deal with the "real" people, organizations and businesses that originate the stories. Call or fax with information related to breaking news stories. Otherwise, they prefer to receive information in the mail.
Booking Contact:
Associate Producer: Meryl Schaeffer, who's in charge of research. Send information on books, authors, and experts to her.

Good Morning, America
147 Columbus Ave., 6th floor
New York, NY 10023
Phone: (212) 456-5900
West Coast Bureau:
4151 Prospect
Los Angeles, CA 90027
Phone: (310) 557-5938
Airs: Monday-Friday, 7-9:00 a.m. ET
Audience: General adult
Profile: General news, information and features program with interviews.
How to pitch: They like audio and video tapes, books and samples of products. Material should be short and to the point.
Booking Contacts:
Senior Program Producer: Kevin McGee, (212) 456-5986—the best overall contact if you're unsure who covers your topic.
Segment Producer: Susan Reichley, (212) 456-6016. Covers environment, technology, and business.
Segment Producer: Peggy Neger, (212) 456-6157. Covers books and authors, parenting, pets, and health.

Hard Copy
Paramount Pictures
5555 Melrose Avenue, E and G Bldg.
Los Angeles, CA 90038-3197
Phone: (213) 956-5808; *fax*: (213) 862-1940

Airs: Monday-Friday, 30 minutes
Profile: Syndicated tabloid program in a magazine format featuring interviews and current news items.
How to pitch: Subjects must be current and of importance to a wide variety of viewers.
Booking Contact:
Assignment Editor: Nancy Moscatiello

Inside Edition
King World Productions
402 E. 76th Street
New York, CA 10021-3104
Phone: (212-737-3399; *fax*: (212) 737-4983
To mail materials:
P.O. Box 1323
Gracie Station, NY 10028
In California, send materials to:
12400 Wilshire Blvd. #1160
Los Angeles, CA 90025
Phone: (310) 447-1187; *fax*: (310) 447-1472
Airs: Monday-Friday, 30 minutes
Audience: General adult
Profile: Syndicated magazine featuring national news stories and related interviews.
How to pitch: Interviews are booked out of both New York and Los Angeles.
Booking contact for LA:
Producer: Adrienne Schwartz is the best overall contact and the best contact for books and authors.

Larry King Live
820 First Street NE
Washington, D.C. 20002
Phone: (202) 898-7690 or 7698; *fax*: (202) 898-7686
Airs: Larry King Live: Monday-Friday, 9:00-10:00 p.m. ET,
          Larry King Weekend: Saturday, 9:00 p.m. ET
Audience: It's the world's only live television phone-in talk show seen in all 24 times zones.
Profile: News-oriented, in-depth talk program concentrating on current issues.

How to pitch: Submit written material by mail or Fedex if it's time sensitive. Do not fax. However, King rarely covers personal growth, how-to, diet/fitness, or individual finance.
Booking Contact:
Segment Producer: Katie Spikes (202) 898-7661

Money Wheel
2200 Fletcher Avenue
Fort Lee, NJ 07024-5005
Phone: (201) 585-2622; *fax*: (201) 585-6393
Airs: Monday-Friday, 10:00 a.m. - 4:00 p.m.
Audience: General adult
Profile: Business, finance, and consumerism show with interviews and guests; takes listener phone-in questions dealing with personal finance; produced by most of the same people who produce Market Wrap on CNBC.
How to pitch: Material should be sent through the mail. The pitch should show how the guest's information can benefit the audience.
Talent:
Correspondent: Sue Herera (201) 585-6465

Moneywise
Produces regular personal and family finance segments for CBS News and CBS This Morning. Producers want everything from personal financing and budgeting to investment information and opportunities.
Senior Producer: James Segelstein (212) 975-8907

NBC Nightly News
30 Rockefeller Plaza, Room 324
New York, NY 10122-0035
Phone: (212) 664-4691; *fax*: (212) 664-6044 (not verified)
Airs: Monday-Friday, 6:30-7:00 p.m.
Audience: General adult
Booking Contact:
Researcher: Tammy Fine. Send her information on experts and authors.

Newshour with Jim Lehrer
WETA-TV
3620 27th Street South
Arlington, VA 22206
Phone: (703) 998-2870

Airs: Monday-Friday, 6:00-7:00 p.m., live ET
Audience: General adult, 3.5 million viewers.
Profile: A very serious, event-driven news program featuring the "hard" news of the day and some guest interviews.
How to pitch: You must be an expert in an area that is newsworthy. Economic stories are run every Friday; each Tuesday features an interview (sometimes with authors).
Booking Contacts:
Senior Producer for Economic Issues: Jeff Brown (703) 998-2105

Nightline (ABC)
Washington Bureau:
ABC News
1717 DeSales Street NW
Washington, D.C. 20036
Phone: (202) 222-7000; *fax*: (202) 222-7976 (not verified)
Airs: Monday-Friday, 11:35 p.m.-12:05 a.m. ET
Audience: General adult
Profile: Hard-hitting news program featuring breaking news stories with an unconventional approach.
How to pitch: They like books that make news and that can be made into shows. Send galleys, manuscripts, and author bios as early as possible.
Booking Contacts:
Associate Producer and Chief Guest Booker (Washington): Sara Just (202) 222-7987

Oprah Winfrey Show
Harpo Productions
110 N. Carpenter
Chicago, IL 60607-2146
Phone: (312) 633-0808
Airs: Monday-Friday
Audience: Primarily adult women
How to pitch: Oprah is doing fewer sensational topics and more shows about positive relationships, family, and home topics. Proposals have to go through research and then be deemed interesting enough to be pitched to a producer.
Booking Contacts:
Senior Producer: Ellen Rakieten
Send book with cover letter to: Oprah Book Club, P.O. Box 617640, Chicago, IL 60661

Prime Time Live
147 Columbus Avenue, 3rd floor
New York, NY 10023-5900
Phone: (212) 456-1600; *fax*: (212) 456-1297
Airs: Wednesday, 10:00-11:00 p.m. ET
Audience: General adult
Profile: Magazine format show concentrating on news, current events, and newsworthy people and guests.
Booking Contacts:
Associate Producer: Jennifer Maguire (212) 456-1573. Send information on books and authors to her.

Today
NBC-TV
30 Rockefeller Plaza
New York, NY 10112-0002
Phone: (212) 664-4602/4249; *fax*: Won't give out
Airs: Monday-Friday, 7:00-9:00 a.m.
Audience: General adult
Profile: News and general interest morning magazine show with interviews.
How to pitch: Best to pitch by mail unless the subject or guest is breaking news.
Booking Contact:
Book/Literary Editor: Andrea Smith (212) 664-4371

Part IV
The Circle of Publicity
Activities

Part IV is where you put it all together, clean up all those loose ends, and make your debut as a recognized expert. It is at this stage in your program that it may be appropriate to hire a public relations firm.

In this part, you'll learn how to get your name out as an expert in your industry and really move into the distinction of expert. Once you're viewed as a credible source, writers, reporters and editors will contact you and you'll gain endorsements from them. Also included is a chapter for finding outside assistance.

Chapter 23
Advertising and Public Relations—How to Make Them Work

In this chapter, you will learn:
• Why traditional advertising doesn't work
• How to make advertising work
• What is public relations
• How to make public relations work

The Advertising Assault

Americans are exposed to an estimated 500 to 1,700 commercial messages daily. From the time you wake up and brush your teeth until you fall asleep to the sound of late night infomercials, you're bombarded with ads. They're everywhere: media, billboards, shop windows, bus benches, and t-shirts. Because there's no escape from them, we have learned to ignore them. The brain creates a buffer that filters out all but the few messages each day that we are really interested in.

Advertising is saying exactly what you want, where you want, and as often you want. But, the cost is huge and the results unpredictable. The vast majority of the billions and billions of advertising dollars spent is wasted money. A decade ago, a $2 million television budget was considered minimal; today, according to some advertising experts, the accepted minimum is closer to $10 million. Meanwhile, Mitsubishi Electric Company is busy marketing a video cassette recorder that automatically edits out commercials.

Print advertisers have only three seconds to grab attention before the reader turns the page. Three seconds. That's a lot of pressure. It takes at least ten seconds for someone to hang up on your cold call. That's why you only see the double-digit performance returns advertised in mutual fund ads—but that strategy can also backfire, as Fidelity recently discovered.

Fidelity Investments was spending millions of dollars a month on full page ads in various financial publications. Then an article appeared in *Business Week* (February 17, 1997). "So Much For Fidelity Loyalty" told of the investment giant's poor performance, that its flagship, Magellan, was one of 1996's worst-performing funds (560 out of 624), and that insiders were staying clear of it. How would you like to spend millions advertising, and then read that? Well, back to the Madison Avenue drawing boards.

Unfortunately, many of today's ads do not reflect the fact that today's upscale, more educated consumer wants to learn more about a product, rather than just last year's performance. The public has to watch an avalanche of $90 billion worth of annual national advertising, yet chooses not to be loyal because few marketers have offered any reason to be loyal. Consumers wait to buy when they're ready, *not* when the marketers would like them to.

The real question is: Why advertise in the first place? Is it because you have no other method of getting your message out? Or because everybody else does? Most advisors do it because they want to elevate their position in their market to ultimately get new business. The idea seems logical; the more you get your name out there, the better off you are. But, not all exposure will result in benefits to you or your company.

If you attempt to use advertising to go up against giants in the industry, you force your customer to compare you to the giant. It's difficult for a small company not to suffer by comparison. Even if you had the money to compete with the giants dollar for dollar, celebrity for celebrity, you're really not elevating your firm.

So How Can You Make Advertising Work?

Create a Perceived Differentiation Between You and All the Rest

What does that mean? It means to define the difference that exists that is not obvious. For instance, you can focus on your local market. You know that market and can respond faster to customer needs and can fulfill those needs better.

You must give people a reason to buy from you. The reason, either real or perceived as real, is why people choose you over competitors and use your services. Otherwise, you're in a commodity position where you're just another banana in the bunch. Maybe they'll pick you; maybe they won't.

Create an Image That You Want to Convey in Your Advertising

Try this exercise: Ask your customers how they feel about what you do. What do they think of your competitors? What do they think about the direction of your company? You want detailed responses, not just sound bites from people you poll. Many customers or clients are quite happy with your level of service and will tell you so. If they're not, it's good to find that out, too.

Use focus groups, opinion polls, sampling of potential customers or prospects. At these meetings, you're not going to try to sell them anything, but you want to find out what they think of you. You also want to develop a visual identity for your company so that whatever you or your employees say is the same. Consistency helps build your image.

What Should You Write About?

Write advertising copy about how your product or service can enhance your prospects' knowledge and expertise. Write ads that educate, solve a problem, or convey a successful or advantageous situation. Reread "Chapter 7 How to Write The Problem/Solution Article".

How do You Structure Your Advertisement?

Structure your ad in the same format as a problem/solution article. An easy format is to state the problem in the first sentence, then tell the reader you are going to explain how to solve it, then solve it. Don't forget to include a call-to-action with a way to find you.

Questions to ask before you write your ad:

1. Who is your target market?
2. What are their financial problems or concerns?
3. What do they read for their own businesses insights?

What About Public Relations?

Public relations is the strategic process of employing a variety of methods and activities to promote a favorable relationship with the public.

However, don't expect to get into the *New York Times* or on *Oprah* or on the cover of *Life*!

In a Golin Harris-Ball State study, public relations marketing was perceived as an effective method in various areas that had traditionally been the responsibility of advertising. There's strong agreement that advertising and public relations marketing should work together strategically. Public relations has been considered more cost effective than advertising; it can complement advertising, increasing the credibility of the message.

The consulting firm of Hill and Knowlton conducted a poll of senior executives at 20 of the top 50 national advertising firms. The H and K Study indicated that public relations is becoming more and more important. In the next five years it will likely become the most important element of marketing.

RJR Nabisco began slashing advertising budgets and eventually eliminated advertising for some products altogether. Using new and specialized media, the company reached local consumers by working closely with retailers to develop special promotions, event sponsorships, and other public relations techniques.

Advertising Age commissioned a study by Northwestern University Medill School of Journalism to find out how many free plugs occurred during an average broadcast day. TV programs are peppered with talk show product mentions, corporate logos, behind newscasters headlines, signage, and visual labels. The study viewed tapes of consecutive 24-hour broadcast days on each of the big three networks, counting every brand name mentioned. In a single day of programming, they found 818 instances of a recognizable product or mention of a brand or corporate name. News programs accounted for 360 mentions, or 44 percent. Variety shows had 199 mentions, and news features 117. The study also showed that the greatest number of mentions of products and brands came during early morning news programs, such as *Good Morning America* or *NBC Today.*

Indirect Media

The means of reaching people through editorials and articles is called "indirect media." Professor Theodore Levitt of the Harvard Graduate School of Business, former editor of *Harvard Business Review*, drew a distinction between public relations and advertising messages in his book, *The Marketing Mode*, pointing out that when the message is delivered by an objective third party, it is much more persuasive.

There's an increased consumer demand for specialized editorial content. Magazine titles have proliferated as a result of publishers targeting their market to niche audiences and special interest groups. The industry's ability to segment its market to reflect new trends facilitates the growth of these consumer magazines. Opportunities to reach consumers in publications focused on particular interests have exploded.

Sunday papers offer a special opportunity to reach more readers because people tend to have more time to read on weekends. There are 1,650 daily newspapers, and over 838 Sunday newspapers. Most people don't have a chance to read daily newspapers thoroughly, but Sunday newspapers have space to fill and provide a great opportunity for public relations placement. *USA Today* has also become a major outlet for public relations material, including new product introduction and sponsorship of events and surveys.

Studies on Advertising and Public Relations

The link between advertising and sales, once accepted as gospel, is now being questioned by the researchers. The American Management Association published a 30-page Management Bulletin measuring the effectiveness of publicity. Overall, the authors found that publicity outpulled advertising for a particular product by 7 to 1.[1] But in some publications, publicity outpulled advertising by 2.5 to 1 ratios; and in other cases, the exact reverse was true. Call the AMA at 212-586-8100 for a copy, or try University Microfilm International in Andover, MI at 800-521-0600.

A study by John Ivison reported in a Scottish publication, *The Scottsman* (September 15, 1995), that publicity outpulled advertising by a 30 to 1 ratio.

Another useful study by Glen T. Cameron, professor of public relations at the University of Georgia is titled, "Does publicity outperform advertising? An experiment and test of third party endorsement." (*Journal of Public Relations*, Vol. 6, Issue 3, 1994). Cameron can be reached by phone at 706-542-5009.

---

[1] The American Management Association, 1601 Broadway, New York, NY 10019, Management Bulletin #110 entitled "Measuring and Evaluating Public Relations Activities."

Can Public Relations be Effective?

Most public relations firms work on a retainer fee, so that you have to pay them a monthly fee plus expenses, and often an upfront fee. For this, they'll develop a press kit, cover letters, press releases, and a list of media contacts. They'll do the contacting for you and try to sell reporters on you or your unique service.

While most public relations firms take all comers, you should make sure the firm you are considering knows your industry. If you can find someone who has expertise in your area, you'll have a better chance of getting the exposure you want. You won't have to explain your jargon to them because they'll already know it. Hiring a public relations firm that doesn't understand your business could be a waste of money.

I've seen good public relations programs scrapped and heard people vow never to use advertising or a public relations firm again. What I discovered was it wasn't necessarily the fault of the public relations or advertising program. The problem was the client's unrealistic expectations. The program didn't respond to the true goal of the financial advisor: to attract pre-qualified prospects.

While public relations efforts may generate hundreds of prospects, the prospects may have little money to invest, so marketing to them is counterproductive. Poor targeting is often a fault of public relations firms. Many of them sell cars and soap and are not aware of the special needs of, say, those in the financial community. Inside, their target market is the lowest common denominator.

The financial services market is the affluent: wealthy business owners, retirees, doctors, etc. Your target market's concerns may not be the primary concerns of the masses. Mass media vehicles are not necessarily the most suitable place to present one's story.

Where to Go For Public Relations Help

The Public Relations Society of America (PRSA), headquartered in New York City, is the world's largest organization for public relations professionals. Its wide-ranging new website has links for PR professionals, journalists, writers, students, job-seekers and others. It provides links to websites of PRSA chapters, though not to PR agencies. It covers environmental communications, section newsletters, case studies, conference updates, leadership contacts, environmental PR audiotapes and videotapes, monographs and eco-pr links. (Public Relations Society of America, 33 Irving Place, New York, NY 10003-2376 (212) 995-2230; hq@prsa.org)

Figure 23-1 Example of Highly Effective Ad

Will You Be Broke When You Retire?

What if your retirement plan funds run out, and you aren't financially stable enough to support yourself or your family? Do you think you can depend on Social Security or hitting the lottery to keep you from going broke?

With so many people living longer, healthier lives, it is even more important than ever to pre-pare yourself for "life after a paycheck." **Michael Lane** will offer great tips on how to build an investment portfolio that you can't outlive. He will reveal valuable tips on how to protect your money and make it last for as long as you need it!

CREDENTIALS: Michael F. Lane is the author of *GUARANTEED INCOME FOR LIFE.*

AVAILABILITY: Kentucky, nationwide by arrangement and via telephone

CONTACT: Michael F. Lane, (502) 560-3194 (KY)

Source: Larry Chambers

This ad is a great example of what works. Lane asks a powerful opening question. This ad placed in *Radio/TV Interview Magazine* landed him multiple interviews.

Figure 23-1 Example of Highly Effective Ad, con't.

Build A Business Worth
MILLIONS!

Investment advisors and financial planners are sitting atop gold mines and they don't even realize it. The source of this amazing undiscovered wealth? Their own businesses—their unique abilities, strengths, and asset base.

Creating Equity shows you how to add value to your business—for your clients and yourself. *Creating Equity* offers step-by-step instructions and proven strategies from financial experts on how you can build a business worth over a million dollars.

Design a business model that will make you a success by:

- **learning to create investment processes that deliver consistent high-quality service to your clients**
- **avoiding thirteen pitfalls that can bring down the value of your business**
- **developing investment strategies that will help clients achieve investment goals**
- **and much more!**

Creating Equity is written by *John J. Bowen, Jr.*, a leader in the asset management industry. He is President and CEO at *Reinhardt Werba Bowen Advisory Services*, which manages over $1.5 billion in assets. *Creating Equity* is brought to you by **Securities Data Publishing**, a producer of leading financial publications—*Financial Planning, On Wall Street* and *Bank Investment Marketing*.

Let the experts show you how you can build a million dollar business. Order your copy of *Creating Equity* and make the investment that's sure to yield high returns.

To place your order, call our Customer Service Department
at 212-765-5311 or 800-455-5844 or use the coupon below.

Mail or fax to: **Securities Data Publishing** **40 West 57th Street, 11th Floor** **New York, NY 10019** Fax **(212) 765-6123** or **(212) 765-3063**	**YES!** I want to learn how I can build a million dollar business. Please rush me ____ copy(ies) of *Creating Equity* for just $39.95 each ($45 outside the U.S.) per copy. *(MA, CT, PA, IL, CA, TX, NJ and NY residents please add applicable sales tax.)*

❑ Check enclosed, made payable to Securities Data Publishing ❑ Bill me (Book will be shipped upon receipt of payment)

❑ Charge my: ❑ Visa ❑ MasterCard ❑ American Express   Card# _____Exp. Date _____

Signature _____ Name _____

Title _____ Company _____

Address _____ City/State/Zip _____

Phone _____ Fax _____

Source: Reinhardt Werba Bowen Advisor Services. Reprinted with permission.

Instead of traditional advertising, this ad cost the author nothing. The author formed a strategic alliance with the trade magazine publisher who shared the same target market. Not only did they print, sell and set up a distribution system for this book, they ran full page ads in three of their magazines.

Chapter 24
How to Turn a Trade
Conference into a
Gold Mine

In this chapter, you'll learn:
• How to locate the gold vein
• How to mine it
• How to maximize your muscle
• The impact this will have on your overhead

Always give your customers more than they expect. Satisfied customers spread the word and are a natural part of your strategic alliance network. Not only are satisfied customers your best advertisement as walking, talking billboards for your services, they are repeat buyers. The best advertising is still word of mouth from satisfied customers.

But to reinforce that, you need to devise a detailed plan to assure successful promotional opportunities happen as well. Promotional events are part of it. These can range from a book signing to sponsoring a Playathon benefit for your favorite charity—it's up to your creativity and imagination. To get additional attention, you might even decide to auction off your books at the event. I recently gave a hundred of my books to the Boys Club of Ventura, which also auctioned off a dinner with an author. Piggyback with events that promote your cause. You can become a part of an ongoing success such as the Boys Club, United Way, Project Red Cross, or the Kiwanis. Provide uniforms for Little League, donate food, or help sponsor a community event. This will give you local visibility.

To really reach your target market, though, you need to join trade or professional associations. Since associations publish trade magazines and newsletters, they help you keep track of news, key people, trends, and coming events. Attend conventions, trade shows, seminars, and other opportunities to network.

If you join an association, don't fade into the woodwork. Become an active member. Get to know CPAs, business owners, and others in that industry. Become familiar with their concerns, needs, and desires—and let them know yours. As part of your active participation, sponsor awards, contests, or scholarships that give others recognition and help them grow in their professions. These activities might not immediately show on your balance sheet, but they will help you gain recognition as a leader in the industry and community—a critical image for you to project.

Most trade associations have a reading list. Some even publish a limited number of books and booklets. I've found they're very receptive when they discover they have as a member an investment expert who understands their particular financial problems. If your book is accepted by a trade organization, you've gained immediate association credibility and an endorsement by the association of your ideas.

Every industry has its trade conference—from the certified public accountants to building and plumbing contractors. Speaking at a conference should be a goal of every marketer to the affluent. Speakers at a conference, by definition, are experts.

You can be on a panel with other marketers of the same service. Or give workshops or seminars at trade shows as well as locally. If you're a keynote speaker at a trade conference, you can have the undivided attention of literally thousands of people about your asset management service. It would take you hundreds of days of traditional prospecting to encounter the number of affluent business owners that you come in contact with at a major conference. The people who attend these meetings are there intentionally to learn. And while ten very wealthy clients could make your year, a hundred very wealthy clients in one room does elevate your chance of great success!

It takes the same hour of time to speak to 100 people as it does to speak to one, so you might as well save 99 hours. If you're a good public speaker, it's a good way to leverage your time. If you're not, either develop the skill required, or find a strategic ally with whom you can share the podium. Public speaking helps to rapidly elevate your credibility as a problem solver. *Caution:* Do not use this speaking opportunity to sell your product! This is generally not allowed by associations and it would not be appropriate anyway. You want to position yourself as a problem solver, not a product pusher!

There are thousands of trade associations around the country. The best source is the *Encyclopedia of Associations*, from Gale Research Company.

Figure 24-1 Encyclopedia of Associations

Figure 24-1 Encyclopedia of Associations, con't.

Gale Directory of Publications & Broadcast Media / 1997   NEW YORK—New York

📖 **20776 Field & Stream**
Times Mirror Magazines, Inc.
2 Park Ave.   Phone: (212)779-5230
New York, NY 10016   Fax: (212)779-5465
Magazine focusing on hunting, fishing, camping, and boating. **Founded:** 1895.
Frequency: Monthly. **Print Method:** Offset. **Trim Size:** 7 7/8 x 10 1/2. **Cols./Page:**
3. **Col. Width:** 27 nonpareils. **Col. Depth:** 143 agate lines. **Key Personnel:** Duncan
Barnes, Editor; Micheal Rooney, Publisher; Paul J. Turcott, Advertising Dir.
ISSN: 8755-8602. **Subscription Rates:** $15.94. $2. single issue.
Ad Rates: BW: $49,905   **Circulation:** Paid 1,750,000
               4C: $73,930

📖 **20777 Film Comment**
Film Society of Lincoln Center
70 Lincoln Center Plaza   Phone: (212)875-5610
New York, NY 10023   Fax: (212)875-5636
Motion picture magazine. **E-mail address(es):** rtjfc@aol.com; rtj-fc@msn.com.
Founded: 1962. **Frequency:** Bimonthly. **Print Method:** Offset. **Trim Size:** 8 5/16 X
10 7/8. **Cols./Page:** 3. **Col. Width:** 27 nonpareils. **Col. Depth:** 137 agate lines. **Key
Personnel:** Richard T. Jameson, Editor; Tony Impavido, Advertising Mgr. ISSN:
0015-119X. **Subscription Rates:** $4.95.
Ad Rates: BW: $720   **Circulation:** ‡47,000
               4C: $1,360

📖 **20778 Film Journal International**
The Sunshine Group
244 W. 49th St., Ste. 200   Phone: (212)246-6460
New York, NY 10019   Fax: (212)265-6428
Magazine addressing interests of the motion picture industry. **Founded:** 1933.
Frequency: Monthly. **Print Method:** Offset. **Trim Size:** 8 1/2 x 11. **Cols./Page:** 3.
Col. Width: 30 nonpareils. **Col. Depth:** 150 agate lines. **Key Personnel:** Robert
Sunshine, Editor and Publisher; Kevin Lally, Managing Editor; Jimmy Sunshine,
Publisher. ISSN: 0199-7300. **Subscription Rates:** $30.
Ad Rates: BW: $1,660   **Circulation:** 10,200
               4C: $2,710

📖 **20779 Films in Review**
National Board of Review of Motion Pictures, Inc.
PO Box 589   Phone: (212)628-1594
New York, NY 10021   Fax: (212)427-9307
Movie magazine containing reviews. **Founded:** Jan. 1950. **Frequency:** Bimonthly.
Print Method: Offset. **Trim Size:** 5 1/2 x 7 1/2. **Cols./Page:** 2. **Col. Width:** 25
nonpareils. **Col. Depth:** 74 agate lines. **Key Personnel:** Roy Fruakes, Editor. ISSN:
0015-1688. **Subscription Rates:** $18.
Ad Rates: BW: $300   **Circulation:** 38,500

📖 **20780 Financial History Review**
Cambridge University Press
40 W. 20th St.   Phone: (212)924-3900
New York, NY 10011   Fax: (212)691-3239
                                                       (800)221-4517
Journal focusing on banking, finance and monetary matters. **Founded:** Apr. 1995.
Frequency: Semiannual. **Key Personnel:** Youssef Cassis, Editor; Philip Cottrell,
Editor. ISSN: 0968-5650. **Subscription Rates:** $39; $79 institutions. $41 single
issue.

📖 **20781 Financial Leadership Speaks**
Williams & Wilkins
208 E. 51st St., No. 224   Phone: (212)753-4806
New York, NY 10022   Fax: (212)480-3705
                                                       (800)222-3790
Subtitle: The Journal and Index of Financial Speeches. **Founded:** 1991. **Frequency:**
Bimonthly. **Key Personnel:** Richard Cook, Publisher. ISSN: 1055-8675. **Subscrip-
tion Rates:** $125 U.S. and Canada; $145 other countries.

📖 **20782 Financial Planning**
SDC Publishing
40 W. 57th St., 11th Fl.   Phone: (212)765-5311
New York, NY 10019   Fax: (212)765-6123
Subtitle: The Magazine for Financial Services Professionals. **Founded:** 1972.
Frequency: Monthly. **Print Method:** Offset. **Trim Size:** 8 1/8 x 10 7/8. **Cols./Page:**
3. **Col. Width:** 2 3/16 inches. **Col. Depth:** 10 inches. **Key Personnel:** E van
Simonoff, Editor-in-Chief; Bruce Morris, Publisher. **Subscription Rates:** Free to
qualified subscribers; $48 individuals. $6 single issue.
Ad Rates: BW: $4,650   **Circulation:** Paid 17,835
               4C: $5,850   Controlled 51,911

📖 **20783 Financial World**
Financial World Partners
1328 Broadway, 3rd Fl.   Phone: (212)594-5030
New York, NY 10001-2116   Fax: (212)629-0021
                                                       (800)829-5916
Magazine focusing on finance and business that provides useful information to
individual and professional investors and corporate managers. **Founded:** 1902.
Frequency: 18x/yr. **Print Method:** Web offset. **Trim Size:** 8 x 10 3/4. **Cols./Page:** 3.
Col. Width: 27 nonpareils. **Col. Depth:** 140 agate lines. **Key Personnel:** Barry L.
Rupp, Chairman and CEO; SEth E. Hoyt, President/Publisher; Stephen Taub,

Editor-in-Chief; John Kennelly, Advertising Mgr. ISSN: 0015-2064. **Subscription
Rates:** $2.95 single issue; $27 annually.
Ad Rates: BW: $28090   **Circulation:** Paid 503,447
               4C: $42130
Alternate Formats: Online, with Dow Jones News-Retrieval; Online, with LEXIS-
NEXIS; Online, with Electronic Newsstand; Internet, at http://
www.financialworld.com.

📖 **20784 Finding Guide to AIAA Meeting Papers**
American Institute of Aeronautics & Astronautics
85 John St.   Phone: (212)349-1120
New York, NY 10038-2823   Fax: (212)349-1283
Comprehensive guide to papers presented at AIAA meetings held each year.
Founded: 1981. **Frequency:** Annual. **Key Personnel:** Geoff Worton, Director. ISSN:
0894-3818. **Subscription Rates:** $60.

📖 **20785 Fire and Materials**
John Wiley and Sons, Inc.
Subscription Dept.   Phone: (212)850-6000
605 3rd Ave.   Fax: (212)850-6799
New York, NY 10158
Journal which focuses on the fire properties of materials. Topics include heat
release, properties of combustion products, and modelling and testing. **Subtitle:**
An International Journal. **Frequency:** Bimonthly. **Key Personnel:** J.D. Redfern,
Editor-in-Chief; S.J. Grayson, Managing Editor; M. Hirschler, Associate Editor;
M. Janssens, Associate Editor; H. Suzuki, Associate Editor; M. Kokkala, Associate
Editor. ISSN: 0308-0501. **Subscription Rates:** $695.

📖 **20786 FIRST THINGS**
Institute on Religion & Public Life
156 5th Ave. Ste. 400   Phone: (212)627-1985
New York, NY 10010   Fax: (212)627-2184
                                                       (800)783-4903
Periodical for academics, clergy, journalists, and others. **Subtitle:** A Monthly
Journal of Religion and Public Life. **Founded:** Mar. 1990. **Frequency:** 10x/yr. **Print
Method:** Web offset. **Trim Size:** 8 1/8 x 11. **Cols./Page:** 2 and 3. **Col. Width:** 2 1/8
inches. **Col. Depth:** 9 and 9 inches. **Key Personnel:** James Nuechterlein, Editor;
Richard John Neuhaus, Land Editor-in-Chief; Richard A. Vaughan, Advertising
Mgr.; Matthew Berke, Managing Editor; J. Bottum, Associate Editor. ISSN: 1047-
5141. **Subscription Rates:** $29. $3.75 single issue.
Ad Rates: BW: $850   **Circulation:** ‡25,000
               4C: $1,450
Alternate Formats: Online.

📖 **20787 Fit Magazine**
GCR Publishing Group, Inc.
1700 Broadway   Phone: (212)541-7100
New York, NY 10019   Fax: (212)245-1241
                                                       (800)877-5368
Health, fitness, lifestyles for women on the go. **Subtitle:** Health, Fitness, Lifestyles
for Women on the Go. **Founded:** 1982. **Frequency:** 7x/yr. **Print Method:** Offset.
Trim Size: 8 1/2 x 11. **Cols./Page:** 3. **Col. Width:** 27 nonpareils. **Col. Depth:** 137
agate lines. **Key Personnel:** Nicole Dorsey, Editor; Charles Goodman, Publisher;
John Damboragian, Advertising Mgr. **Subscription Rates:** Newsstand sales only.
Ad Rates: BW: $1,785   **Circulation:** Paid 100,000
               4C: $2,680

Variant Name(s): Formerly: New Body Magazine.

📖 **20788 Fitness Diet and Exercise Guide**
The Family Circle, Inc.
110 5th Ave.   Phone: (212)463-1673
New York, NY 10011
Magazine suggesting ways to eat healthier and exercise better. **Founded:** Apr. 1987.
Frequency: 5x/yr. **Key Personnel:** Barbara Winkler, Editor; John Hillock, Publish-
er. **Subscription Rates:** $2.25 single issue.

📖 **20789 Flavour and Fragrance Journal**
John Wiley and Sons, Inc.
Subscription Dept.   Phone: (212)850-6000
605 3rd Ave.   Fax: (212)850-6799
New York, NY 10158
International journal on essential oils and related products for organic chemists,
food scientists, toxicologists, flavour chemists, and technologists. **Frequency:**
Bimonthly. **Key Personnel:** R. Stevens, Editor; J.J.C. Scheffer, Editor. ISSN: 0882-
5734. **Subscription Rates:** $455.

📖 **20790 Fluid Dynamics**
Plenum Publishing Corp.
233 Spring St.   Phone: (212)620-8000
New York, NY 10013   Fax: (212)463-0742
Scientific journal translated from Russian. **Frequency:** Bimonthly. **Print Method:**
Offset. **Key Personnel:** G.G. Chernyi, Editor; Sophia Conyers, Advertising Mgr.
Subscription Rates: $1,075; $1,260 other countries.

📖 **20791 Fluid Mechanics Research**
John Wiley and Sons, Inc.
Subscription Dept.   Phone: (212)850-6000
605 3rd Ave.   Fax: (212)850-6799
New York, NY 10158
Journal publishing translations of research papers from Russia and the Ukraine.
Topics include compressible fluids, slurry flow, and boundary layers. **Frequency:**
Bimonthly. **Key Personnel:** Novak Zuber, Editor; Ivan Catton, Editor. ISSN:

Ad Rates: GLR – general line rate; BW – one-time black & white page rate; 4C – one-time four color page rate; SAU – standard advertising unit rate;
CNU – Canadian newspaper advertising unit rate; PCI – per column inch rate.
Circulation: ★ – ABC; △ – BPA; ◆ – CAC; ● – CCAB; □ – VAC; ⊕ – PO Statement; ‡ – Publisher's Report; Boldface figures – sworn; Light figures – estimated.
Entry type: 📖 – Print; 📻 – Broadcast.   **1515**

Source: Gale Research. Reprinted with permission.

If you haven't already, put *Encyclopedia of Associations* on your list of books to buy. It provides important details on key trade associations in almost every industry, with membership, location, dates of annual conferences, and important publications as well as who's who. *Association Management* is a magazine that provides information to the officers of associations.

You should try to attend at least one trade show as soon as possible just to get a feel for it. For a complete list of professional meetings and seminars, read the appropriate trade and professional magazines. Or look into these directories, some of which should be available at your local library:

- *Association Meeting Directory* – Lists 9,000 meetings. Available from Association Meeting Directory, 1001 Connecticut Avenue NW #1035, Washington, DC 20036; (202) 296-7400; (800) 541-0663; Fax: (202) 296-7565. $245.00.

- *Exhibits Directory* – Lists 250 book shows worldwide. From the Association of American Publishers, 220 East 23rd Street, New York, NY 10016-5825; (212) 689-8920; Fax (212) 696-0131. $90.00

- *Trade Shows Worldwide* – Lists 4,500 trade shows and conventions. From The Gale Group, 835 Penobscot Building, Detroit, MI 48226-4094; (313) 961-2242; (800) 877-GALE; Fax: (313) 961-6083. $169.95. Gale also publishes and distributes many other valuable directories and provides mailing lists. Call for their catalog.

- *Tradeshow Week Data Book* – Lists 4,200 international trade shows. Available from R. R. Bowker, P.O. Box 31, New Providence, NJ 07974; (908) 665-2818; (800) 521-8100; Fax: (908) 665-6688. $299.00.

- *Trade Shows & Exhibits Schedule* – Features 11,000 exhibits and trade shows. From Successful Meetings, 355 Park Avenue South, New York, NY 10011; (800) 253-6708. $170.00

You may also get the information you need from The Trade Show Bureau, 1660 Lincoln Street, Suite 2080, Denver, CO 80264; (303) 860-7626.

Marketing yourself at a trade association is not difficult; however, it does take planning, time, and energy, and there is some cost.

Trade Show Budget Worksheet

Use this worksheet to project the variety of expenses that you may incur in connection with a trade show or convention.

Expenses
Show registration fees   _____
Booth-related expenses (furniture, give-aways, etc.)   _____
Phone and Fax   _____
Postage   _____
Courier services (e.g., Federal Express, UPS)   _____
Printing   _____
Stationery   _____
Envelopes   _____
Press kit covers   _____
Travel and entertainment   _____
Meals with reporters   _____
Travel to and from airports   _____
Taxis   _____
Incidentals   _____

Press Conference
Room rental   _____
Food   _____
Beverages   _____
Equipment rental/delivery   _____
Slide show/presentation materials   _____

                                        Total Costs   _____

Checklist of Trade Show Tactics

There are a number of things you can do to make your trade show appearance more effective:

- Place press kits in the Press Room, and be sure your booth location is included on the press kit or on your press release inside. (*Warning*: If you are not a registered exhibitor, materials you leave in the Press Room will probably be thrown away. If you're sharing a booth registered in another company's name, notify the Press Room attendant so your kits won't be thrown out.)
- Post a press release on the bulletin board in the Press Room.
- Post fliers announcing your press conferences, hospitality suites, or booth locations in or near the Press Room.
- Keep a supply of press kits at your booth for visiting reporters.
- Carry a handful of press kits with you. You never know when you'll run into a reporter.
- Collect business cards and write notes for follow-up on them.
- Locate the rooms where reporters congregate (Press Room, press conference rooms) and frequent these places yourself.

Scheduled Meetings
- Call the reporter's hotel the night before and leave a message to confirm your meeting.
- Arrive at the meeting site 10 minutes before the appointment is scheduled.
- Wait at least 15 minutes after the appointed time for late reporters.

Unscheduled Meetings
- Conduct on-the-spot interviews/demos with reporters you encounter.
- Stand outside the Press Room with press kits to "bump into" reporters.
- Read badges/faces for key press people. Introduce yourself and gain their interest.

Parties
- Ask reporters with whom you've built rapport where the parties are.
- Go to booths rented by publications you advertise in and ask for an invitation to their parties.
- Attend parties. Be low key.

Chapter 25
How to Turn Your Expertise into a College Course

In this chapter, you'll learn:
- You don't need a degree to teach
- What to teach and how
- How teaching can bring in millions
- A course proposal

How can you make sure that hungry prospects find you?

One successful financial advisor, Lucinda Fairfield, answers, "Leave a trail of marketing clues, strategically placed, so seekers have a trail to follow."

Fairfield teaches a continuing education course at the University of New Mexico. She's one of the most popular teachers there—in fact, Fairfield was voted teacher of the year—plus she runs a successful investment advisory business. How did she accomplish all this? Well, it all started with Fairfield proposing a course on investing to the university in the fall of 1985.

Her background: from the time Fairfield began working for a large Wall Street firm, Boettcher & Company, she realized she would have to find a way to market herself that would be more efficient than cold calling. The branch manager mentioned she should see if the local university might be interested in offering a new investment course, but Fairfield found the university already offered a course by an advisor from a competing firm.

Fairfield didn't give up. Instead she decided to do some research into what courses were taught in other colleges around the country, and particularly what courses were popular in her own region. Next, she familiarized herself with the Division of Continuing Education at the local university.

225

Fairfield discovered the division was seeking to increase enrollment. She went back to the drawing board and designed classes that would complement the interests of that division. She prepared a preamble that demonstrated she understood their goals were to increase enrollment, bring in tuition, and increase community participation. She stated that she believed she could assist them and presented four or five different class ideas. They were so impressed, their enthusiastic response was "Great! Let's get on with it!"

What to Teach

Now Fairfield concentrates on three different topics. The first is estate planning—how to create, build, and preserve wealth. She teaches this subject in conjunction with an attorney, a CPA, and an insurance specialist.

The second course, her most successful, is an introduction to the stock and bond market. The third is a new class titled "The Guide for the Prudent Investor—How to Beat the Market." See Figure 25-1 on page 227. (Remember John Bowen's book—it really *is* getting around.)

Fairfield states, "There may be a class that's a raging success in Denver but, for whatever reason, that same class might not work in Albuquerque – or vice versa. You have to be willing to experiment and repeat a class more than one semester to give it time to catch on. Because one class doesn't work, that doesn't necessarily mean there isn't any interest in what you have to say. It may mean that today people are simply in the mood for a certain type of topic to be discussed."

How to Teach

Lucinda Fairfield's Teaching Outline:
   1. Overview: The first night of class she gives a preview of the material that will be covered. Then the students are asked to state their names, what they do for a living, and what their goals are for the class. She makes a conscious effort to remember everybody's name from that point on and to refer to each one by first name. The class enrollment is a minimum of 12 and a maximum of 25 students.

Figure 25-1 How to Beat the Market

708   A GUIDE FOR THE PRUDENT INVESTOR-HOW TO BEAT THE MARKET

In 1990 Modern Portfolio Theory won the Nobel Prize. However, this management strategy that has had the most positive impact on portfolio performance has not been widely available to individual investors . . . until now.

A Guide for Prudent Investors is the first class that offers individual investors true insights to beat the "Best-of-the-Best" mutual funds in both good and bad markets. Using the techniques in "Asset Class Investing," you can secure a solid financial future for you and your family.

This class brings academic research and some of the more sophisticated strategies to Main Street. This easy to use investment strategy has historically beaten professional managers as a group. This class combines ground breaking research with real world applications for prudent investing. A materials fee of $25 is payable aaat the FIRST CLASS MEETING.

$50	UNM Cont. Educ.
A: Mon, 6:30-8:30pm	Carlisle Center
Aug 26-Sept 23	4 Weeks
(no class Sept 2)	

Lucinda Fairfield, CFP, Securities America

"People usually come to class with insecurities about handling money, and they often feel intimidated," Fairfield comments. "Once students discover that the other people in the room are like them – a nurse, a computer tech, a teacher – they relax. The personal introduction session breaks the ice and puts everyone at ease, so they're better able to learn the material. I then talk about myself - what I do for a living, and what my goals and objectives are for the class. Then we begin the learning process."

2. Introduction: As an introduction to the class, Fairfield tells the students a personal story. At the beginning of her career, she was very proud of herself for having passed the securities test on the first try. In fact, she felt extremely smug, smart, and clever—that is, until she stepped into the professional world of finance. She then found that she'd learn something new one day, but it was contradicted the next day. She became very confused and unsure of herself. After a couple of weeks, she wasn't feeling so bright any more, but rather humble and overwhelmed by the amount of information.

Three or four months later, at a securities dinner, a colleague who had been in the business many years asked how she was doing. Fairfield replied, "I feel like I have some kind of learning disability. Every day I feel even more overwhelmed than the day before." The seasoned professional slapped her on the back and said, "Don't worry, kid, the first 20 years are the hardest."

She shares this true story with students to let them know up front that the introduction class is not going to give them every single bit of information that they'll ever need to skillfully manage their portfolios. The class is designed to help students discover where to get answers to questions and from what resources. The story also gives them an inkling of just how much information there is in the world of finance and portfolio management, and starts them off with a realistic perspective.

3. Introduce New Concepts: In the first full class, Fairfield begins talking about basic money concepts. She first describes the three ways to make money: income, growth, and tax savings. She then leads students to examine how their portfolios are currently designed relative to income, growth, and tax savings. The class then investigates ways to generate income: employment, savings accounts, CDs; ways to generate growth: business, real estate, collectibles, stocks; then ways to generate tax savings: pensions, profit sharing plans, municipal bonds, estate planning, life insurance, etc.

At the conclusion of that class, Fairfield gives her students an assignment. "Go home and get in touch with your portfolios; bond with your money," she tells them and gives them tools for analyzing their current money practices.

Each subsequent class examines a single topic; for instance, how a portfolio is divided between income, growth, and tax savings. She has students examine their own portfolios relative to risk. "I give my students a number of assignments, but I don't collect or grade them. The assignments are designed to help students become more aware of what they have done to date with their own money, whether they have consistently followed good plans, whether they have examined and kept within their risk tolerance ranges, what their return expectations are, and so on."

In This for You?

Considering Teaching? Fairfield has Some Tips

The first requirement is a sincere desire to teach. Second is a commitment to prepare information in a way that's meaningful and understandable to students. Third is a willingness to put ego aside, to be sensitive and keenly aware of the needs of the students. For instance, when a student states, "I'm not understanding this," or asks, "Could you please explain that in another way?" it's very important that the instructor not judge the student. It's only an indication that the teacher needs to look for another way to convey the message. Some instructors have the attitude, "Look how bright I am. Look how much I know." The point is to not use esoteric phraseology in order to show off. If students are not getting it, the teacher has failed them.

When a person undertakes teaching, the commitment is to teach, not to advertise. As soon as the message sounds like advertising, respect and attention are lost. You will be perceived by others as having a hidden agenda. The student is not there to hear about how wonderful the teacher is. The student is there to learn about investing, not to become your client or devotee.

How Does This Contribute to Your Business?

The description of Fairfield's classes in the catalog states, "Tuition includes one individual session with the instructor for portfolio evaluation and planning." On the first night of class, there's a calendar on the table of available dates and times for students to schedule an hour or half-hour meeting with Fairfield. In that session, she will answer any personal or private questions relating to the student's portfolio or the market in general. This meeting is private, confidential, and held in her closed office. In class itself, Fairfield does not give specific recommendations on mutual funds, or on which way she thinks the market's going, or how she feels about CDs versus annuities. The personal time can be used by students to explore these areas with Fairfield. If a student raises a hand in class and asks, "What do you think of Fidelity?" her answer is, "If you'd like to discuss that, here's the schedule. I'll give you 30 minutes. This class time is not the time or place for me to give you my personal opinion."

Trust is built in the class environment that would ordinarily take months. It's been a successful means of building a solid practice for Fairfield. By the time students show up for the personal appointment, they've already had at least three contacts with her in the classroom. Out of 25 people, 70 to 75 percent make appointments.

Fairfield's closing rate is very high—68 percent. The average portfolio under her management is in excess of $400,000. Her closing rate would be even higher but many prospects don't qualify, either because of a lack of assets to work with or because they expect her to simply trade stocks. That's not the kind of advisor she is.

Outstanding Effort Brings Benefits

In 1987, Fairfield was named Instructor of the Year for her division and was interviewed on TV and radio. Now people recognize her on the street and identify her as an expert.

There have, in fact, been many side benefits. Two years ago, Jazzercise Corporation was looking for someone to make a presentation on managing a portfolio as part of their employee benefit program. The university recommended Fairfield. Jazzercise called and asked how much she would charge. When she replied, "Six weeks, $5,000," they said, "No problem," and she was on.

Jazzercise set it up—desks, chalkboard, everything. She taught the class twice to about 20 women each time. As a result, she was asked by an influential attendee to become a city sponsor, a very prestigious position. As city sponsor, Fairfield then gave a talk to 600 women about financial investing. It snowballed from there. These are just some of the spin-offs from teaching at the university.

There have been marketing advantages, too. The university takes care of printing and sending catalogs out, about 50,000 a term, containing her course description. It also takes care of the registration process and provides the facilities. She picks up the list of students, shows up, and delivers. What could be better?

Proposing a Course: A Checklist

1. Research the school's philosophy, goals, and current course offerings.
2. Compare its catalog with other college catalogs.
3. Write descriptions for several new courses.
4. Find out who the decision maker is.
5. Get your materials together.
6. Send in your proposal or deliver it personally.
7. Follow up with a phone call.

Chapter 26
Yellow Gold: Revisit the Yellow Pages

In this chapter, you'll learn:
• How effective the Yellow Pages can be
• Mistakes to avoid
• How to get the most for your money
• Where to go for help

According to a recent survey by financial researcher Dalbar, Inc., "Because the volume of advertising and mass mailing in the financial securities industry is so overwhelming, many people turn to the Yellow Pages when they need an investment advisor." This may not be true for your business—a lot depends on where you live. In a small town in the Midwest, they use the Yellow Pages. The big-city affluent will not look for you there.

Forget what you think you know about the Yellow Pages. Once again, Big Yellow has emerged as a viable source for getting your message out effectively. But, there are both effective and ineffective ways to advertise in the Yellow Pages. For example, if you look through your local Yellow Pages, you'll see lawyers advertising they can do everything from wills, probate, and divorces, to handling accidents. They're telling you "come one, come all." Not very effective.

Though many financial advisors have the misconception that the Yellow Pages is the aluminum siding version of advertising, the Yellow Pages is the fifth largest advertising medium in the country—after direct mail, TV, newspapers, and radio—with $10.4 billion spent each year on directory advertising.

According to Statistical Research, Inc., in a study commissioned by the Yellow Pages Publishing Association, average Yellow Page usage among all adults is 1.9 references per week—a total of 19.4 billion references a year. Local Yellow Page advertising by small services and retail establishments makes up 86 percent of all directory ads. But local advertisers often miss something that national advertisers know intimately: You don't just run any ad. You first need to consider the objective of advertising in a particular medium. What is the ad expected to produce? What is the strategy? What are you trying to get out of it? Start from there and work toward creating the ad that will work for you. The Yellow Pages is a much more sophisticated medium than most people realize. Results can be tracked to find out what you're really getting from your advertising.

Figure 26-1 The Value of Yellow Pages

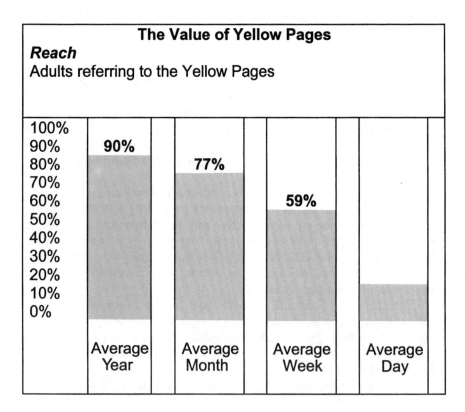

The Wrong Way

Most local advertisers look at the amount of money they spent on advertising the previous year and ask themselves how much they can afford to spend this year: "Business was good. I can spend more." Or "Business was tough. I'll cut back." That's the classic mistake. When times are rough, advertising should be increased, not cut back. But even that's not approaching it the right way.

The point is what directory advertising can do for local advertisers. It can't do everything. It can only reach certain types of prospects. Depending on what service or business you're in, the Yellow Pages can play either a very important role or a very minor role. Once you understand that role, you can decide the type of competitive presence you want to have there. Only then should you work on an appropriate ad budget—not the other way around, starting with the dollars and then figuring out what size ad to buy.

Another mistake is thinking that because you're known in the community, you don't need to advertise. As society is becoming increasingly transient, however, people must depend more on the media for direction. In parts of the country where people tend to move a lot, like Connecticut and New Jersey, Yellow Pages referrals are much higher than in places like Nebraska, Arkansas, or Mississippi where the population is less transient. People who are not familiar with an area use the directory much more often than those who have resided in the area for a long time.

When you move into a new house in a new unexplored neighborhood, you look forward to getting the phone book. It puts you in touch. You have a hundred things you have to do that first week in the new house—find the gas company, get your long distance service connected, find a new bank, a new pharmacy. The directory is not viewed as an intrusive medium the way direct mail is.

If one well-placed ad picks up one managed account, it was worth it.

The Main Purpose of the Yellow Pages

People use the Yellow Pages to locate services. The directory is the number one way that people find a dentist, for example. The challenge, however, is not only to get your name out, but to explain why a potential customer should choose you. Statistics that track customers show that directory ads have a greater response rate than any other medium, second only to personal referrals.

Only 23 percent of people who use directories know the name of the company they're looking for before they open the book. Most people simply have a need, whether it be for tutoring services or a plumber. Most people are familiar with names in a particular category, but they're still considering which one to go with. They're influenced by what they see and what they don't see. If they don't see you in there, or they see your competitor before they see you, you are likely to miss out on that opportunity. You don't have to outspend everybody, but you do have to be specific in your goals and understand the role Yellow Pages advertising can play in your industry.

Sophisticated national advertisers look at a Yellow Pages directory's ability to reach their customer profiles. You should evaluate a directory by its ability to reach your target customers. For example, your target customer might be female, with a college degree, a household income of $70,000 and above, and children. *A word of advice*: Don't make assumptions. Don't base your customer profile on seat-of-your-pants type thinking. Do some real research.

"Who You Gonna Call?"

"I would suggest that you avoid Yellow Page consultants," says Mark O'Halloran, marketing and creative director for O'Halloran Advertising, Inc. "These people are, in my opinion, dangerous. They tell customers that they will cut all the fat out of their program for a fee of perhaps 30 percent of whatever they cut out, with an additional 30 percent the next year. And of course, they come in and cut—whether fat or bone, they cut it out."

O'Halloran recommends sticking with your phone company representative. Go in knowing what you're trying to accomplish and how you want to approach it, then hold your position. Tell your sales representatives that you want to look at studies. Ask your representatives to come up with a plan aimed at your target market and to recommend directories that will reach that market. Sales representatives have access to demographic information; if pressed, they'll give this information to customers.

Note from Figure 26-2 (on the following page) that of adults whose household income is $60,000 or more (close to that target of $70,000), 69 percent use the Yellow Pages at least once in an average week (col. 2). The average number of uses per week is 2.4 (col. 3).

Figure 26-2 Demographics

DEMOGRAPHICS		Column 2	Column 3	Column 4	Column 5	Column 6
		Weekly Usage (Reach)	Average Frequency (Pop.)	% of Uses (Pop.)	% of Population	Usage Index
Total	Adults 18+	58	2.0	100	100	100
Sex	Males	58	2.0	49	48	103
	Females	59	1.9	51	52	97
Age	18-24	64	2.4	15	13	119
	25-34	66	2.4	26	21	120
	35-49	65	2.3	36	31	115
	50-64	56	1.8	17	19	88
	65+	40	0.9	7	16	45
Education	<H.S. Grad.	36	1.2	8	14	60
	H.S. Grad.	56	1.8	34	37	92
	Some College	66	2.3	27	23	118
	College Grad.	67	2.3	31	26	117
Income	Under $10,000	44	1.3	6	10	61
	$10-$24.9	51	1.9	20	22	88
	$25-$39.9	65	2.2	24	23	104
	$40-$59.9	69	2.3	27	24	111
	$60,000 or more	69	2.4	24	21	113
Census Region	Northeast	52	1.6	17	20	83
	Midwest	61	2.1	27	24	110
	South	57	1.9	34	35	98
	West	64	2.1	22	21	109

Column 2	The average weekly usage or "reach" by the demographic subgroups.
Column 3	The average number of uses per week for each demographic subgroup.
Column 4	The distribution of uses in a typical week within each subgroup.
Column 5	The distribution of the adult population within each subgroup.
Column 6	The result of dividing column 4 by column 5. As an index, it is used to compare strength of Yellow Pages usage by demographic subgroup.

Research conducted by Statistical Research, Inc., commissioned by Yellow Pages Publishers Association.

This group's share of Yellow Pages uses is 24 percent (col. 4); however, within the distribution of household income, $60,000 or more represents 21 percent of the population (col. 5). The resulting index of 113 (col. 6) means that adults whose income is $60,000 or more account for 13 percent more references to Yellow Pages than the average adult.

Heavy User Profile: The study by Statistical Reseaerch, Inc., shows that among users of the Yellow Pages, heavy users—those who made five or more references in the past seven days—are more likely to be males under 50 years old, who earn $40,000-$60,000 annually, with at least some college education, living in one of the 21 largest metropolitan areas.

If you're a business-to-business service, you might have certain sectors that you want to reach. Ask your phone company about the numbers of those businesses resident within the directory area. It might be advantageous to pool your money and buy a larger, more effective ad in one book that reaches a higher concentration of your target customers, rather than spreading your budget out to include a greater number of directories.

Offer a Solution to a Problem

A common mistake is to talk about who you are in the ad and to feature your logo prominently, as if those are the most important features. The most important thing you offer in a Yellow Pages ad (or any other marketing option) is the solution of a problem that's on the mind of the person looking in the directory. A person who didn't have a need or a problem wouldn't be opening the phone book. So don't address prospects with your logo; address them with the solution to their problem. "Transmissions fixed in 24 hours," not "A-1 Transmissions."

You have to understand how Yellow Pages ads work. With a few exceptions, people who look to the directory are already in the process of buying. That's not the case with other media, such as newspapers, magazines, and broadcasts, that must generate a need, then an awareness, and then an interest in a product line.

A Dalbar study showed that people were looking for financial advisors who could solve their financial problems, so your advertising should focus on solving a problem. Instead of advertising every service you perform, which is everyone's first inclination, you want to narrow your focus by covering just one topic in your ad. If you must cover more topics, create a separate ad for each area you want to represent. The best advertising and marketing plans are the ones that are easily understood and acted upon.

Nobody goes out shopping for anything any more unless the cereal box is empty. When do most people buy a new car? When their lease is up. The days of seeing an ad on TV and thinking, "You know, that's a pretty nice car. I'd like to buy one," are over. Nearly every purchase is becoming a 'critical purchase'. Life is so busy that people don't have the time to act on advertising influences. When prospects are actually in the purchase process is when you have to reach them. "Yellow page advertising does that very well," asserts O'Halloran.

Since people referring to a directory are in the process of making a purchase, directories have an audience that's already interested. That's a huge advantage. It puts you in the selection set. People say that directory advertising is expensive and complain that competitors are side by side. But having your competitors right next to you can be an advantage. People may be looking for your competitor, not you; it's an opportunity to present your case. For instance, a customer may have been referred to Merrill Lynch, but right next to Merrill Lynch in the directory is Smith Barney. Smith Barney's ad may answer the question that this potential customer wants answered. He makes the call to Smith Barney.

Most people referring to directories do not have their minds made up, and will call an average of three references per heading. In some cases, they call as many as eight. These people are shopping. They're looking for the best choice. Make sure you are one of those selections.

Extra Added Benefits

One new Yellow Pages option is to include a RCF (Remote Call Forwarding) number in an ad. This means that you can run a phone number in your ad that does not appear anywhere else, and the calls can be forwarded to your normal number. This is a great tool because you can track the number of calls you received from your ad. You can receive a list of the phone numbers of people who called, the length of the phone call, and the time of day each call came in. You can analyze that data in-house to find out how many calls it took to generate one sales lead, how many sales leads to generate a sale, the average revenue of the sale, the profit, etc. You can thereby determine the return on your directory investment.

It's not as complicated as it sounds. If I were going to spend $5,000 on an ad, or even $500, I'd want to know something about what I was getting for my money.

Soon we'll be able to get a monthly print-out from the telephone company on every call that comes into an office. We'll be able to get a customer's name, household income, number of children, number of cars registered to an address, lifestyle category, education level, etc. That's all going to be public information. For the first time, an advertiser will be able to get a clear indication of what a company's customer profile looks like and just who's using what media.

Expand Your Market Share

National Security Guard Company, for instance, has 500 locations nation-wide, with 100,000 guards working for the company. Its biggest customers are organizations like the New York Port Authority and the World Trade Center. Those customers obviously don't come through the phone directory. What does come through the directory are smaller customers, such as a jewelry store that's been broken into and needs a guard for a few days until the window glass gets repaired; or a college hosting a concert that wants to supplement campus security for two nights. The Yellow Pages customers are companies that may never have used security guard services before but now have a need for a guard on the premises. Their typical customer is a totally different animal.

The point is, don't make the assumption that whatever your typical customer profile is would be your *directory* customer profile. A different segment of your business may use a directory to find you.

For example, your typical customers might be people who've lived in your town for many years. You've built a relationship with them and now they're your biggest clients. However, those people are eventually going to move away or die out. You need to expand into a new market share, whether that's new people moving into town, or people who are dissatisfied with their current service. You need to give customers an opportunity to find your company.

Discounts

There are specific requirements to qualify for a national service. A company has to be in three states, with at least two different Yellow Pages publishers, in 20 directories, with not more than 70 percent of Yellow Pages placement (dollar wise) in any one state. (California counts as two states—northern and southern.) A company that meets those qualifications can use a Yellow Pages specialist like O'Halloran Advertising, Inc. (116 Danbury Road. Wilton, CT 06987; 800-762-0054; www.ohallorana-gency.com.)

Everybody who qualifies should be using a national agency. A large number of companies that do qualify still place their ads locally, which makes no sense at all. Often, these companies are spending much more money than they need to on directory advertising.

A specialist service is like having a person on staff who is an expert in this particular advertising medium, yet there's no additional cost to the advertiser, namely, you.

Effective Reach

O'Halloran's company uses a formula called Effective Reach: "Reach times visibility equals effective reach." Reach refers to the number of directories you're in and the number of target customers that you're reaching—how many customers open that phone book to the heading you're listed under.

The second part of the equation is visibility. If they open a book you're listed in, can they find your ad? If you're running very small ads that customers easily miss in 300 books, you have reach, but you don't have *effective* reach. Effective reach is the combination of the number of target customers you're reaching and the visibility.

Sometimes it's better to be in fewer books with a more visible ad than to be in many books. When you choose one directory over others, make it the book that best reaches your target customers and go for the most effective reach you can afford. You don't have to be the largest if you use creative graphics.

Yellow Pages Advertising Checklist

Research. Before you start designing your ad, know who your readers and potential customers are and what they want. Think about placement before design.

Don't use color. It's a waste of money. You're better off funneling the money into a larger ad or another book.

Take the time to design the ad well. It doesn't cost any more to run a good-looking ad than an ugly one. Put some time and effort into your graphics. You'd be surprised how many advertisers run hideous ads. They'll let the telephone company local sales rep design the ad right there on a laptop. They're going to buy a $5000 ad and run the ad for three years, spending $15,000 for space, but they're not going to put any money into decent graphic design and layout.

Instead, think of it as a TV commercial. It costs a lot of money to shoot a TV commercial; you wouldn't just wing it. Think through what you want to say and the image you're trying to portray and design an ad to convey that.

Tell 'em what you want to tell 'em. When you write ad copy, remember the point of advertising is to get somebody to *do* something, so tell them what they're supposed to do. Don't just create a delightful little ad with your phone number. You've got to stand up and shout at the reader to call or come in for something. The goal is to get that reader, your potential customer, to contact you by mail, fax, phone, or (best of all) in person.

Chapter 27
Speak Like an Expert—
Unforgettable
Presentations

In this chapter, you'll learn:
• Why the combination of speaking and writing is so powerful
• How to organize a speech
• Calendar of industry events to speak at

"The mind is a wonderful thing. It starts working the minute you're born and never stops until you get up to speak in public," says Roscoe Drummond. But there are ways to get around that natural tendency.

If you want to make unforgettable presentations, don't sell your product or service. Sell the result that they produce. Sell the solution: "What this means, Mr. Client, is that you can lengthen your time horizons in a variable annuity by having a higher after-tax return. That means you don't have to take as much risk."

A lot of advisors think that selling intangibles like the stock market would be a lot easier if they were tangible, like real estate. They're certain that if somebody could touch the product, they could sell it a lot quicker. That really isn't true. People always buy an end result, a solution, a lot faster than they'll buy a product or service. People don't buy stock for the sake of owning pieces of paper with pictures of the corporation's building on them. They buy for a specific result, like a comfortable retirement or a college education.

Emphasize the special advantages resulting from your product or service. An advantage is always related to the consumer's "hot button." These hot buttons are connected to the senses of sight, hearing, smell, touch, and taste.

Why is an oral presentation supplemented by written presentations becoming geometrically important in your PR efforts? Because people respond to the senses in the following percentages:

243

Sight	87.0 percent
Sound	7.0 percent
Smell	3.5 percent
Touch	1.5 percent
Taste	1.0 percent

By combining appeals to sight and sound your rate of response increases to 94 percent. What Someone Remembers:

	After 3 hours	*After 3 days*
If you tell something to someone:	70 percent	10 percent
If you show something to someone:	72 percent	20 percent
If you both tell and show:	85 percent	65 percent

That 65 percent retention after three days is a dramatic increase over the impact of the written word alone. You must make an auditory as well as a visual impact. Speaking puts you in the limelight; it raises your head above the crowd. A person who can speak effectively is usually given credit out of proportion to what he or she really knows.

Can you remember the day General Schwarzkopf made his famous 'Hail Mary' presentation about surprising Iraq and smashing through their lines? You can—why? Because the military knows how to make a presentation. During the CNN news coverage of operation Desert Storm, the military used visual aids such as charts and graphs during every briefing. The US Army has always realized the importance of the art of a good presentation.

The ability to make a successful presentation has become a prerequisite for advancement in business as well as in the military. In today's competitive business world, highly developed presentation skills add up to a bankable career advantage, an advantage you need.

Twenty years ago, a skillful presentation for a manager was a nice plus, but as in the military, you didn't need it to get ahead. Years ago, it was technical job-related skills that helped you get ahead. Today, technical skills are still important, but communication skills have become the ultimate weapon.

Revisit our old problem: How do you get seen and heard in our over-communicated society? Prospects who hear you speak for the first time begin to form opinions about you, and you soon become positioned in their minds either as a salesperson or as a trusted advisor. To occupy the trusted advisor "space," the smartest thing for you to do is behave like a trusted advisor from the beginning. It's much easier to create an impression than to change one.

Our extravagant use of communications to entertain and solve a host of business and social problems has jammed our media so much so that only a fraction of all messages actually get through. We will require exceptional skills in communications as we move into a generation that is experiencing a sensory overload of messages.

The following is a simple seven-step presentation plan that can help you get your point across and ensure success at your next meeting:

1. Plan what you're going to say.
2. Know the frame of reference for your audience
3. Pull your audience in with a strong opening statement about your—and their—point of view.
4. State what you want to say, then tell your audience what you said.
5. Use visual aids.
6. Anticipate any questions and present the answers in your speech; make your points again while answering questions.
7. Create a "call to action" in your closing.

Conceptually, a presentation is divided into three sections: beginning, middle, and end. Grab a pad and pen; you're ready to start creating your presentation.

I. The Beginning

First, write down your selling points, your recommendations, and your action plan. You'd be surprised how many presenters never really tell their audience what their point is. Formulate your message so that it's absolutely clear what it is you want to impart.

The Opening

The function of your opening is to clearly state your message, to outline the argument that supports it, and to prepare listeners for the detailed discussion that will follow.

It has another function as well. In addition to introducing your message, your opening is your chance to really get your listeners to listen.

Grab Their Attention

Tell a story that is a memorable insight or incident that grabs your audience's attention:

> I can still remember the way I felt the day my dad retired from the service. After 30 years of hard work, two wars, and many personal sacrifices, he handed my mother a pension check for $800.
>
> "This is it?!" She actually pulled on the check in an attempt to make it stretch longer. "This is what they expect us to live on!" Tears filled her eyes as if she suddenly realized an irreversible mistake. My dad hung his head, dropped his shoulders, and walked out of the kitchen. I felt her pain and his bitter disappointment, but at the time I didn't understand there was something they could have done differently.
>
> My dad had trusted the system, depended on someone else's plan for his retirement, and ended up working as a security guard at K-Mart until the day he died. I supplemented their income as well. They never understood how to invest.
>
> When it comes to retirement planning, most people have overly ambitious goals, inadequate funding, and either no investment strategy or the wrong kind of strategy, as we have seen. In the unlikely event that you stay with the same employer all your working years (although statistics say you won't), the best you can hope for is to retire on half your average annual earnings. You can't expect Social Security to fill in the gaps, since most employers' retirement formulas count half of the monthly Social Security benefit as part of your pension income.
>
> To reach your financial goal, you will have to develop a dependable income stream, control costs, and beat the inflation robber.
> Get the idea?

Attention is a prerequisite to communication. The more of the audience's attention you have, the more communicating you can do. An introduction that captures your listeners' attention is a necessity. A presenter needs an oral equivalent of hitting the audience over the head with a two-by-four. You want not merely to capture your listeners' attention but to really engage their minds.

The Lead

Introduce the topic in a catchy, arresting, or amusing manner, or introduce yourself, creating a connection between you and your listeners. At its very simplest, you need to grab your listeners' attention with a pertinent thought, insight, or observation that gets your point across.

II. The Middle

The middle of your presentation is the guts. It's where the information is imparted and the persuasion takes place.

List the selling points that support your conclusion. Very often a strong selling point makes an excellent grabber; especially effective selling points are those that stimulate the intellect, provoke a "gee-whiz" response, appeal to our sense of self-interest or well-being, or touch one of our emotional buttons—hitting us in the heart, or our pocketbooks. Here's where you use supporting data, statistics, evidence, research, findings, and proof.

If you get lost or feel you're wandering, reiterate your point to get you back on track.

Before your presentation, lay out those 3 x 5 cards and write down the points you want to make and write a list of articles, books, or reprints that will support those points. Throughout the demonstration there must be impact. To get the full impact, use all of the proof statements that you can. The inflection of your voice can produce impact, along with visuals of your proofs.

Visual Aids

Remember that typical listeners forget 40 percent of what they've heard within half an hour, 60 percent by the end of the day, 90 percent after a week. Every accomplished presenter knows this secret: use visual aids!—whether they're overhead transparencies, color slides, videotapes, or, like General Schwarzkopf, large color charts. A visual aid can help you make your point—a point your audience will remember.

Without good, hard information in the middle, all the audience profiling and message tailoring in the world isn't going to accomplish much.

III. The Ending

You've told 'em what you're gonna tell 'em. Now it simply remains to tell 'em what you told 'em—and to drive it home. The whole ending should take no more than a minute. The end of your talk is the last thing your audience will hear, and the last thing heard is the thing most likely to be remembered.

Have a "call to action." Make a request, or give them the option of buying your book, or making an appointment with you. The more clearly and forcefully it's stated, the greater the likelihood that it will be remembered accurately.

Rehearse your speech. The more you practice, the better you'll sound.

Once you're perceived as an expert, you will most likely be asked to speak in public. If the idea worries you, take a Dale Carnegie course in public speaking (800 342 7787). It's worth it!

Figure 27-1 Speaking Calendar

SPEAKING CALENDAR

FEBRUARY	MAY	JULY

FEBRUARY

Early February
Investment Management
Consultants Association (IMCA)
Regional Consultants Conference
Contact: IMCA 303/770-3377
www.imca.org

Mid February
The Institute of Certified Financial
Planners (ICFP)
Practice Management Conference
Contact: ICFP 800/322-4237, ext. 146;
www.icfp.org

Mid February
Securities Industry Association
(SIA)
Internet Update Conference
Contact: Mary Ann Battista
212/618-0577; www.sia.com

Mid February
National Association of Personal
Financial Advisors (NAPFA)
Advanced Planner Conference
Contact: NAPFA 847/537-7722,
800/366-2732; www.napfa.org

Late February
SIA
Securities Industry Institute
Western District Conference
Contact: Mary Ann Battista
212/618-0577; www.sia.com

MARCH

Early March
SIA
Securities Industry Institute
Contact: Geri-anne Cascio
212/618-0561;www.sia.com

Mid March
IMCA
Regional Consultants Conference
Contact: IMCA 303/770-3377
www.imca.org

APRIL

Late April
IMCA
Spring National Conference
Contact: IMCA 303/770-3377
www.imca.org

MAY

Early May
SIA
Southern District Conference
Contact: Mary Ann Battista
212/618-0577;www.sia.com

Mid May
SIA
Management Conference (formerly
Regional Firms)
Contact: Mary Ann Battista
212/618-0577; www.sia.com

Mid May
NAPFA
National Conference
Contact: NAPFA 847/537-7722,
800/366-2732; www.napfa.org

Mid May
International Association for
Financial Planning (IAFP)
Advanced Planning Conference
Contact: IAFP 800/945-4237
www.iafp.org

JUNE

Early June
NAPFA
National Conference
Contact: NAPFA 847/537-7722,
800/366-2732; www.napfa.org

Early June
SIA
Savings and Retirement Conference
Contact: Mary Ann Battista
212/618-0577;www.sia.com

Mid June
Institute for Investment
Management Consultants (IIMC)
Sales and Marketing Conference
contact: IIMC 602/922-0090
www.theiimc.org

Late June
SIA
Technology Management Conference
Contact: Mary Ann Battista
212/618-0577; www.sia.com

Late June
Morningstar
Mutual Fund Conference
Contact: Morningstar
312/696-6000, 800/735-0700
www.morningstar.net

JULY

Late July
ICFP
ICFP Retreat
Contact: ICFP 800/322-4237
www.icfp.org

Late July
The College for Financial Planning
National Conference
Contact: The College for Financial
Planning
303/220-4800; www.fp.edu

AUGUST

Mid August
NAPFA
Advanced Planners Conference
Contact: NAPFA 847/537-7722,
800/366-2732; www.napfa.org

SEPTEMBER

Mid September
SIA
Retail Managmenet Conference
(formerly Sales & Marketing)
Contact: Mary Ann Battista
212/618-0577; www.sia.com

OCTOBER

Early October
IIMC
Annual Conference
Contact: IIMC 602/922-0090
www.theiimc.org

Early October
SIA
Mid-Atlantic District Conference
Contact: Mary Ann Battista
212/618-0577; www.sia.com

Early October
IAFP
Annual Convention and Exhibition
Contact: IAFP 800/945-4237
www.iafp.org

Source: Larry Chambers

Chapter 28
Help!

In this chapter, you will learn:
- Where to find a ghostwriter/writer-for-hire
- An effective way to work with a ghostwriter
- How much is it going to cost
- Where to get *Cooperative Publishing*
- Reference books

At this point in the book, you may be thinking, "This all sounds good, but frankly I don't have the time or talent to write."

I understand. You have the expertise, but putting words down on paper is not for you. You may need to hire a ghostwriter; someone you can talk to and say, "Here are my ideas. Shape them into a story for me."

A ghostwriter is a person who is hired to write for another person who then takes credit for authorship. You'd be surprised how many of today's best sellers have used a ghostwriter. Mega-sellers, such as *Reengineering the Corporation* by Michael Hammer and James Champy, *The Pursuit of Wow* by Tom Peters, and *The Discipline of Market Leaders* by Michael Treacy were all ghostwritten (*Business Week*, Publishers Row, Sept. 18, 1995). Today, ghostwriters discreetly write, edit or even research a book. They can be expensive—typically $60,000 for a book proposal, or $300,000 to produce a title from scratch, but you may not need this kind of help.

Where Can You Go for Help

So where can you get a writer-for-hire or a ghostwriter who doesn't cost you an arm-and-a-leg? The first reaction that most advisors have is, "I'll have my secretary do it or my [significant other]". *Not* a good idea. There is a big difference between writing something grammatically correct and something that will get published.

A better idea would be to hire a professional freelance writer who would do ghostwriting on the side for two reasons. First, they make their living writing and know the process; and second, they can possibly help get your manuscript into the right magazine or the hands of the right publisher.

Call the editor of the trade magazine you'd like to have print your article. Editors know established writers who may be looking for extra work. The editors already have relationships with these writers, and that can work in your favor when it comes time to submit your story.

Try your local high school English department or University writing programs or City College continuing education department. One phone call to the job placement center and you could be interviewing candidates by nightfall.

I use a variation of pure ghostwriting which I call *coach*-writing. It's been a very successful approach because my clients become active participants in the writing process. My clients' thoughts and feelings are the written material. I am merely the facilitator who gets the words down on paper and in the hands of the publishers.

For the do-it-yourselfer you might consider the new speech recognition software. After your article is in your software you can either rewrite or have your editor make changes.

Speech Recognition

The three software programs currently available are Drago Systems' *Naturally Speaking*™, IBM's® *Via Voice*™ and Kurzweil's *VoiceXpress*™ *(Plus)*. For the latest details, here are the addresses:

Dragon Systems, Inc.
Tel: 800-4DRAGON, 617-965-5200
info@dragonsys.com
http://www.naturalspeech.com
http://www.dragonsys.com

IBM
Tel: 800-IBM-2255, ext. SA093
talk2med@vnet.ibm.com
http://www.ibm.com/viavoice
http://www.software.ibm.com/is/voicetype/

Kurzweil
Tel: 800-380-1234; 781-203-5000
sales@kurzweil.com
http://www.lhs.com/kurzweil

Speech-Recognition Web Sites, Resources and Support

Here are some great web sites on dictation software and its use. Some have links to many more sites.

Joel Gould of Dragon has an unofficial *Naturally Speaking* site with lots of helpful information. Log on to http://www.synapseadaptive.com/joel/default/htm

Computing Out Loud is Susan Fulton's site: http://www.outloud.com

Books on Speech Recognition

The Essential Simply Speaking Gold by Susan Fulton, ISBN 1-888725-08-7, 8.5 x 8, 124 pages. How to use IBM's popular speech recognition package for dictation rather than keyboarding. Dozens of screen shots and illustrations. $18.95.

The Computer Speech Book by Esther Schindler. 312 pages with disk. 1996. $39.95

Speech Recognition: The Future Now! by Michael Koerner. 306 pages. 1997. $49.95.

Write & Grow Rich, Using Speech-Recognition To Dictate Your How-To Book by Dan Poynter. Para Publishing Tel: 800-PARAPUB; orders@ParaPublishing.com.

Multiple Submissions

Another place to get help and leverage your efforts is to repackage your articles. After your original article has been published, look to other target industries that may take it. I've found many times that all I have to do is change the doctor to accountants or small business owners and you find the trade magazine for that industry. It can be a company publication, a regional publication, a national publication or newspaper. You can send your article around yourself or hire someone to help.

Where and what it will cost for repackaging reprint service: Anne Bachrach, 800-232-4429 or email anne@bachrach.vbs.com. Cost is $1,000 a month plus expenses: phone, postage, and copying.

How to Work With a Ghostwriter

Following is my "how to work with a ghostwriter format" which includes
a few tricks I've found along the way that make the process easier.

Using this method will enable you to write your books as fast as possible. The more prepared you are the less it's going to cost you and the
less time you waste.

Step One—Plan Your Subject Matter

Contemplate the subject you wish to address. What are four or five major
problems related to your subject? How can you help resolve those
problems?

Step Two—Organize Your Thoughts in Writing

Use 3 x 5 cards to briefly layout your story. Write a different chapter title
on each card. Then, on the reverse side, list the points that will go inside
that chapter.

a) *Identify the problem*
Write down your topic or chapter problem

_____

_____

_____

b) *Identify three related problems that support the main problem*
1._____

_____

2._____

_____

3._____

_____

c) *Have a powerful story that relates to your topic*
You can illustrate your point through personal experience or with an
anecdote which forms a practical explanation of the effect your point will
have on the reader. This can establish a strong initial connection between
you and your readers. Even if you are working with a professional writer,
it's up to you. You need to grab attention by relating a pertinent thought,
insight or observation that gets your main point across.

Descriptions trigger emotions. Look at one of the ways using your investment product resolves the problem and create a story that explains it. Here's an example:

> I can still remember the way I felt the day my dad retired from the service. After 30 years of hard work, he handed my mother a pension check for $800.
> "This is it?!" She actually pulled on the check in an attempt to make it stretch longer. "This is what they expect us to live on!" My dad dropped his shoulders, and walked out of the kitchen. I felt her pain and his bitter disappointment, but at the time I didn't understand there was something they could have done differently. I made up my mind that night. I was going to learn how to invest for my future. I'd like to share with you the steps I took.

See how that brings the reader into the story? Authenticate the story with something that you actually experienced—maybe a mistake you made until you learned about this particular product or methodology and how it changed you life. Describe your experience.

_____

_____

_____

_____

_____

_____

_____

_____

d) *Provide the solution to the problem*
This is not intended to pitch your service or product, but to provide the reader with the answer to the problem you described. This is why the reader continues to read your article or book. List your ideas:

_____

_____

_____

e) *List the steps to reach the solution*
These can be how-to components of the solution that build on each other, or a listing of resources, or examples of the results (such as a case study).

I like to move my readers through a sequence of instructions that can help solve the problem in the same order they would perform them.

_____

_____

_____

_____

_____

_____

f) *Summarize your article or chapter*
A bad ending can ruin all your hard work. Sum up your conclusion with information your reader can use. The more clearly and forcefully stated, the greater the likelihood that what you say will be remembered accurately.

Remember the goal is to achieve a professionally written investment article or book that inspires the readers to want to put the ideas into action. The main purpose is to use your ghostwritten article or book in your seminar programs to help build your businesses and to help you stand out in the midst of competitive clutter. Your objective in conveying your ideas should be to instill a sense in the reader that he or she has discovered something new and useful.

Step Three—Assemble Your Reference Material

Organize your research material before you start writing, so that you know what you are including and where to find it. Don't call a writer until you have all of this organized.

Step Four—Telephone Interview

Tell your story, referring to your cards to keep you on track and covering all the aspects. Either you or your writer should record this material.

Step Five—Polishing the Manuscript

Have your writer send you the first draft to edit and polish. The more time you spend polishing the manuscript, the better the book is going to look in the readers' hands.

Have an Agreement

What can go wrong? Two financial advisors who were partners wrote an article together. They split up and each started sending the article out under his own name without the partner's name. As luck would have it, they each submitted the same article to Tom Johnson, senior editor at *Financial Planning* magazine. "I had already accepted it from the first guy when I received it from the second guy. I had to toss a good article."

From a credibility standpoint, you don't want someone saying that they wrote your article or book. You can avoid these problems with an agreement that spells out the terms and costs. Most ghostwriters are independent contractors and will already have a contract. If not, you are welcome to use mine.

Costs & Fees

There's quite a range of fees and methods of billing, but there are some guidelines you can find in the 1999 *Writers Market*. Ghostwriting for business, usually trade magazine articles or columns: $25-$100 an hour, $200 or more per day plus expenses.

Author Advances & Royalties vary, but not by much. An advance is the amount of money paid to an author before the book is published; usually half upon signing a book contract and half when the completed manuscript is delivered. Royalties must match the advance before the author starts receiving distributions on any future royalties. There are standards in the industry: 10% of the cover price on hardcover books, 60% on paperback. There are usually escalators and an increase on the royalty rate if the book has sold a certain number of copies.

Most business books are going to receive advances anywhere from $5-$10,000, unless the author is a well-known commodity. Then they might command upwards of $100,000, but those cases are rare. A big name ghostwriter is going to charge around $60,000 and will want half the royalties on the sale of the book.

Client Service Agreement

1.00   AGREEMENT

This Client Service Agreement ("Agreement") dated January 9, 1998, is by and between Larry Chambers ("Chambers"), P.O. Box 1810, Ojai, California, 93024-1810, and XXXXXXXXX ("Client"), address.

2.00   PROJECT SERVICES

Chambers agrees to formulate a 230/275-page book, which includes interviewing and rewriting/editing contributors' prepared materials for each chapter, the writing and editing of the book, writing the foreword, and preparation, if necessary, of a book proposal.

Chambers will provide a final draft of each chapter to its individual author for editing and obtaining approval from their firm's compliance department. Upon return of compliance approved, edited drafts, Chambers will then prepare a final edit to be delivered to Client.

Chambers will use his best efforts to locate a commercial publisher, and will coordinate publishing contract.

3.00   CONFIDENTIAL INFORMATION

Chambers shall not disseminate or use for his own purposes, either during or after the term of this Agreement, any confidential information imparted to Chambers by the Client.

4.00   INDEMNIFICATION

Chambers assures the Client that best efforts will be made to ensure that any books produced for the Client are free from inaccuracies. Client shall hold Chambers harmless from and against any claims, suits, liabilities, damages, costs, expenses (including attorney's fees) arising from any publicity, programs, or statements approved by the Client, and arising from the acts or omissions by Client or from Client's contractual relations with others.

5.00   TIME TO COMPLETION

Chambers estimates the book will take three (3) months for completion, not including time required by contributors for individual chapter editing and compliance approval. Chambers will not be responsible for any delays or extensions caused by untimely response to interviews, submission or return of materials from contributors, or compliance approval processes.

Publishing is not included in time estimate.

Client Service Agreement, *con't.*

6.00 AUTHORSHIP

Client will own the book and Client's name(s) will be the only author(s) to appear on the inside cover. Chambers will be acknowledged in the book as the writing coach.

7.00 FEES

Ghost-writing book (250/300 pages): **$45,000**
Fee to be paid in (3) equal installments of $15,000, commencing on execution of Agreement, and at time book is completed. Checks should be made payable to Larry Chambers.

Commercial publishing bonus: **$5,000**
Fee due when publishing contract is obtained.

Expenses for any approved travel will be reimbursed to Chambers.

Fees for any additional services not outlined in this Agreement will be negotiated at such time as those services are requested or become necessary.

Xxxxxx will serve as Client's coordinator and primary contact with Chambers; with full and final responsibility for all fees due under Agreement.

Please sign and return one copy of Agreement, along with initial payment, in self-addressed envelope provided.

AGREED:

_____Date:_____

_____
Larry Chambers

Table 28-1 Schedule of Fees and Costs

• Ghostwriting professional and trade journal articles under someone else's byline	$1000-$6000
• Permission fees to publishers to reprint articles or stories	$75-$500
• Copy editing	$13-$30/hour
• Editing, general	$500/day
• Fact checking	$17-$25/hour
• Writing a financial presentation for a corporation 20-30 minutes	$1500-$4500
• Ghostwriting in general	$25-$100/hour, $200 per day plus expenses
• Ghostwriting a corporate book, 6 months' work	$20,000-$50,000
• Newsletter editing Some writers charge on a regular or monthly basis	$50-$500 per issue. $25-$150 per published page
• Newsletter ghostwriting	$10-$800/published page, $5-$5,000/issue
• Article query letter	$250/letter
• Book query letter	$250/letter to publisher
• Outline of book	$100-$500/outline
• Book Proposal	$2,500-$25,000/proposal
• Copy editing Rates are generally higher end of scale for reference material	$35/hour, $6/1000 words, or $2/page
• Ghostwriting a business book as *told* to	Full advance and 50% of royalties or $10,000-$50,000 plus research time for 200-300 page book
• Ghostwriting without as *told* to credit for clients who are either self-publishing or have no royalty publisher lined up	$15,000-$40,000 plus expenses with ¼ down payment; ¼ when manuscript completed; ¼ at ¾ mark; and ¼ when book is finished, or you can negotiate chapter by chapter
• Proofreading	$12-$25/hour and up
• Research for writers and book publishers	$40/hour and up; $50-$500/per day and all expenses – some quote a flat fee of $300-$500 for a completed job

Table 28-1 Schedule of Fees and Costs, *con't.*

• Rewriting Some writers have combined ghostwriting and rewriting short-term jobs for which they get paid $350/day and up; some participate in royalties for book rewrites	$18-$50/hour; sometimes $5/page
• Book Summaries for Business People 4-8 pages	$500-$1000
• Business Letters such as form letters to improve customer relations	$100/letter business letter $500 up/form letter for corporation
• Business Meeting Guide and Brochure	4 pages/$500 8-12 pages
• Business Plan	$2/word; $200/manuscript page; $500-$2500/project
• Business Writing. May be advertising, copy, collateral materials, public relations or other jobs.	$25-$60/hour; $200-$500/ day plus expenses
• Book Proposal consultation	$20-$70/hour; flat rate $500 depending on length and whether client provides full information or writer must do research and whether sample chapter is required
• Sales Letter for business or industry	$350-$1000 for 1 or 2 pages
• Service Brochure	12-18 pages, $2500- $4000
• Trade Journal ad copy	$250-$500
• Radio Advertising Copy	$500-$1000/script
• Press Kit	$500-$3000
• Press Release	$500-$1500, 1-3 pages

Where Can You Go for Help

On-Line Services

National Writer's Union (212 254-0279)

Contact Kenya Briggs, Job Hotline (510) 839-6092, or post your requests on their website, jobhotline@nwu.orgJobhotline@nwu.org
They have on-line resources and markets, etc. The National Writers Union is the trade union for freelance writers of all genres publishing in

U.S. markets. The Job Hotline is a nation-wide, non-profit alternative to job shops, temp agencies, and brokers. The Hotline is a project of the National Writers Union and is run by, and for, the writers who use it. Employers list contract jobs for free. W2-type staff positions may be listed for a nominal charge. Writers contact and deal with employers directly.

The Hotline is not involved in, or party to, employment agreements. For employers who require that contractors and temporary employees work through a third-party or payroll service, the Hotline has a recommended list of such companies that meet writer-approved fairness standards and fee guidelines.

Writers who find a job through a Hotline listing agree to pay the service a finders fee of 10 percent of their first four months' income. This low fee attracts a great many professional writers searching for an alternative to the 30-35 percent, life-of-the-contract commissions typical of most brokers and job shops. Writers using Hotline services must be members of the National Writers Union. Union membership is open to all working writers.

Society of American Business Editors & Writers

Headquartered in the University of Missouri, School of Journalism, www.sabew.org Contact the Executive Director, Carolyn Guniss (573) 882-7862.

They can run an inquiry in the job section of their newsletter. If you are interested in writing a text book, Carolyn can hook you up with an academic at the School of Journalism.

Society of Professional Journalists (765 653-3333)

www.spj.org
One of the most complete sources of information about freelance journalists on the Web. Information from all 50 states. The latest news, plus regular Alerts from SPJ's Freedom of Information chair.

The Society of Professional Journalists' *Jobs for Journalists* weekly newsletter is your source for journalism-related job openings around the country. The 10-page newsletter averages more than 100 listings each week. Individual listings run about three weeks and include entry-level and advanced openings. The newsletter accepts listings from around the country which are organized by categories. Past fees have included $20 for 6 mos. (members, e-mail); $30 for 6 mos. (members, US Mail); $100 for 6 mos. (non-members, either method).

American Society of Journalists and Authors (212 997-0947)

Founded in 1948, a coast-to-coast and overseas membership of more than 800 independent freelance writers who have met ASJA's exacting standards of professional achievement. Call their Dial-A-Writer (212) 393-1934 referral service. Fees are negotiated directly with the writer. E-mail *asja@compserve.com*

Editorial Freelance Association (212 929-5400)

EFA has 900+ members that can do everything in the communications business. Their members are writers of all sorts: editors, line editors, copy editors, researchers, proofreaders, picture researchers, indexers, desktop publishers, designers, translators, and other publishing professionals.

They can produce anything from a book-length project to an annual report to a short newsletter article. Members also write magazine and journal articles, advertising and catalogue copy, speeches, technical manuals, and anything else. They can also create original material, rewrite or rework existing material, collaborate with others, or ghostwrite.

To hire the EFA member with the skills you need, place an ad on their Job Phone service. An ad costs US$30 for six weeks or until you fill the position, whichever comes first. Just e-mail, call, or fax them with a description of your job. They'll list it on their Job Phone tape and bill you $30. Job Phone members call the tape, hear the listings of available jobs, and contact you if they're interested. The tape is updated twice a week, so your job listing is targeted quickly to the people who can help. If you'd like to hear the current Job Phone listings, call (212) 929-5411. (Fax: 212 929-5439 and e-mail *info@the-efa.org*)

Or, purchase their Membership Directory to help you find the writers and editors with the expertise you need. Members and contact information are indexed alphabetically and by geographic location, with descriptions of skills and interests categories. Directory and listing are free with membership. Price: US$28

Cooperative Publishing

Okay, you've found your ghostwriter and know what you want to write, but you can't get anyone to publish your book. Self-publishing has become an accepted practice when you have the means to market your own book. But there are still pitfalls to avoid and more favorable ways to approach self-publishing.

Cooperative publishing is an emerging publishing trend. Technology has made it possible for skilled professionals with many years experience in publishing and graphic arts to generate regional press efforts on a profitable or quasi-profitable basis. It's generally a very selective process and does require the author to help underwrite the cost of the project. The publisher contributes through time, effort and in some cases, additional publishing funds. The result is a cooperative effort that the publisher and the author each markets on his or her own.

Unlike with many major publishers, with a cooperative publisher, the author retains all their rights and are always in control of their work. The author is free, once the book is published, to continue to market it to major publishers.

The costs can run between $7,500 and $20,000 depending on the level of customized effort. So, if the author receives 1,000 copies of the book, the cost per book is between $7 to $20.

While they have the capability of distributing selectively to bookstores, in all except a handful of cases where ad budgets are in the high six figures, the marketing and success of the book do not come down to the placement in bookstores. Instead, the success is the result of the efforts of the author and the individual publisher to market the book. You can get individual placements for vanity purposes or for marketing purposes in local bookstores. Barnes and Noble will make its store available to local authors. The bottom line is there is little advantage to placing a book in a bookstore.

My recommendation for a cooperative publisher is:
Palisade Business Press, 102 Palisades Avenue, 4th Floor,
Jersey City, NY 07306, Contact Mark Fadiman, FAX: 201-222-6403.

Palisade Business Press is a specialized cooperative publisher which is set up to work with selected professionals. They prefer to receive an author's query over the phone so they can speak to you directly and find out if your business profile and your way of approaching publishing actually fit with them. Palisade Business Press runs 6" x 9" books, between 128 and 140 pages, with a high gloss, full color dust cover and a nice cream matte interior paper.

A few words of caution: Don't mistake cooperative publishing with vanity press. A vanity press basically places your manuscript on a printing press at a cost of $15 to $20 a book. They don't automatically edit what they print. The author, for the most part, must supply an entirely polished product. They make their money not from selling books to the public, but selling books to the author. They may use inferior quality paper, inks, graphics and colorists, and the results can look *self-published*.

Another approach is the new *publish* on demand service. I recently came across one on the Internet, Xlibris, or www.xlibris.com. For a one-time fee, Xlibris will electronically store your manuscript using a proprietary digital technology. They can then manufacture a hardback book on demand. The author shares in the gross profit of the sales, approximately $4 per book, and retains ownership and control. The initial cost may be lower, but the only marketing effort is through Xlibris' Internet bookstore.

Reference Books for Help

Writing with a Collaborator

Is There a Book Inside You? Writing Alone or with a Collaborator by Dan Poynter and Mindy Bingham. $14.95. Para Publishing. Also available in a six-cassette audio album. Also see http://www.ParaPublishing.com.

Journal Writing

How to Get Published in Business/Professional Journals by Joel J. Shulman. $28.95. Jelmar Publishing Co., PO Box 488, Plainview, NY 11803. Tel: (516) 822-6861.

Magazine Writing

Freelance Writing for Magazines and Newspapers by Marcia Yudkin. A plan for selling your work. Resources. $11.00. HarperColling Publishers.

Magazine Writing That Sells by Don McKinney. $16.95. Writer's Digest Books.

Complete Guide to Magazine Article Writing by John M. Wilson. $17.99. Writer's Digest Books.

Beginner's Guide to Writing & Selling Quality Features by Charlotte Digregorio. A simple course in freelancing for newspapers and magazines. $12.95. Civetta Press, PO Box 1043-P, Portland, OR 97207-1043. Tel: (503) 228-6649.

Newsletter & Newspaper Writing and Publishing

Publishing Newsletters by Howard Penn Hudson. 224 pages. $39.95. H&M Publishing, 44 West Market Street, PO Box 31I, Rhinebeck, NY 12572. Tel: (800) 572-3451; Fax (914) 876-2561; e-mail: HPHudson@aol.com.

The Newsletter Handbook; How to Produce a Successful Newsletter by Wesley Dorsheimer. 194 pages, $14.95. Hippocrene Books. Tel: (201) 568-5194; Tel: (201) 894-5406.

Newsletter Sourcebook by Mark Beech. 137 pages. $29.95. Writer's Digest Books.

Editing Your Newsletter by Mark Beech. $22.95. Writer's Digest Books.

Success in Newsletter Publishing; A Practical Guide by Frederick D. Goss. $39.50. Newsletter Association, 1401 Wilson Blvd., #403, Arlington, VA 22209. Tel: (800) 356-9302.

How to Do Leaflets, Newsletters & Newspapers by Nancy Brigham. $14.95. Writer's Digest Books.

A Beginner's Guide to Getting Published by Kirk Polking. $11.95. Writer's Digest Books.

The Writer's Handbook. How and where to sell magazine articles, poetry, greeting card verses, fillers, scripts and book manuscripts. An anthology of helpful chapters with a lengthy directory of resources. $30.70 ppd. The Writer, 120 Boylston Street, Boston, MA 02116. Tel: (617) 423-3157 or (888) 273-8214; Fax: (617) 423-2168; e-mail: writer@user1.channel1.com; Web: www.channel1.com/thewriter/.

Book Publishing

The Self-Publishing Manual, How to Write, Print & Sell Your Own Book by Dan Poynter. The complete manual on book production, marketing and distributing. Tenth revised edition, 464 pages. $19.95. Para Publishing, Tel: (800) PARAPUB. See http://www.ParaPublishing.com.

Financial Feasibility in Book Publishing by Robert Follett presents a step-by-step method for evaluating the financial future of new book projects. Worksheets, guidelines, projection methods, rules of thumb and estimating methods with explanations to help you decide whether your book will make money. 39 pages. $14.95. Para Publishing.

Self-Publishing to Niche Markets by Gordon Burgett. $14.95. Communications Unlimited. Para Publishing.

How to Get Happily Published by Judith Appelbaum. How to write, find a publisher, or locate an agent. $11.95. Harper & Row. Para Publishing.

Mastering the Business of Writing: A Leading Literary Agent Reveals the Secrets of Success by Richard Curtis. $18.95. Allworth Press. 10 East 23rd Street, New York, NY 10010. Tel: (212) 777-8395; Fax (212) 777-8261; e-mail: PUB@allworth.com; Web: http://www.allworth.com.

Book Prospects

How to Write a Book Proposal by Michael Larsen. Examples and resources to help you approach a publisher or agent. $14.99. Writer's Digest Books.

Nonfiction Book Proposals Anybody Can Write: How to Get a Contract & Advance Before You Write Your Book by Elizabeth Lyon. $14.95. Blue Heron Publishing, 24450 NW Hansen Rd., Hillsboro, OR 97124.

Directories

Literary Marketplace. Very important. Lists associations, book clubs, reviewers, exporters, magazines, newspapers, news services, radio and TV, and many other services. Annual.

Conclusion

Whew! Not bad for a day's work! You have learned how to:

• Build your publicity program
• Write and publish an article
• Write and promote a book
• Shorten the sales process
• Build your image and credibility
• Position yourself as an expert

Just a few reminders and then you're on your way...

Surprisingly, most advisors ignore how much they already know about their existing customers and their work culture, but some of your most powerful resources are your relationships with your existing customers and strategic allies. This information can be readily put to use in your marketing campaign,

Do six promotional things every week. That might include calling, letter writing, mailing a review copy, working on a magazine article, or writing a book. Times when your particular service is at a low are times to work on your public relations. If you put it out of your mind or off your schedule, you might miss opportunities.

Collect other people's good ideas. Clip articles about people whose media coverage catches your eye and makes you marvel out loud. People in the advertising business call this a "swipe file." Of course, you won't steal and you won't copy exactly—you'll borrow and adapt.

Lastly, remember this story about John Bowen and his credibility marketing campaign: One of his articles explaining his managed money methods appeared in a small trade magazine. The article was copied and sent to an advisor who read it closely. In fact, he liked what Bowen had to say so much that three months later, he transferred over $60,000,000 dollars worth of assets to Bowen's firm.

We said we were going to help you become a recognized expert. We addressed the fact that to stand out, you have to decide you want to be an expert. This book gives you the game, showing you how to play it and make it work to create an endless stream of pre-qualified, pre-endorsed prospects.

The ball is in your court and the odds are on your side. Keep in touch. Let me know how this is working for you. Contact me on the Internet at LChamb007@aol.com or visit my website, www.LarryChambers.com.

Good Luck!

Appendix I
Marketing Studies

Following are the results of a survey conducted among members of the IAFP (International Association of Financial Planners). The point of presenting the study here is for you to see what other professionals are doing to build their business.

Telephone Solicitation: Warm Calls: the "Dial-and-Smile" Method.

Cold calling is never anyone's favorite marketing method, but almost everyone still uses it. Yet it's been demonstrated that it takes 13 calls to generate a prospect and an additional two calls before that prospect becomes a client (though skill on the phone can reduce this number greatly).
The survey results:

39% call existing clients
30% cold call
11% have others solicit (a secretary, an assistant)

It takes an average of 13 cold calls to generate one new client?

Public Speaking (Other than Seminars):

Speaking before civic groups seems to be a good way to generate new clients. You can also contact the convention bureau in your city to get a schedule of upcoming conventions. Write the organizations and companies and volunteer to be a speaker. Local members of the company or organization may become your clients as a result of the appearance.

Prospects: Best Time to Call

Chemists and engineers	Between 4 p.m. and 5 p.m.
Clergymen	Thursday or Friday
Contractors and builders	Before 9 a.m. and after 5 p.m.
Dentists	Before 9:30 a.m.
Druggists and grocers	Between 1 p.m. and 3 p.m.
Executives	After 10:30 a.m.
Prospects at home	Monday between 7 p.m. and 9 p.m.
Lawyers	Between 11 a.m. and 2 p.m.
Merchants, and department heads	Between 9 a.m. and 11 a.m.
Physicians and surgeons	After 4 p.m.
Professors and school teachers	At home, between 6 p.m. and 7 p.m.
Accountants - any time during the day	Avoid between Jan. 15 and April 15
Publishers and printers	After 3 p.m.
Bankers	Before 10 a.m. and after 3 p.m.

Where do your colleagues serve as guest speakers?

56% speak at meetings of civic organizations
25% at conventions
21% elsewhere

What training courses are most helpful in developing public speaking skills?

1. Toastmasters
2. Experience
3. College
4. Dale Carnegie
5. Former teacher

Seminars

New advisors deliver a lot of seminars; the average is 11 a year. Breakfast seminars are becoming more popular; this meal is less expensive than lunch or dinner.

Our survey showed that seminars generate 31 new clients for every 100 persons in attendance - a very positive result. Incorporate reprints and problem/solution techniques into your seminars to further market your credibility.

Favorite location for holding seminars?	28% favor hotels
How many seminars in a series?	Average: 3
The most important single aspect of giving seminars to attract new clients?	*Credibility*

What advertising techniques for seminars are most effective?

1. Bold type
2. Photo
3. Special wording
4. Graphs and charts
5. Seminar invitation

The average number of seminars given:

5% weekly
23% monthly
16% quarterly
24% other

What percentage of the attendees became clients?　　　18%

Teaching

Giving adult education courses is another great way of developing new clients. Submitting a course outline to the department or division director is the best way to get on the faculty.

Advertising

Of all the media used for advertising, the respondents were overwhelmingly in favor of newspapers, though many also recommended the use of the Yellow Pages (telephone directory). Nearly all suggested that advertising is most effective if done consistently rather than sporadically. Writing skills and using targeted problem/solution techniques can also increase your advertising results.

Media most advertised in?

30% newspaper
16% flyers, brochures
8% magazines
9% radio
4% TV

Best media – top 5 responses:

1. Newspapers
2. Flyers
3. Magazines
4. Radio
5. Yellow Pages

Direct Mail

Nearly half of the financial advisors polled believe in the effectiveness of direct mail, though few use a professional direct mail service. Direct mail is relatively easy and inexpensive, but this method of prospecting does not provide many new clients on the average, generating responses of only about 1.5 percent or less of direct mail contacts, according to the survey results. However, by including a targeted problem/solution piece and following up with a phone call, it's possible to increase your results. In fact, some advisors have made such an art of this style of direct mail that they are converting 30 percent of all names on their direct mail lists to clients.

What percentage uses direct mail to prospect for new clients?   46%

From direct mail responses, what percentage result in appointments with a prospective client?   50%

From the appointments, what percentage become clients?   53%

What functions does a mailing service perform for you?

8% provides mailing list
3% provides list maintenance service
10% collates, stuffs, meters and mails
3% receives Business Reply Mail

Top three responses for turning direct mail leads into clients:

1. Phone call
2. Immediate follow-up
3. Invitation to seminar

The average service company or professional practice loses 10 to 20 percent of its customers each year due to attrition, making it important to have a continuing number of prospects to replace those lost customers. Half of these customers leave because they feel that no one cares about them any more.

Many marketing professionals suggest maintaining contact with clients at least 12 to 15 times a year. Yet, since it costs five to ten times as much to attract a new customer as it does to keep an old one, less than two-thirds of business inquiries are followed up. The minimum period for maintaining follow up to inquiries should be two years.

Appendix II
Media Comparison:
Pros & Cons

MEDIA	PROS	CONS
Television	*Viewership* • 98.6% of U.S. households own televisions. • Average viewership is 6 hours and 57 minutes a day. *Impact* Television's color and motion are perfectly suited for impacting product demonstrations and brand recognition on viewers.	*Lack of Retention* The TV message is perishable and easily forgotten without expensive repetition. *Audience Fragmentation* • Cable, independent stations, and VCRs all contribute to the fragmentation of television's audience. • A particular concern of the industry is confusing commercial clutter, especially with the arrival of the 15-second commercial. *Cost* Production costs for TV commercials continue to escalate.
Radio	*Reach* • Radio reaches 96.9% of Americans • Adults listen an average of 2 hours and 53 minutes a day.	*Lack of Retention* • Radio is often "background" for listeners, so commercials must be run often to achieve an acceptable impact.

MEDIA	PROS	CONS

Radio, *Flexibility/Mobility*
con't.
- Quick production time
- Low production costs
- Radio goes with the listener, giving advertisers close proximity to the sale.

Targetability
- Programming and promotions reach carefully defined audiences.
- Radio can target a specific kind of lifestyle.

Creative Limitations
Use of radio is limited by the fact that ads are heard and not seen.

Ad Clutter
Radio can be confusing due to ad clutter.

Newspapers *Reach*
- Newspapers have a wide exposure, especially to the upscale, over 35 audience.

Daily Reader
College Graduates	75%
Professional/Mgr	71%
$75K+ Income	76%

Sunday Reader
College Graduates	83%
Professional Mgr.	80%
$75K+ Income	83%

Flexibility
- Today's technology has shortened lead times for ad preparation – transmitting to hundreds of newspapers simultaneously, by satellite and by phone.

Declining Readership
Daily newspapers have seen a continuing decline each year.

Failure to Target Niche Markets
Newspapers have always been able to reach a mass audience, but if that continues to be its primary benefit, they will be deemed media dinosaurs.

MEDIA	PROS	CONS
Direct Mail	*Selectivity* • Direct mail can identify select customer niches according to specific factors, such as occupation, earnings, or interests. *Measurability* • A direct campaign can clearly account for advertising dollars concerning how many potential customers view an ad through coupon redemption, response cards, and call back options. *Targetability* • Direct mail can convey highly detailed messages and deliver product samples.	*Low Penetration* Although the number of shoppers at home who respond to direct mail advertising has increased from 36% in 1983 to 52.5% in 1994, direct mail ads are usually thrown away after one reading or a partial reading and they are rarely seen by anyone other than the one reader who opens the mail. *Negative Image* • Perceptions that direct advertisers are less honest than other businesses occur in 56% of consumers polled. • The average American household receives 11 pieces of direct mail a week, amounting to 65 billion mail solicitations nationwide each year.
Magazines	*Ease of Use* Magazines can be carried anywhere. *Targetability* Specialized publications allow advertisers to reach narrowly targeted audiences. *Long Shelf Life* Magazines provide long life for the ads and offer a prestigious, quality environment for advertisers.	*Long Lead Time* Deadlines occur long before publication, making it difficult to react to fast-changing markets. *Titled Clutter* The number of magazines in the U.S. increased from 7,000 in 1950 to 20,000 in 1997 and continues to grow. *Audience Fragmentation* • 2.2 new magazines are launched every day.

MEDIA	PROS	CONS

Magazines, *con't.*

• As newsstands become more crowded and consumers more selective, publishers are being challenged to find new ways to bring their product to market.

Internet

Flexibility
Web sites can be updated often. No other advertising medium is so quickly and economically changeable.

Interactivity
Games, surveys, and e-mail are ways the business can interact with the customer. The average person spends approximately 5½ hours per week on the Internet.

Direct Response
With a web site, you can get instant feedback from your customers. E-mail can be built into Web pages giving you the answers while they're fresh in your customers' minds and for a fraction of the cost.

Complements Print Advertising
• If your company's Web site is mentioned in a print ad, customers will be able to look at your Web site, buy your products, and learn more about your services.

Geographical Targetability
Although the Internet is accessible the world over, you may reach more people in your area using local advertising vehicles than you would on the Internet.

Measurement Standards
No one can agree on how to measure the traffic visiting the ever-proliferating number of Web pages, or even, at this early juncture, whether it is absolutely necessary to know the exact head count.

Computer Ownership
Only 35% of American households own a computer, making the potential audience that actually sees your ad very limited

MEDIA	PROS	CONS

Yellow Pages

Targetability
It's a medium where your best prospects seek you out. Simply stated, in all other print advertising, you must gain the attention of the reader before you even have a chance to tell your story; with Yellow Pages, those who need your products and services come to you.

Usage
A Yellow Pages telephone directory is found in 96.9% of all U.S. households. The average among adults is nearly 2 references per week, which results in 19.4 billion references by U.S. adult consumers per year.

Awareness
• 99% of all adults are aware of the Yellow Pages as a reference source.
• Yellow Pages directories are distributed to every home and business with a telephone, as well as pay telephones for public use and convenience.

Inflexible
Generally, Yellow Pages books are only published once a year, so the information can't be changed very frequently.

Saturation
Markets are getting saturated with sometimes three or more telephone directories.

Ad Clutter
Yellow Pages advertising presents challenges not found in other mediums. It is very competitive, and you are surrounded by your competition on the same page.

Source: Statistical Research, Inc. Reprinted with permission.

Appendix III
Sample Client Letters

Letter 1

Date

Name
Address
City

Dear

I normally don't write such long letters to complete strangers but feel this is important. I want you to be aware of my services and how I might help solve some of the most talked about investment problems facing us today: what to do now about retirement, CDs, and other financial investments.

The rules of investing have changed dramatically and most investors are overwhelmed and bewildered by the sheer number of investment choices—most of which are not very compelling. Before I go on, see if you identify with one of the following types of investors:

The investor who regards the stock and bond markets as casinos. To protect their principal, these people invest primarily in CDs and money market funds. These types of investments offer stability of principal (CDs offer guaranteed repayment of principal up to $100,000). But with CD rates around 2 to 3 percent, these investors are looking for higher returns—without going out on a limb.

The second type of investor wants aggressive growth. These people usually have a brokerage account and call their own shots—often with the help of an advisor. These investors would like to continue earning double-digit returns. But the stock market may be testing its upper limits, plus bonds have just completed their biggest rally in history. If these investors make the wrong decisions, they'll get battered when interest rates move against them.

The third group of investors is the largest group. These investors fit somewhere between the first two extremes. They're basically conservative and safety conscious, but they want to earn a fair return on their investments. I call these people "prudent investors."

So, (_____) here's the question: Is there really some happy medium between extremes? Is there an intelligent solution in today's confusing investment climate for all types of investors? In my opinion, the answer is yes, absolutely! I believe the answer is professional money management.

Let me tell you the good news first: These days you don't have to be fabulously wealthy to qualify for your own investment manager. Because of the number of fee-based money management programs available, almost any investor can access private investment management firms.

Now for the bad news: While you can hire someone to maneuver you through the investment minefield, it's up to you to choose the right person. And after you do that, you need to monitor how you're doing so you don't get stuck with below par results. That's where my firm can help. I am an investment management consultant and my only job is to find investment advisory firms that can achieve my clients' desired results.

Most importantly, (_____) my goals are the same as yours—to make you as much money as possible—within your risk comfort level. I call this risk appropriate investing.

Over the years, I've found that informed investors are my best clients. That's why I'm writing to you. I believe you would work with me if you understood my investment philosophies and strategies.

Once you understand the benefits of professional money management strategies, I don't think you'll be satisfied with any other method.

I would like to invite you to call or come to my office to learn about professional money management.

If you decide to make an appointment, here's what will happen when you arrive at my office. I'll introduce you to the basics of professional investment management. You'll quickly understand why these practical ideas set the standards for prudent investing.

I'll start by explaining fundamental investment risks that all successful investors must overcome. Most people are concerned about just one or two of these key risks. Ignoring them won't make them go away.

You'll learn how professionals identify and *quantify* investment risks. You will see clearly the historical risk/reward relationship between different types of investments. You'll learn why some investments have consistently outperformed others.

You will also discover why, over time, there is a strong probability that owning CDs will erode your purchasing power (despite U.S. government insurance up to $100,000).

I will also explain why most investment advice isn't worth the paper it's written on.

Then you'll learn about the hidden costs of investing in mutual funds. You will understand why most no-load mutual funds chronically underperform against industry or market benchmarks. You'll also discover an institutional tactic for slashing your administrative and transaction costs.

I want this to be the best use of your time, and promise that it will be. Rest assured that this is truly an educational experience. There's no hidden agenda. I am not here to sell investment products, only a professional investment service.

If you're interested in learning how I can help you implement these concepts, that's great.

Spouses are encouraged to accompany you because financial security is a family affair. If you want more information about professional money management, please call my office at _____ for an appointment or return the enclosed response sheet for a free copy of my latest article, _____.

Sincerely,

Letter 2

Date

Name
Address
City

Dear Mr. Smith,

Managing your money is a lot like playing golf; and finding the right
money manager, in many ways, is like finding the club best suited to your
style. Let me explain.

I once watched (name someone you watched, like Arnold Palmer)
give a demonstration to about twenty media people one very hot after-
noon. He was hitting a seven iron about 175 yards out, while explaining
how he intended to play the course, as well as answering endless questions. I watched each ball hit within a target circle that was no more than
ten feet wide. I walked down the hill and found fifty or so balls almost on
top of each other. (Arnold) hadn't seemed to pay much attention to how
well he was doing. He just answered questions and chatted. His discipline
and his groove were so well rehearsed that he could hit a small circle over
and over almost 200 yards down a hill that he had never seen before. Most
of us could only hope to duplicate the same shot once in a game. At best
we would call it luck.

Professional money managers and professional golfers develop the
same kind of discipline and exactitude.

When a political event takes place, like the invasion of Kuwait, professional managers don't panic. They take advantage of a market correc-
tion the same way a professional golfer takes advantage of terrain.

But how do you find the right manager to direct your financial future?
An Investment Management Consultant can help by constantly screening
investment managers across the country and across investment disciplines. Specially trained Broker Advisors are able to responsibly recommend those managers who match your particular financial situation. They
not only monitor money managers on an ongoing basis, they help you
monitor and evaluate your personal portfolio through a quarterly performance report.

Professional portfolio managers adhere to a strategy. Their discipline
enables them to catch trends while avoiding fads, maximize potential
profits, and minimize possible losses.

Investment firms have immediate access to important market information. They know the impact that a changing political situation or economic shift may have on a client's portfolio and are able to respond immediately. Like professional golf, professional portfolio management is a skilled full-time job.

The secret to both professions is discipline. A hacker plays in a state of panic. A pro never panics. Some investors think that because they have proven themselves in business, they should be able to compete in the stock market with the pros. But after a few poor rounds in the stock market, many investors simply give up.

You may not be able to find a professional PGA tour member who is willing to play a round of golf with you, but with the help of someone like myself, an investment management consultant, you can find a top money manager to manage your money professionally.

If you want more information about professional money management, please call my office at (your number) for an appointment. Or return the enclosed response sheet for your complimentary copy with no obligation of my latest booklet, _____.

Warm regards,

Letter 3 (Latest article)

Date

Name
Address
City

Dear

Should you hire a professional money manager? The answer is "yes" for anyone who has a long-term investment orientation, does not have adequate time to devote to investment, has difficulty making investment decisions, or simply wants a professional approach as used by large pension funds and other institutions.

Five years ago I became very frustrated over the reshaping the securities industry had experienced. I perceived the investment public had changed. What the investing public wanted was fee-based, rather than commission-based, money management. That was when I changed my business orientation and became an investment management consultant.

I now help my clients select a money manager after consideration of a host of relevant issues, including investment objectives (such as retirement), desired levels of return, and risk tolerance. A good investment executive will remain totally objective during this process to determine the most appropriate money managers for a client's particular set of circumstances.

If you want more information about professional money management, please call my office at (your number) for an appointment; or return the enclosed response sheet for your complimentary copy with no obligation of my latest article, _____.

Warm regards,

Letter 4 (Booklet)

Date

Name
Address
City

Dear Mr. Smith,

In recent years, the money manager has become a viable alternative to directly investing in stocks, bonds, or mutual funds. Simply put, a professional money manager is a person who will make investment decisions on a regular basis on your behalf.

The professional money manager has been managing mutual funds, retirement plans, and personal assets of the super wealthy for more than 60 years. Within the past decade, this kind of manager has gained in popularity. Today, there are thousands of registered investment managers nationwide serving investors from all walks of life.

Investment portfolios, whether for individuals or institutional investors, require well-informed and timely investment choices. A professional money manager can handle the day-to-day investment decisions.

But the investor must decide what type of manager is most appropriate, select one with a track record, and then monitor the results regularly.

Who should hire a professional money manager? The answer is simple: Anyone who has a long-term investment orientation, does not have adequate time to devote to investment, has difficulty making investment decisions, or simply wants the same professional approach as that available to large pension funds and other institutions.

Just as doctors and lawyers specialize, money managers can be retained to fulfill objectives in almost any desired niche or specialty—such as auto and entertainment. In addition, there are minority and women managers to choose from.

You might want to work with your broker/investment executive in selecting a money manager. He or she will present two to four managers that fit your objective, and together you can consider a host of relevant issues: investment objectives (such as retirement), desired levels of return, determination of risk tolerance, and other important matters. A good investment executive will remain totally objective during this process.

The final step in a successful money management program is the review or monitoring of the manager's performance.

The review or monitoring should involve a report—usually issued quarterly by the broker or investment executive—that details investment returns, comparison of returns to appropriate benchmarks, comparison to other similarly managed portfolios, as well as discussions of current market trends.

Good results do not happen overnight; they require time and patience.

If you want more information about professional money management, please call my office at (your number) for an appointment or return the enclosed response sheet for your complimentary copy with no obligation of my latest booklet, (title here).

Warm regards,

Letter 5

Date

Name
Address
City

Dear

How do you find reliable information about the top investment managers in the country—the ones who consistently out-performed their peers as well as the stock market? Answer: You hire an investment management consultant to do the homework for you. The consultant looks at hundreds of investment managers and narrows down the selection to a workable group that passes professional financial scrutiny.

An investment management consultant acts like a marriage broker, helping you find an investment partner compatible with your objectives. A consultant stays narrow in focus as he or she screens investment managers across the country and across investment disciplines in order to recommend those managers who best match your financial requirements. The consultant not only monitors your money manager on an on-going basis, but also helps you monitor and evaluate your personal portfolio with a quarterly performance report.

If you seek the help of an investment management consultant, finding a firm to manage your money will become less confusing and much more rewarding.

If you want more information about professional money management, please call my office at (your number) for an appointment or return the enclosed response sheet for your complimentary copy with no obligation of my latest article/book, _____.

Warm regards,

Letter 6

Date
Name
Address
City

Dear

How does the average investor cope with the investment product explosion? Not very well. Studies on the sensitivity of the human brain have established the existence of a phenomenon called "sensory overload."

Scientists have discovered that a person is capable of receiving only a limited amount of input. Beyond a certain point, the brain goes blank and fails to function normally. Many individual investors today are having trouble processing the vast quantity of information available on investment products.

Because we are in such a hurry these days and have so many investment vehicles, we tend to invest 'conservatively,' and go on to attend to the many other important matters in our complex lives.

Consequently, we invest in short-term CDs, money market mutual funds, U.S. Government bonds, or other high-yielding instruments that produce income but little or no growth.

Sure, fixed income securities have been a safe way for you to invest in the past. And over the last ten years, certain high-yield securities have been disastrous.

The solution: hire an investment consultant who understands the investment management process. This solution can reduce the risk of inappropriate investment decisions and keep your personal emotions out of your investment choices.

If you want more information about professional money management, please call my office at (your number) for an appointment or return the enclosed response sheet for your complimentary copy with no obligation of my latest article, _____.

Warm regards,

Glossary

abstract	A brief description of chapters in a nonfiction book proposal (also called a synopsis); a point-by-point summary of an article or essay. In academic and technical journals, abstracts often appear with (and may preface) the articles themselves.
advance	Money paid (usually in installments) to an author by a publisher before a book is published. The advance is paid against royalties: If an author is given a $5,000 advance, for instance, the author will collect royalties only after the monies due exceed $5,000. A good contract protects the advance if it exceeds the royalties that are ultimately due from sales.
advance orders	Orders received before a book's official publication date, and sometimes before actual manufacture of the book.
agent	The person who acts on behalf of the author to handle the sale of literary properties. Good literary agents are as valuable to publishers as they are to writers; they select and present manuscripts appropriate for particular houses or of interest to particular acquisitions editors. Agents are paid on a

percentage basis from the monies due their author clients.

American Society of Journalists and Authors A membership organization for professional writers, ASJA provides a forum for information exchange among writers and others in the publishing community, as well as networking opportunities.

authorized biography A history of a person's life written with the authorization, cooperation, and, at times, participation of the subject or the subject's heirs.

author's copies/ author's discount Author's copies are the free copies of their books that authors receive from the publisher; the exact number is stipulated in the contract, but it is usually at least 10 hardcovers. The author will be able to purchase additional copies of the book (usually at a 40 percent discount from the retail price) and resell them at readings, lectures, etc. If large quantities are bought, author discounts can go as high as 70 percent.

author tour Travel and promotional appearances by the author to market a book.

autobiography A history of a person's life written by the person, or, as is typical, composed with a collaborative writer ("as told to" or "with") or a ghostwriter.

best-seller Based on sales or orders by bookstores, wholesalers, and distributors, best-sellers are those titles that move in the largest quantities. Lists of best-selling books can be local (newspapers), regional, national (*Publishers Weekly* or the *New York Times*), and international. Fiction and nonfiction are usually listed separately, as are hardcover and paperback, and sometimes additional classifications (such as how-to/self-improvement) are used; in addition, bestseller lists can be keyed to particular genres or specialty fields (such as mysteries, science fiction, or romance novels, or historical works, business books, or religious titles).

bibliography   A list of books, articles, and other sources that have been used in the writing of the text in which the bibliography appears. Complex works may break the bibliography down into subject areas, such as General History, the Twentieth Century, or Trade Unions.

binding   The materials that hold a book together (including the cover). Bindings are generally denoted as hardcover (featuring heavy cardboard covered with durable cloth or paper) or paperback (using a pliable, resilient grade of paper). In the days when cloth was used more lavishly, hardcover volumes were conventionally known as clothbound; in the very old days, hardcover bindings sometimes featured tooled leather and real gold- and silver-leaf ornamentation.

blues (or bluelines)   Photographic proofs of the printing plates for a book, used to inspect the set type, layout, and design before it goes to press.

blurb   A piece of written copy or extracted quotation used for publicity and promotional purposes, as on a flyer, in a catalog, on a book jacket, or in an advertisement.

book club

A book-marketing organization that ships selected titles to subscribing members on a regular basis, sometimes at greatly reduced prices. Sales to book clubs are negotiated through the publisher's subsidiary rights department (in the case of a best-seller, they may be auctioned off). Terms vary, but the split of royalties between author and publisher is often 50/50. Book club sales are seen as blessed events by author, agent, and publisher alike.

book contract

A legally binding document that sets the terms for the advance, royalties, subsidiary rights, advertising, promotion, publicity, and a host of other contingencies and responsibilities related to publication of a book. Writers should be thoroughly familiar with the concepts and terminology of the standard book-publishing contract.

**book producer or
book packager**

An individual or company that can assume many of the roles in the publishing process. A book packager or producer may conceive the idea for a book (most often nonfiction) or series, bring together the professionals (including the writer) needed to produce the book(s), sell the individual manuscript or series project to a publisher, take the project through to manufactured product – or perform any of those functions as commissioned by the publisher or other client (such as a corporation producing a corporate history as a premium or giveaway for employees and customers). The book producer may negotiate separate contracts with the publisher and with the writers, editors, and illustrators who contribute to the book.

book review

A critical appraisal of a book (often reflecting a reviewer's personal opinion or recommendation) that evaluates such aspects as organization and writing style, possible market appeal, and cultural, political, or literary significance. Before the public reads book reviews in the local and national print media, important reviews have been published in such respected trade journals as *Publishers Weekly, Kirkus Reviews, Library Journal,* and *Booklist.* A rave review from one of these journals will encourage booksellers to order the book; copies of these raves will be used for promotion and publicity purposes by the publisher and will encourage other book reviewers nationwide to review the book.

Books in Print

Listings, published by R. R. Bowker, of books currently in print. These annual volumes (along with periodic supplements such as Forthcoming Books in Print) provide ordering information including titles, authors, ISBN numbers, prices, whether the book is available in hardcover or paperback, and publisher name. Intended for use by the book trade, *Books in Print* is also of great value to writers who are researching the markets for their projects. Listings are provided alphabetically by author, title, and subject area.

bound galleys

Copies of uncorrected typesetter's page proofs or printouts of electronically produced pages that are bound together as advance copies of the book. Bound galleys are sent to trade journals as well as to a limited number of major reviewers who work with long lead times.

bulk sales

The discounted sale of many copies of a single title (the greater the number of books, the larger the discount).

byline

The name of the author of a piece, indicating credit for having written a book or article. Ghostwriters, by definition, do not receive bylines.

co-author

One who shares authorship of a work. Co-authors have bylines. Co-authors share royalties based on their contributions to the book.

collaboration

A writer can collaborate with professionals in any number of fields to produce books outside the writer's own areas of expertise (for example, a writer with an interest in exercise and nutrition may collaborate with a doctor on a health book). Though the writer may be billed as a co-author, the writer does not necessarily receive a byline (in which case the writer is a ghostwriter), and royalties are shared based on proportionate contributions to the book (including expertise, promotional abilities, and the actual writing).

copy editor

An editor responsible for the final polishing of a manuscript, who reads primarily in terms of appropriate word usage and grammatical expression, clarity, and coherence of the material as presented, in addition to factual errors and inconsistencies, spelling, and punctuation.

copyright

The legal proprietary right to reproduce, have reproduced, publish, and sell copies of literary, musical, and other artistic works. The rights to literary properties belong to the authors from the time the work is produced – regardless of whether a formal copyright registration is obtained. However, for legal recourse in the event of plagiarism, the work must be registered with the U.S. Copyright Office, and all copies of the work must bear the copyright notice.

cover blurbs
Favorable quotes from other writers, celebrities, or experts in a subject that appear on a book jacket and are used to enhance the book's point-of-purchase appeal to potential book buyers.

deadline
In book publishing, this not-so-subtle synonym for the author's due date for submission of the completed manuscript to the publisher can be as much as a full year before the official publication date, unless the book is being produced quickly to coincide with or follow up a particular event.

delivery
Submission of the completed manuscript to the editor or publisher.

display titles
Books that are produced to be eye-catching to the casual browser in a bookstore are sometimes termed display titles. Often rich with splashy cover art, these publications are intended to pique the book buyer's senses. Many display titles are stacked on their own freestanding racks; a book shelved with its front cover showing is technically a display title. Promotional or premium titles are likely to be display items, as are mass-market paperbacks and hardbacks with enormous best-seller potential.

distribution
The method of getting books from the publisher's warehouse into the reader's hands - traditionally via bookstores, but including

such means as telemarketing and mail-order sales. Publishers use their own sales forces as well as independent salespeople, wholesalers, and distributors. Many large and some small publishers distribute for other publishers. A publisher's distribution network is extremely important, because it not only makes possible the vast sales of a best-seller but also affects the visibility of the publisher's entire list of books.

distributor   An agent or business that buys books from a publisher to resell, at a higher cost, to wholesalers, retailers, or individuals. Skillful use of distribution networks can give a small publisher greater national visibility.

dust jacket   (also dustcover or book jacket) The paper wrapper that covers the binding of hardcover books, designed especially for the book by either the publisher's art department or a freelance artist. Dust jackets were originally conceived to protect books during shipping, but now their function is primarily promotional – to entice the browser to reach out and pick up the volume by means of attractive graphics and sizzling promotional copy.

editor   Editorial responsibilities and titles vary from publisher to publisher (usually being less strictly defined in smaller houses). In general, the duties of the editor-in-chief or executive editor are primarily administrative: managing personnel, scheduling, budgeting, and defining the editorial personality of the firm or imprint. Senior editors and acquisitions editors acquire manuscripts (and authors), conceive project ideas and find writers to carry them out, and may oversee the writing and rewriting of manuscripts. Managing editors have editorial and production responsibilities, coordinating and scheduling the book through the various phases of production. Associate and assistant editors edit; they are involved in most of the rewriting and reshaping of the manuscript. Copy editors read the manuscript and style its punctuation, grammar, spelling, headings and subheadings, etc. Editorial assistants, laden with extensive clerical duties, perform some editorial duties as well – often as springboards to senior editorial positions.

endnotes

Explanatory notes and source citations that appear either at the end of individual chapters or at the end of a book's text; used primarily in scholarly works.

epilogue

The final segment of a book, which comes "after the end." In both fiction and nonfiction, an epilogue offers commentary or further information, but does not bear directly on the book's central design.

footnotes

Explanatory notes and source citations that appear at the bottom of a page. Footnotes are rare in general-interest books, the preferred style being either to work such information into the text or to list informational sources in the bibliography.

foreword

An introductory piece written by the author or by an expert on the topic of the book. A foreword by a celebrity or well-respected authority is a strong selling point for a prospective project or, after publication, for the book itself.

fulfillment house   A firm commissioned to fill orders for a publisher; services may include warehousing, shipping, receiving returns, and mail-order and direct-marketing response. Although more common for magazine publishers, fulfillment houses also serve book publishers.

galleys   Printer's proofs (or copies of proofs) on sheets of paper, or printouts of the electronically produced setup of the book's interior that are the author's last chance to check for typos and make any (usually minimal) revisions or additions to the copy. (*See* bound galleys.)

ghostwriter   A writer without a byline, and often without as much remuneration and recognition as bylined authors receive. Ghostwriters typically get flat fees for their work, but even without royalties, experienced ghosts can receive respectable sums.

glossary   An alphabetical listing of special terms used in a particular subject area, often with more in-depth explanations than would be provided by general dictionary definitions.

hardcover   Books bound in a format that uses thick, sturdy, relatively stiff binding boards and a cover composed (usually) of a cloth spine and finished binding paper. Hardcover books are conventionally wrapped in a dust jacket. (*See* binding, dust jacket.)

hook   The distinctive concept or theme of a work that sets it apart as being fresh, new, or different from others in its field. A hook can be an author's special point of view, often encapsulated in a catchy or provocative phrase intended to attract or pique the interest of a reader, editor, or agent. One important function of a hook is to present what might otherwise be seen as dry though significant subject matter (academic or scientific topics; number-crunching drudgery, such as home bookkeeping) as an exciting, commercially attractive package.

how-to books

An immensely popular category of books ranging from purely instructional (arts and crafts, for example) to motivational (popular psychology, self-improvement, inspirational) to get-rich-quick (real estate and investment).

imprint

A separate product line within a publishing house. Imprints may be composed of just one or two series or may offer large, diversified lists. Imprints enjoy varying degrees of autonomy from the parent company. An imprint may have its own editorial department (possibly consisting of only one editor), or house acquisitions editors may assign particular titles for release on appropriate specialized imprints. An imprint may publish a certain kind of book (juvenile or paperback or travel), or have its own personality (such as a literary tone).

index

An alphabetical directory at the end of a book that references names and subjects discussed in the book and the pages where such mentions can be found.

introduction

Preliminary remarks pertaining to a piece. Like a foreword, an introduction can be written by the author or an appropriate authority on the subject. If a book has both a foreword and an introduction, the foreword will be written by someone other than the author; the introduction will be more closely tied to the text and will be written by the book's author. (*See* foreword.)

ISBN

(International Standard Book Number) A 10-digit number that identifies the title and publisher of a book, used for ordering and cataloging books and appears on all dust-covers, on the back cover of the book, and on the copyright page.

lead

The crucial first few sentences of a query letter, book proposal, novel, news release, article, advertisement, or sales tip sheet in which the writer must hook the reader, consumer, editor, or agent.

lead title

book featured by the publisher during a given season – one the publisher believes should do extremely well commercially. Lead titles are usually given the publisher's maximum promotional push.

letterpress

A form of printing in which set type is inked, then impressed directly onto the printing surface. Now used primarily for limited-run, books-as-fine-art projects. (Compare offset.)

Library of Congress

The largest library in the world, in Washington, DC. As part of its many services, the Library of Congress will supply a writer with up-to-date sources and bibliographies in all fields, from arts and humanities to science and technology. For details, write to the Library of Congress, Central Services Division, Washington, DC 20540.

Library of Congress Catalog Number

An identifying number issued by the Library of Congress to books it has accepted for its collection. The publication of those books, which are submitted by the publishers, are announced by the Library of Congress to libraries, which use Library of Congress numbers for their own ordering and cataloging purposes.

mass-market paperback   Less-expensive, smaller-format paperbacks that are sold from racks (in such venues as supermarkets, variety stores, drugstores, and specialty shops) as well as in bookstores. Also referred to as *rack editions*.

option clause/right of first refusal   In a book contract, a clause that stipulates that the publisher will have the right to publish the author's next book. However, the publisher is under no obligation to do so.

outline   Used for both a book proposal and the actual writing and structuring of a book, an outline is a hierarchical listing of topics that provides the writer (and the proposal reader) with an overview of a book's ideas in the order in which they will be presented.

permission   The right to quote or reprint published material, obtained by the author from the copyright holder.

preface   An element of a book's front matter. In the preface, the author may discuss the purpose of the book, the type of research upon which it is based, its genesis, or its underlying philosophy.

press kit   A promotional package that includes a press release, tip sheet, author biography and photograph, reviews, and other pertinent information. The press kit can be put together by the publisher's publicity department or an independent publicist and sent with a review copy of the book to potential reviewers and to media professionals responsible for booking author appearances.

price

There are several prices for a single book. The invoice price is the amount the publisher charges the bookseller; the retail, cover, or list price is what the consumer pays.

proposal

A detailed presentation of the book's concept, used to gain the interest and services of an agent or to sell the project to a publisher.

publication date (or pub date)

A book's official date of publication, customarily set by the publisher to fall six weeks after completed bound books are delivered to the warehouse. The publication date is used to schedule the promotional activities on behalf of the title, so there is time for books to be ordered, shipped, and received in the stores to coincide with the appearance of advertising and publicity.

public domain

Material that is uncopyrighted, whose copyright has expired, or that is uncopyrightable. The last category includes government publications, jokes, titles, and, it should be remembered, ideas.

publicist (press agent)

The professional who handles the press releases for new books and arranges the author's publicity tour.

publisher's catalog

A seasonal sales catalog that lists and describes a publisher's new books; it is sent to all potential buyers, including individuals who request one. Catalogs range from the basic to the glitzy, and often include information on the author, on print quantity, and on the amount of money slated to be spent on publicity and promotion.

publisher's discount The percentage by which a publisher discounts the retail price of a book to a bookseller, often based in part on the number of copies purchased.

Publisher's Weekly (PW) The publishing industry's chief trade journal. PW carries announcements of upcoming books, respected book reviews, interviews with authors, and news (such as publisher mergers and personnel changes).

query (letter) A brief written presentation to an agent or editor, designed to pitch both the writer and the book idea.

remainders Unsold books. Remainders can include titles that have not sold as well as anticipated, in addition to unsold copies of later printings of best-sellers. Remaining stock is purchased from the publisher at a huge discount and resold to the public.

reprint A subsequent edition of material that is already in print, especially publication in a different format—the paperback reprint of a hardcover, for example.

résumé A summary of an individual's employment experience and education. When a résumé is sent to prospective agents or publishers, it should contain the author's publishing credits, specialty credentials, and pertinent personal experiences. Also referred to as the curriculum vitae or, more simply, vita.

returns

Unsold books returned to a publisher by a bookstore, for which the store may receive full or partial credit (depending on the publisher's policy, the age of the book, and so on).

reversion-of-rights clause

In a book contract, a clause stating that if the book goes out of print or the publisher fails to reprint the book within a stipulated length of time, all rights revert to the author.

review copy

A free copy of a (usually) new book sent to print and electronic media that review books for their audiences.

royalty

The percentage of a book's retail cost that is paid to the author for each copy sold after the author's advance has been recouped by the publisher. Some publishers structure royalties as a percentage payment against net receipts.

sales conference

The semiannual meeting of a publisher's editorial and sales departments and senior promotion and publicity staff members, during which the upcoming season's new books are introduced and marketing strategies are discussed.

sales representative (sales rep)

A member of the publisher's sales force or an independent contractor who, armed with a book catalog and order forms, visits bookstores in a certain territory to sell books to retailers.

SASE (self-addressed stamped envelope)

It is customary for an author to enclose SASEs with query letters, proposals, and manuscript submissions. Many editors and agents do not reply if a writer has neglected to enclose an SASE.

self-publishing A publishing project wherein an author pays the costs of manufacturing and selling his or her own book and retains all profits from the book's sales. This is a risky venture but can be profitable (especially when combined with an author's speaking engagements or imaginative marketing techniques); if successful, self-publication can sometimes lead to distribution or publication by a commercial publisher. (Compare with *subsidy publishing*.)

serial rights Reprint rights sold to periodicals. First serial rights include the right to publish the material before anyone else (generally before the book is released, or coinciding with the book's official publication) – either within the United States or a wider territory. Second serial rights cover material already published, either in a book or in another periodical.

shelf life The amount of time an unsold book remains on the bookstore shelf before the store manager pulls it to make room for newer incoming stock with greater (or at least untested) sales potential.

signature A group of book pages printed together on one large sheet of paper that is then folded and cut in preparation for being bound, along with the book's other signatures, into the final volume.

simultaneous publication The issuing at the same time of more than one edition of a work, such as hardcover and trade paperback editions. Simultaneous releases may also include mass-market

paper versions and, rarely, deluxe gift
editions.

**simultaneous (or multiple)
submissions**   The submission of the same material to
more than one publisher at the same time.
Although simultaneous submission is a
common practice, publishers should always
be told when it is being done. Multiple submissions by an author to several agents is,
on the other hand, a practice that is frowned
upon.

slush pile   The morass of unsolicited manuscripts at a
publishing house or literary agency, which
may fester indefinitely awaiting (perhaps
perfunctory) review. Some publishers or
agencies do not maintain slush piles –
unsolicited manuscripts are slated for
instant return without review (if an SASE is
included) or may otherwise be literally or
figuratively pitched to the wind. Querying
a targeted publisher or agent before submitting a manuscript is an excellent way of
avoiding, or at least minimizing, the possi-
bility of such an ignoble fate.

spine   The portion of the book's casing (or binding) that backs the bound signatures and is
visible when the volume is aligned on a
bookshelf.

stamping   In book publishing, the impression of orna-
mental type and images (such as a logo) on
the book's binding, using a die with raised
or intaglio surface to apply ink or metallic-
leaf stamping.

subsidiary rights   The reprint, serial, movie, television,
audiotape, and videotape rights deriving
from a book. The division of profits

between publisher and author from the sales of these rights is determined through negotiation. In more elaborately commercial projects, such details as syndication of related articles and licensing of characters may ultimately be involved.

subsidy publishing

A mode of publication wherein the author pays a publishing company to produce his or her work, which may thus appear superficially to have been conventionally published. Subsidy publishing (also known as vanity publishing) is generally more expensive than self-publishing, because the subsidy house makes a profit on all its contracted functions, charging fees well beyond basic costs for production and services.

syndicated column

Material published simultaneously in a number of newspapers or magazines. The author shares the income from syndication with the syndicate that negotiates the sale.

synopsis

A summary in paragraph form, rather than in outline format. The synopsis is an important part of a book proposal. For fiction, the synopsis hits the key points of the plot. In a nonfiction book proposal, the synopsis describes the thrust and content of the successive chapters (and/or parts) of the manuscript.

trade books

Books distributed through the book trade—meaning bookstores and major book clubs—as opposed to, for example, mass-market paperbacks, which are also sold at magazine racks, newsstands, and supermarkets.

trade discount

The discount from the cover or list price that a publisher gives the bookseller. It is

	usually proportional to the number of books ordered (the larger the order, the greater the discount), and is typically between 40 and 50 percent.
trade list	A catalog of all of a publisher's books in print, with ISBNs and order information. The trade list sometimes includes descriptions of the current season's new books.
trade publishers	Publishers of books for a general readership – that is, nonprofessional, nonacademic books that are distributed primarily through bookstores.
university press	A publishing house affiliated with a university. The press is generally nonprofit and subsidized by the university. Generally, university presses publish noncommercial scholarly nonfiction books written by academics, though their lists may include literary fiction, criticism, and poetry. Some university presses also specialize in titles of regional interest, and many acquire limited numbers of projects intended for broader commercial appeal.
unsolicited manuscript	A manuscript sent to an editor or agent that has not been requested.
vanity press	A publisher that publishes books only at an author's expense—and will generally agree to publish virtually anything that is submitted and paid for. (*See* subsidy publishing.)
word count	The number of words in a document. When noted on a manuscript, the word count is usually rounded off to the nearest 100 words.

Suggested Resources

Bly, Robert W. *Targeted Public Relations* (Henry Holt and Company 1993). How to get thousands of dollars of free publicity.

Boswell, John. *The Awful Truth about Publishing: Why They Always Reject Your Manuscript... and What You Can Do about It* (New York: Warner Books, 1986). A view from the other side—that is, the view from within the large publishing house.

Burgett, Gordon. *The Writer's Guide to Query Letters and Cover Letters* (Rocklin, CA: Prima, 1992). Sound and pointed advice, from an expert's perspective, on how to use query and cover letters to sell your writing.

Collier, Oscar, with Frances Spatz Leighton. *How to Write and Sell Your First Nonfiction Book* (New York: St. Martin's, 1994). Practical, encouraging how-to from industry professionals. Topics include choosing a subject, targeting an audience, proposal writing, effective researching, conducting interviews, dealing with agents and editors, understanding contracts, and marketing your book.

Curtis, Richard. *How to Be Your Own Literary Agent: The Business of Getting Your Book Published* (Boston: Houghton Mifflin, 1984). Insights and how-to; a personal point of view from one who knows the ropes.

Dustbooks (editors). *The Directory of Small Press Editors & Publishers; Directory of Poetry Publishers; The International Directory of Little Magazines and Small Presses; Small Press Record of Books in Print* (Paradise, CA: Dustbooks, all volumes published annually). This set of literary references is put out by the publishers of the industry journal *Small Press Review*. These resources for market exploration provide writers with editorial requirements and procedures for manuscript submission, keyed to the individual publishers and periodicals listed.

Henry, Rene Jr. *Marketing Public Relations* (Iowa State University
Press). Tells the reader how to make it work.

Herman, Jeff, and Deborah M. Adams. *Write the Perfect Book Proposal:
10 Proposals That Sold and Why* (New York: Wiley, 1993). Analysis
of successful nonfiction book proposals with pointed commentary
from New York literary agent Jeff Herman and book-proposal doctor
(and author) Deborah Adams. Doesn't just tell you how to do it – this
book shows you in detail how it was done effectively.

Horowitz, Lois. *Knowing Where to Look: The Ultimate Guide to
Research* (Cincinnati: Writer's Digest Books, 1984). An invaluable
tool for anyone who has to dig up elusive facts and figures.

Kremer, John. *Book Publishing Resource Guide* (Fairfield, IA: Ad-Lib
Publications, 1990). Comprehensive listings for book-marketing
contracts and resources; contains a vast bibliography and references
to other resource guides.

Kremer, John. *101 Ways to Market Your Books – For Publishers and
Authors* (Fairfield, IA: Ad-Lib Publications, 1986). Sensible, innovative, and inspiring advice on, first, producing the most marketable
book possible, and then, on marketing it as effectively as possible.

Larsen, Michael. *How to Write a Book Proposal* (Cincinnati: Writer's
Digest Books, 1985). A clear and no-nonsense – even inspiring –
step-by-step guide to the book proposal. The author is a West Coast-
based literary agent and writer.

Luey, Beth. *Handbook for Academic Authors* (revised edition) (New
York: Cambridge University Press, 1990). This reference pinpoints
key (and perhaps unsuspected) considerations in the field of
academic publishing; valuable information with strategic implications for players in the publish-or-perish game.

Parinello, Al. *On the Air: How to Get on Radio and TV Talk Shows and
What to Do When You Get There* (Hawthorne, NJ: Career Press,
1991). Exciting guide to the electronic media and their use for
promotional purposes. Ties in marketing aspects of seminars, social
activism, and professional training and advancement. Especially
appropriate for entrepreneurial authors.

Poynter, Dan. *The Self-Publishing Manual* (Santa Barbara, CA: Para
Publishing, 1989). Informative and complete step-by-step how-to by
the principal of one of the most successful one-person publishing
firms.

Preston, Elizabeth, Ingrid Monke, and Elizabeth Bickford. *Preparing Your Manuscript* (Boston: The Writer, 1992). A contemporary guide to manuscript preparation. Provides step-by-step advice for professional presentation of work for submission to editors, publishers, agents, television producers. Covers punctuation, spelling, indexing; gives examples of proper formats for poetry, prose, plays; offers essential information on copyright, marketing, mailing manuscripts.

Writer's Market (Cincinnati: Writer's Digest Books, published annually). A directory of thousands of markets and outlets, best known for its listing of the hundreds of consumer and trade periodicals. Also includes book publishers, book packagers, greeting-card publishers, syndicates, and more.

Index

48 Hours, 201-202

A

ABC. *See* Nightline.
ABC World News Tonight, 199
Abstract, 293
Advance, 293
orders, 293
Advertisements, 23, 198, 217
Advertisements, writing, 83
subject, 211
Advertisers, 15, 71, 235. *See also*
National advertisers; Print
advertisers.
Advertising, 27, 60, 209-215, 229,
238, 273-274
assault, 209-210
checklist. *See* Yellow Pages.
image creation, 211
messages, 212
structuring process, 211
studies, 213
usage, 210-211
volume, 233
Advertising Age, 212
Agent, 293-294. *See also* Press agent.
American Bookseller, 185
American Management Association
(AMA), 129, 213
American Society of Association
Executives, 100

American Society of Journalists and
Authors (ASJA), 263, 294
Anecdote/analogy, writing, 86
Anecdotes, 161
usage, 98
Appearances, preparation, 181-185
Appendix. *See* Book template.
ARS. *See* Associated Release Service.
Articles. *See* Print publications.
checklist, 91-93
leverage process, 125-128
multiple submissions, 253
research, 48
responses, response rate, 102
reuse, 165-167
structuring process, 83-84
summarization, 256
writing. *See* Sample articles.
ASJA. *See* American Society of
Journalists and Authors.
Associated Press, 185
Associated Release Service (ARS), 44
Association Meeting Directory, 221
Atlanta Journal/Constitution, 185-186
Attention, 246, 247, 254
Author tour, 294
Authorized biography, 294
Authors. *See* Book proposal; Book
template.
Autobiography, 294

B

Background sheet, 27
Back-up copy, 134
Bacon's Mailing Services, 43
Bacon's Media Directories, 45
Bacon's Newsletter Magazine
    Directory and Radio and TV
    Directory, 182
Bacon's Publicity Checker, 110, 179
Bandwidth, 132
Beach, Mark, 141
Before Hours/Business Day, 201
Benefits. *See* Business; Yellow Pages.
    cost-effective communication,
    57-60
Best-seller, 294-295
Bibliography, 295
Bickham, Jack, 84
Binding, 295
Biography, 27, 100, 179, 195. *See
    also* Authorized biography; Book
    proposal.
Block diagram, 88-91
Bloomsbury Review, 186
Bluelines, 295
Blues, 295
Blurbs, 295. *See also* Cover blurbs.
Bly, Robert W., 36
Book
    covers, 177
    manuscript, 154
    prospects, 267
    reviews, sources, 185-192
    sample, 195
    selling. *See* Publisher.
    success story, 179-180
    target, 169
Book club, 296
Book contract, 296
Book List, 182
Book packager, 296
Book producer, 296
Book promotion, 177-192
    ideas, 182-185

Book proposal, 153-157
    authors, biography, 156
    competition section, 156
    cover letter, 154
    guidelines, 154
    marketing/promotional section, 156
    outline, 155
    overview, 155
    sample chapters, 156
Book publishing, 266-267
    tips, 161-163
Book review, 297
Book template, 147-152. *See also*
    Master investment book template.
    appendix, 152
    author, 152
    current trends, 148-149
    diversification, 149
    glossary, 152
    introduction, 147-148
    preface, 147
    pull-it-together chapter, 151
    subject index, 152
    summary, 151
    tools, 150
Book template, investments, 149
    solutions, 151
    steps, 150
    strategies, 149-150
Booking contact, 197
Booklet, 181. *See also* Stay-behind
    booklet.
BookNotes, 199
Books in Print, 297
Boston Globe, 186
Bound galley, 297
Bowen, John, 19, 114, 162, 179, 226,
    269, 270
Bradley Communications Corp., 45
Briefing sheet, 27
Browser, 131. *See also* Internet
    browser.
    software, 130
Bulk sales, 298
Burrelle, 43

Burrelle's Media Directories, 45
Business
  contribution. *See* Teaching.
  efforts, benefits, 230-231
  insights, 63
  readers, 83
Business Week, 186, 210
Business Wire, 42
Business-to-business service, 238
Byline, 298

C

Cable News Network (CNN), 200-201, 244
Calls. *See* Cold calls; Warm calls.
  effectiveness. *See* Phone calls.
CBS This Morning, 199-200
Chapter. *See* Book template; Sample.
  summarization, 256
Characterization, 98
Charity events, 181
Charts, 91
Chicago Sun-Times, 186
Chicago Tribune, 186
Chicago Tribune Book, 182
Cliches, avoidance, 97
Clients
  core groups, 116
  education. *See* Key clients.
  identification, 63
  letters, 283-292
  needs, 21
  organizations, 102
  reading material, 110-113
  referrals, 79
CNBC Business Tonight, 193, 194
CNBC Network Programs, 200
CNN. *See* Cable News Network.
Coach-writing, 252
Co-author, 298
Cold calls, 15, 60
Collaboration, 298
Collaborator, writing, 265
College courses. *See* Teaching.
Columnists, 178

Comments, 31, 32
Commercial magazines, 125
Competition, 16, 117
  section. *See* Book proposal.
  separation, 73
Compliance file, creation, 49
Conferences. *See* News conferences.
Confidence, 29
Contacts, information supply, 74
Content, 97
Controversy. *See* Press releases.
Cook, Scott, 19
Cooperative publishing, 251, 263-265
Copy, spacing, 93
Copy editor, 298
Copyright, 173, 298-299
  permission request, 174-175
Cover blurbs, 299
Cover letters, 51, 97, 195. *See also*
  Book proposal.
Credibility, 15, 25, 26, 28, 51, 79,
  110, 116, 127, 218
  marketing, 10, 55, 57, 60
Credibility marketing strategies,
  57-75
  ideas, 71-75
Cross-connections, 48
C-Span, 199
Customer feedback, 133
Customer profile, 240

D

Daily marketing events, 55
Danko, William, 147
Data bank, 119
Database, 132, 133
Deadlines, 299
Delivery, 299
Dial-and-Smile method, 271
Dialog Information Service, 42
Differentiation, 210-211
Direct mail, 59, 274-275
  contacts, 274
  pros/cons, 279
Direct marketing, 57, 60

Directories, 267
Discounts, 240-241
Display titles, 299
Distribution, 299-300
Distributor, 300
Diversification. *See* Book template.
Double-pocket portfolio, 26
Dow Jones Industrial Average, 9
Dow Jones News Retrieval, 42
Draft, writing. *See* First draft.
Dust jacket, 300

E

Editing, 94
  checklist. *See* Self-edit checklist.
Editorial Freelance Association
  (EFA), 263
Editors, 24, 25, 27, 91, 96, 100, 108,
  115, 153, 155, 183, 197, 300-301.
  See also Copy editor.
  letter, 44
  opinion, 113
  preferences, 121
Editor's and Publisher's International
  Yearbook, 179
EFA. *See* Editorial Freelance
  Association.
Effectiveness, maximization tips, 198
Encyclopedia of Associations, 179
Endnotes, 301
Epilogue, 301
Equal Time (television program), 201
Event sponsorships, 212
Excerpts, 127
  usage, 180
Exhibits Directory, 221
Experts, 52, 61, 194
  alignment, 49
  definition, 20
  positioning, 65-67
  speaking, 243-249

F

Fact sheet, 26
Fairfield, Lucinda, 21, 225-230
Family Circle, 187
Favors, return, 71
Feedback, 27. *See also* Customer
  feedback.
File, Karen Maru, 66
Financial advisors, 23, 29, 58-60, 95,
  233
Financial Planning (magazine), 110,
  126, 257
Financial specialists, 65
First draft, writing, 85-90
Focus groups, 211
Follow up, 72-73
Footnotes, 301
Forbes (magazine), 24, 44, 109, 110
Foreword, 301
Fortune (magazine), 24, 109, 113
FrontPage, 130
Fulfillment house, 302

G

Gale's Directory, 179
Galleys, 302
Ghostwriters, 93, 251-263, 302
  cooperation process, 254-257
  costs/fees, 257-261
Globe (magazine), 187
Glossary, 293-312. *See* Book
  template.
Good Morning, America, 202, 212
Goss, Frederick, 141
Graphic designers, 133
Graphs, 91

H

Hard Copy, 202-203
Hardcover, 302
Head shot, 26

Headlines, 81-82, 91
Home page, 133
Hook, 302-303
How To Get On Radio Talk Shows, 45
How-to books, 303
HTML, 130
  code, 132, 134
Hudson's Subscription Newsletter
  Directory, 45

I

IAFP. *See* International Association of
  Financial Planners.
Ideas, 81-82
  testing, 165
Image creation. *See* Advertising.
Imprint, 303
Index, 303
Indirect media, 212-213
Industry expert, 28
Influence, centers, 117
Information
  gathering, 48-49
  library, building, 49-52
  sheet, 179
Inside Edition, 203
Interest, appearance, 73-74
Interests, 72
International Association of Financial
  Planners (IAFP), 271
International Standard Book Number
  (ISBN), 304
Internet, 129, 132, 160
  advertising, 130
  pros/cons, 280
Internet Explorer, 130
Internet Service Provider (ISP), 132, 134
Interviews, 23, 29-33, 178, 179, 196.
  See also Media; Radio; Telephone
  interview.
  preparation, 181-185, 198
Introduction, 303-304
Investment advisor, 10, 86, 92

Investment Advisor (magazine), 110
Investment book, writing, 143
Investment products, 80
ISBN. *See* International Standard
  Book Number.
ISDN service, 134
ISP. *See* Internet Service Provider.

J

Jargon, avoidance, 97
Job Hotline, 262
Journal writing, 265

K

Key clients, education, 68-69
Kirkus Reviews, 182, 187
Knight Brothers Press Line, 42
Knowledge Index, 42

L

Language, 97
Larry King Live, 203-204
Lead title, 304
Leads, 38, 304. *See also*
  Presentations.
Legal file, creation, 49
Letterpress, 304
Letters. *See* Clients; Editors; Pitch
  letter.
Levitt, Theodore, 212
Library of Congress, 304
  Catalog Number, 304-305
Listening, value, 73
Literary Marketplace, 179
Los Angeles Times, 185
Los Angeles Times Book Review,
  182, 188

M

Magazine articles, writing, 48
  process. *See* Problem/solution
  magazine article.
Magazines. *See* Commercial

magazines; Mass market
  magazines; Trade magazines.
  editors, 178
  feature, 38
  guidelines, 106, 114
  pros/cons, 279-280
  writing, 265
Mahoney, Ann, 100
Mailing list, 138
Mailing service, 275
Management philosophy, 22
Manuscript, 95-97, 127, 153. See also
  Book; Unsolicited manuscript.
  appearance, 159-160
  pages, 147
  polishing, 256
  preparation, 77
  title, 160
  troubleshooting list, 163-164
Market. See Niche market.
  place, positioning, 15-22
  share, 240
Marketing, 11, 71, 221. See also
  Credibility; Credibility marketing;
  Direct marketing; Public
  relations; Relationship marketing.
  advantages, 230
  challenges, 2-3
  events. See Daily marketing events.
  goals, 137
  ideas, 64
  section. See Book proposal.
  strategies. See Credibility
    marketing strategies.
  studies, 271-275
  weapons, 82
Marketing plans, 3-5, 60, 104
  media addition, 23-33
  national exposure integration, 198
Mass mailings, 60
Mass-market magazines, 110
Mass-marketing, 66
Mass-market paperback, 305
Mass-marketing techniques, 52
Master book plot, 145

Master investment book template,
  145-152
  outline, 145-146
  polish, 146
  reorganization, 146
  writing, 146
McCall's, 188
MDS. See Media Distribution
  Services.
Media. See Indirect media.
  appearances, 195, 196
  briefings, 41
  campaigns, 136
  comparison, 277-281
  contact, 29
  entering. See Print media.
  interviews, 60
  kit, usage. See TV media kit.
  location, 45
  opportunity, 9-13
  outlets, 33
  packet, building, 24-27
  relations, 119-120
  relationship building, 27-33
  release, 26
Media Distribution Services (MDS),
  43
Mediamatic System, 43
Merrill, Charles E., 52
Message, 91. See also Titles.
  finding, 170
  quick release, 35-45
Messenger, becoming, 52-54
Midwest Book Review, 188
Mini-feature, 38
Model permissions letter, 175
Money Magazine, 15
Money (magazine), 16, 24, 100, 109
Money Wheel (television program),
  204
Moneywise (television program), 204
Monthly column, 99-100
Multiple submissions, 310. See also
  Articles.

N

NAPS. *See* North American Precis Syndicate.
NASD Regulation, 141
National advertisers, 210, 236
National exposure, integration. *See* Marketing plan.
National television talk show
    angle, 194
    homework, 194
    pitch, 194
    scheduling, 197
    spot, 193-206
National Trade Professional Association Directory, 179
National Writer's Union, 261-262
NBC Nightly News, 204
NBC Today, 212
Netscape Navigator, 130
New Woman, 188
New York News Day, 182
New York Review of Books, 182, 189
New York Stock Exchange, 9
New York Times, 185
    bestseller list, 193
New York Times Book Review, 182, 189
News conferences, 41
News release, 183
Newshour with Jim Lehrer, 204-205
Newsletters, 49, 137-141
    writing/publishing, 266
Newspapers, 127
    editors, 178
    pros/cons, 278
    writing/publishing, 266
Newsweek (magazine), 189, 196
Nexis, 42
Niche
    finding, 110-116
    market, 62
Niche opportunities, 62-65
    starting, 63-65
Nightline (ABC), 205
Non-competing publications, 126

Non-writers, 91, 145
North American Precis Syndicate (NAPS), 43-44
Nouns, 98, 163

O

O'Halloran, Mark, 236, 239
On-line ordering systems, 132
On-line services, 261-263
Opinion leaders, 80
Opinion polls, 211
Oprah Winfrey Show, 205
Option clause, 305
Outline, 305. *See also* Book proposal; Master investment book template.
Outservice, 72
Overview. *See* Book proposal.

P

People, 189
    preemptive calling, 74-75
Permissions, 166, 305
    file, preparation, 174-176
    letter. *See* Model permissions letter.
    request. *See* Copyright permission request.
    writing, 173-176
Philadelphia Inquirer, 190
Phone call, effectiveness, 51
Photographs, 26, 38, 100, 179. *See* Professional photograph.
Pitch letter, 183
Point-of-purchase display, 198
Position statement, 18
Positioning. *See* Market place.
    distinction, 17
    theory, 16
Positioning statement, 29, 85, 141
    elements, 18-22
Power words, 98
PR Newswire International, 42
PR Research and Education, 15-16
Preface, 305. *See also* Book template.
Pre-publication reviews, 179

Present tense, 92-93
Presentations, 243-249. *See also*
    Website presentation.
    attention, 246
    beginning, 245-247
    ending, 248
    format, 166
    lead, 247
    middle, 247
    opening, 245
    plan, 245
    visual aids, 247
Press agent, 306
Press kit, 305-306
Press releases, 24, 35, 36, 113-114,
    179, 195, 197. *See also*
    Problem/solution press release.
    checklist, 37-45
    controversy, 37
    distribution process, 41-45
    information, 37
    news, 37
    timeliness, 37
Price, 306
Prime Time Live, 206
Prince, Russ Alan, 11, 66
Print advertisers, 209
Print media, 10
    entering, 105-108
Print publications
    articles, 195-196
    printing, 195
    program, building, 7-8
Printing. *See* Publicity.
Problem, 91
    identification, 86, 170, 254
    research, 55
    solution, 19, 21, 31, 41, 87, 238-
    239, 255-256
Problem/solution articles, 79, 83, 92,
    165
    writing process, 84-90
Problem/solution magazine article,
    writing process, 79-94
Problem/solution press release, 24

Problem/solution techniques, 273
Problem-solving article, 145
Problem-solving capabilities, 117, 119
Product sample, 195
Professional appearance, 95-104
Professional photograph, 196
Professionalism, 30, 70
Promotional events, 217
Promotional section. *See* Book
    proposal.
Promotions, 212. *See also* Book.
Proof statements, 148
Proposals, 99, 306. *See also* Book
    proposal.
    previews, 153
Prospects, 51, 52, 64-67, 88, 137,
    211. *See also* Book; Qualified
    prospects.
    contacting, 55
PRSA. *See* Public Relations Society
    of America.
Public domain, 306
Public relations, 33, 36, 84, 125, 137,
    209-215, 269
    effectiveness, 214-215
    efforts, 37, 243
    firms, 214
    help, 214-215
    marketing, 212
    module, 119
    studies, 213
    success, 181
    wire services, 42
Public Relations Society of America
    (PRSA), 214
Public speaking, 118, 218, 271-272
Publications, 48, 184, 195, 221. *See
    also* Non-competing publications;
    Simultaneous publication; Target
    publication.
    announcements, 179
    date, 306
    identifications, 117
    relations campaign, 178-179

research process. *See* Target.
shortcuts, 114-115
Publicists, 36, 37, 306
Publicity, 180
  activities, 207
  increasing, 197-198
  library, 47
  printing, 195
Publishable article, writing, 77
Publishers, 95. *See also* Trade
  publishers.
  book selling, 153-157
Publisher's catalog, 306-307
Publisher's discount, 307
Publishers Weekly (PW), 182, 190,
  307
Publishing. *See* Book publishing;
  Cooperative publishing; Newsletter
  writing/publishing; Newspaper
  writing/publishing; Subsidy
  publishing.

Q

Qualified prospects, attraction, 65-67
Queries, 97, 126, 307
Query letters, 106-108, 113-114, 141
Questions. *See* Sample questions.
Quick start, 84

R

Radio
  interviews, 184
  pros/cons, 277-278
RCF. *See* Remote Call Forwarding.
Reader's Digest, 126, 190-191
Reciprocation, 73
Redundancies, 98
Reference books, 265-267
Reference materials, 146
  assembly, 256
Referral sources, 67-69, 74, 138
  acknowledgment, 71
Referrals, 57, 63, 79. *See also* Clients.
  approaching, 70-71

asking, 67-75
earning, 68
requests, making, 69-70
response, 70
Registered Investment Advisors
  (RIAs), 58, 60
Registered Representatives
  (magazine), 110, 126
Relationship marketing, 57
Relationship-based marketing, 60
Relationships, building. *See* Media.
Release form, 176
Reliability, 72
Remainders, 307
Remote Call Forwarding (RCF), 239
Reorganization. *See* Master
  investment book template.
Reporters, 25, 29, 114, 181
  calls, 27-28
Reprints, 141, 307
Resources, 313-315
Response tracking system, 102-104
Resume, 307
Returns, 308
Reversion-of-rights clause, 308
Review copy, 308
Revision, keys, 98
Rhythm, 92, 97
RIAs. *See* Registered Investment
  Advisors.
Right of first refusal, 305
Rotary Club, 17
Royalties, 257
Royalty, 308

S

Sales
  conference, 308
  increasing, 197-198
  opportunity, 197
  plan, 119
  presentations, 114, 151
  representatives, 236, 308
Sample. *See* Book.
  articles, writing, 108

chapters, 156, 195
    questions, 195
San Francisco Chronicle, 191
San Francisco Chronicle Book
    Review, 182
San Francisco Review of Books, 182
SASE. See Self-addressed stamped
    envelope.
Self (magazine), 191
Self-addressed stamped envelope
    (SASE), 308-309
Self-editing checklist, 97-99
Self-education, 21
Self-publishing, 263, 264, 309
Seminars, 55, 181, 272-283
Sentence structure, 97
Serial rights, 309
Service groups, speaking, 180-181
Set-up costs, 133
Shelf life, 309
Sidebars, 99-104
Signature, 309
Silicon Valley, 17
Simultaneous publication, 309-310
Simultaneous submissions, 310
Sincerity, 72
Slant. See Writing.
Slush pile, 310
Society of American Business Editors
    & Writers, 262
Society of Professional Journalists
    (SPJ), 262-263
Solution, reaching, 87
Source acknowledgment. See
    Referrals.
Speaking. See Public speaking.
    engagements, 55
Specialist, 116
Speech recognition, 252-253
    books, 253
    websites, 253
Spine, 310
SPJ. See Society of Professional
    Journalists.
Stamping, 310

Stanley, Thomas, 147
Statistical Research, Inc., 233
Stay-behind booklet, 100-104
Story, power, 254-255
Style, 98
Subject
    index. See Book template.
    matter, planning, 123, 254
    research, 123
Submission, professionalism, 159-164
    avoidance items, 160
Submissions. See Articles; Multiple
    submissions; Simultaneous
    submissions.
Subsidiary rights, 310-311
Subsidy publishing, 311
Subtitles, usage, 171-172
Success story. See Book.
Sulton, Jack, 15
Summary, 87-88
Swipe file, 269
Syndicated column, 311
Synopsis, 311

T

Talk show. See National television
    talk show.
Target
    audiences, 125
    choice, 82-83
    group, 61
Target markets, 12, 21, 55, 80, 99,
    109, 118
    choice, 60-62
    publications, 48
Target publication, 105
    research process, 116-117
Teaching, 273
    business contribution, 229-230
    college courses, 225-231
    concepts, 228
    course proposal, checklist, 231
    decision, 229
    process, 226-229
    subject matter, 226

Telephone
  interview, 256
  solicitation, 271
Television
  pros/cons, 277
Television contacts, 199-206
Tense. *See* Present tense.
  changes, 98
  unity, 92-93
Third-party endorsements, 82
Thought stimulators, 70
Thoughts, organization, 254-256
Time (magazine), 191, 196
Timelessness. *See* Writing.
Titles, 91-92. *See also* Display titles;
  Lead title.
  message, 169-172
  usage. *See* Subtitles.
Today (television program), 206
Tone, 98
Top-of-mind awareness system
  building, 47-55
  strategy, 48-54
Trade associations, 113, 116, 218
Trade books, 311
Trade conference, usage, 217-223
Trade discount, 311-312
Trade journals, 49
Trade list, 312
Trade magazines, 16, 105, 110, 115,
  125, 217
  guidelines, 121-123
Trade publication
  location research, 109-120
  research, summary, 117-120
  writing style, 113
Trade publishers, 312
Trade shows, 118
Trade Shows & Exhibits Schedule,
  221
Trade Shows Worldwide, 221
Tradeshow Week Data Book, 221
Transitions, 97
Trends, 66

TV media kit
  appearance, 196
  follow-up, 196-197
  usage, 195-197
Typeface, 96, 159
Typos/mistakes, 96

U

United Press International, 191
University press, 312
Unsolicited manuscripts, 312
  sending, 154
USA Today, 182, 185, 192, 213
User profile, 238

V

Vanity press, 264, 312
Verbs, 98, 163
Visibility, 241
Visual aids. *See* Presentations.
Voice, 84, 98

W

Wade, John, 30
Wall Street Journal, 185, 192, 196
Warm calls, 271
Washington Post, 185
Washington Post Book World, 182,
  192
Website presentation, 129-136
  checklist, 132-133
  costs, 133-135
  starting process, 130-132
Website software package, 132
Websites, 136, 138, 141, 253
Who's Who in Association
  Management, 45
Win-win attitude, 64
Word count, 312
Wordiness, 98
World Wide Web, 129
Writer's Market, 105, 110, 154, 173,
  257

Writing. *See* Advertisements;
  Anecdote/analogy; Collaborator;
  First draft; Investment book;
  Journal writing; Magazine
  articles; Magazines; Newsletter
  writing/publishing; Newspaper
  writing/publishing; Permissions;
  Sample articles.
  chances, 115-116
  escape route, 93
  examples, 81
  final advice, 93
  focus, 82
  process. *See* Problem/solution
    articles; Problem/solution
    magazine article.
  slant, 80-82
  style. *See* Trade publication.
  subject choice, 80
  timelessness, 92

X

Xlibris, 265

Y

Yellow Pages, 233-242
  advertising checklist, 241-242
  benefits, 239-240
  calls/consultants, 236-238
  pros/cons, 281
  purpose, 235-236
  reach, 241
  research, 241
Yellow Pages Publishing Association,
  233

Z

Ziglar, Zig, 72